A MOTORCYCLE QUEST FROM LANCASHIRE TO CAPE TOWN

ALAN WHELAN

AFRICAN BREW HA-HA

Summersdale Publishers Ltd
46 West Street
Chichester
West Sussex
PO19 1RP
UK

www.summersdale.com

Printed and bound in Great Britain

ISBN: 978-1-84953-044-6

For Olive, with love

CONTENTS

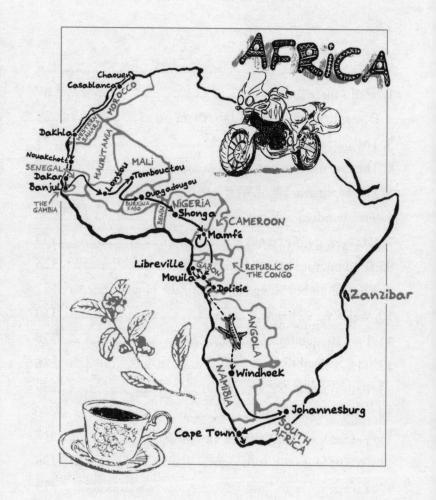

1
'HELLO THERE'

Right, let's have tea.
Margaret Francis

The wonder, and perhaps a little envy, on the faces of the businessmen on the forecourt of the motorway services coming in out of the rain confirms how I must look to others. I'm certainly not going to work. These besuited Audi drivers – who already look foreign to my eyes – get a fleeting glimpse of a life about to be lived; a fleeting, imaginary escape from the quotidian.

I'm drenched through so I have a warming cup of vending-machine tea in a privately ironic nod to my immediate future, and as a souvenir I leave a puddle on the floor of the service station.

I get back on the Triumph and gingerly ease my way out of the services onto the M6. Unused to the immense weight of the luggage on the bike, I squirm between the lanes of motorway traffic. I have so little control I feel more like a passenger. Despite battling with the steering, the amazing, mind-expanding thought is that this road I'm on will eventually take me to Cape Town – the same road these people around me are taking to get to their offices and factories and call centres on this wet October morning.

The adrenalin pumps through my veins, transmits itself through the bars to the forks and the tyres to the tarmac. I may be swaying all over the road like a drunk coming home from a Christmas party, but the road is mine, all mine.

It takes a week to reach the southern Spanish port of Algeciras, skimming along the surface of the washed-out autoroutes. The town has the feel of North Africa about it: the dark-skinned men walking about the city in slippers and djellabas, the unruly moustaches, the tea served in miniature glasses, the hostel that doubles as a brothel. The view from a hill overlooking the port serves to heighten the excitement of tomorrow's ferry to Morocco. I'm here for one of the reasons this city exists – to disgorge the helpless, curious European, in above his head, to AFRICA.

I'm going not because I think I belong but rather because I want to belong. Since I got married to Olive, a South African, in Johannesburg in 1984, I have felt something dragging me back to the continent. The pull has been strong enough for me to want to get close up, to experience Africa outside of my usual frustratingly clinical arrivals at Jo'burg or Cape Town airports. I feel as though I'm on a ten-metre diving board about to take the plunge for the first time. I want to immerse myself in Africa on my quest for the ultimate cuppa, but more of that later. I know the continent is out there waiting for me and I can barely contain myself. As a family catchphrase goes, 'I'm so happy, I envy myself.'

Less than a hundred kilometres from the ferry, I decide to have an easy first day in Africa and ride up to Chaouen in the Rif Mountains. The whitewashed village, aglow in brilliant sunshine, welcomes me to the continent with a warm breeze as I turn away from Europe and face south towards the rest of Africa.

Later, at five o'clock, the hungry villagers will soon be going home to the family evening meal they've been looking forward to since sun-up. The market in the Moroccan village is heaving, and the sale from the stalls of live and recently deceased chickens, dates and festival cakes is peaking. A bird is chosen from the holding pen behind the head of an unshaven man in a once-white coat; then another man wrings its neck and feeds it whole into the de-feathering machine, covering himself with soft down and warm blood. Chicken tajine for supper tonight, I think.

Mohammed and I take an aimless walk through the streets. One building with a huge pile of roughly cut logs leaning against it catches my eye. We approach and I see that the wood is used to fuel the furnace for a hammam. We descend into the furnace room, a small dark space with a man dozing in his cot, a pot of tea beside him.

'He is furnace man,' Mohammed tells me, redundantly. 'Twenty-four hours in a day.'

The furnace stoker must get through gallons of rehydrating tea each day to combat the debilitating effects of the unbearable heat, which I cannot tolerate for more than a few seconds. We emerge, gratefully, back up into the light.

The sight of the tea brings on a thirst and I suggest to Mohammed that we find a café for some mint tea of our own. He gives me a quizzical look. Nonchalantly, he clears his throat and coughs up a large spit ball which lands at his feet.

'Guide' would be too grand a description of Mohammed's services, but he is available to aid the stranger in town, interpret and answer questions. He has an impressive habit of hacking up great gobs of phlegm to punctuate his conversation. Much as I might 'erm' and 'umm' my way through a dialogue, he uses throat clearing to emphasise the importance of a particular point, to critique the ways of the world, to clear his airways and just to amuse himself.

We skip up a narrow staircase to an empty rooftop tea room.

'There are forty thousand peoples in this village; it is very old but lots of poor here and around,' *hack*, 'but we live in beautiful place. Look around.' *Spit*. 'Many Berber people come and sell food in the medina but *I*,' says Mohammed, stressing the distinction, '*I* am *Arab*.' *Big garggly hack*.

Mohammed leans back on the low wall tracing the perimeter of the roof and shows off his Nike T-shirt with its slogan 'Hello There'. We look out over the town clinging to the hillside. Chaouen is a beguiling place full of gracious, slippered people scuffing along the dusty streets and immaculately dressed children skipping home from school, their angelic faces rimmed by coloured head scarves. Occasionally, old women walk by dressed in four-cornered straw hats with blue pompoms attached. They all squint into the late afternoon sun, some stopping to look up and observe the stranger.

Mohammed tells me he is penniless – he pulls out his trouser pocket linings as some sort of proof, then dredges up a document from his back pocket from the Court of Justice administering a fine of 1,000 dirhams which must be paid by a date, conveniently, a few days hence.

He says, 'If not I find the money at this date,' he holds out his upturned wrists in mock shackles, 'How you say? The jail is for me.'

He neglects to confess how the fine was incurred.

'I have son, Ahmed, he six years. I cannot pay one thousand dirhams,' he looks pleadingly at me.

I don't believe a word. We look out over the rooftops to the mountains beyond until Mohammed breaks the silence.

'I wait for six o'clock to arrive for some soup, some tajine, maybe some kif. You want kif?'

He's determined to get some cash out of me one way or the other.

He pulls a great oyster-like gob from the depths of his chest into his mouth, rolls it around his tongue, tastes it and lobs it in a graceful arc to the street below. *Ppboompff*. He is pleased with its trajectory and its dusty landing.

'I should bring for you, kif. Many people come for kif; they eat, they smoke, they sleep, they feel good. But many people they just smoke... and dream...'

'No, I don't want any kif, thanks.'

'And I cannot drink this mint tea, my friend.'

'Why not?'

'I wait for the call from the mosque, for it is Ramadan. No food... no drink.'

Damn. I've started a tea tour in the middle of the Islamic month of fasting! My first African Tea Encounter is a non-event. I sip my own tea and prepare to take a photograph of Mohammed.

Hoick, spit.

He may be unable to ingest anything during daylight hours but it's certainly busy one-way traffic in the opposite direction.

'OK, I hold it.' He grabs the glass, leans back on the low wall and repeats the phrase on his T-shirt, 'HELLO THERE!'

Although my tea with Mohammed yielded none, I am collecting tea bags where I can as a promise to a Cape Town upliftment project – a cross between a charity and a going concern that helps disadvantaged people get a foothold in the job market and gain employable skills. I like to think of each tea bag as a milestone. You could mark out your life in the stories that tea bags tell.

For many years the notion of riding a motorcycle through Africa seemed to me to answer the continent's call; it was as if I missed something I had never known. Since my earliest childhood in London, like many others, I'm sure, I have dreamed of far-off lands and exotic cultures. But it was not until 2005 that I started taking the whole idea of riding to Cape Town seriously. Nobody else did, of course, but that's the thing with hare-brained schemes, they wouldn't be hare-brained if everybody wanted to do them. The impulse for the trip also fed into the enduring idea of escape and, in common with many guys with a job, a mortgage and a CD-buying habit to support, as I get older there seems more to escape from.

As with the notion for an African journey, it feels like I have always loved tea, not only as a thirst-quencher but also as an important, and undervalued, social ritual – that welcome interlude that punctuates the events of the day. My Irish family help make their country the biggest per-head consumers of tea in the world, using the amber liquid to commemorate, commiserate and celebrate, so I'm used to turning to the teapot to help me through every occasion. It's a democratic drink – the Morris Minor of the drinking classes. I am sure world summits and peace negotiations would be resolved more quickly over a nice pot of tea – pouring the precious liquid into a waiting cup breaks down perceived barriers and stimulates conversation; you feel closer to your host in a way that sharing a pint in a pub can never achieve. The ritual is in your own hands; you create the encounter and make it what it is, and each one is different.

In 2005, my thoughts on tea got me wondering, do Africans perform the tea ritual? Do they even *drink* tea? Is it enjoyed with the same formality with which it is occasionally served in Britain? Does the phrase 'I'll put the kettle on' have the same connotations at times of crisis? Is it used as a soother, a pick-me-up or a consolation?

The journey began to take shape in my mind. I just needed a little push to make it a reality... and I got it from a most unexpected place. During a holiday with Olive to Cape Town I visited the township of Imizamu Yethu, a shambolic creep of humanity spreading like a rash up the side of a mountain. Compared to the desirable homes on the other side of the gorgeous valley, it was a blot on the landscape. And it was a lot worse close up. Our guide, a well-informed man called Afrika Moni, introduced us to people who were struggling to meet the basic necessities of life: food, fresh water, shelter, employment. The township was home to around 15,000 people, the vast majority of whom lived in simple dwellings to say the least – precarious structures made of odd bits of tin, wood and plastic sheeting nailed together to keep the rain off.

During the second week in the Mother City, Olive noticed a newspaper article about a project called Original Tea Bag Designs that was running out of their raw materials – used tea bags! Natural curiosity forced us to check it out.

'Hello! Welcome to Tea Bag Designs. The kettle's just boiled,' said the smiling woman in an English accent. We had barely stepped inside the workshop before two steaming mugs of tea were offered.

'I'm Jill.'

Jill told us that the project, which had grown to employ fifteen people from the township, made tourist gifts and souvenirs featuring painted tea bags: coasters and trays, bookmarks and jewellery, trinket boxes and candle holders, all featuring a mini tea bag work of art.

'We dry the tea bag, empty the leaves then paint on it. All the designs are the artists' own work and each one is unique. You could say they're painting their way out of poverty.'

The products were terrific: delicately crafted, eye-catching and original in every way. I found it inspiring that someone had found a way of extending the life of the humble tea bag – the very epitome of the throwaway society – to create such a success.

'The wages are higher than the local average and working conditions are good, as you can see,' said Jill. 'We have one woman who works here called Nomsa who recently moved out of her shack into a brick-built house because of the wages she's earning. She'll be the first to tell you it's transformed her life.'

On our return to Britain we began sending all our used tea bags to the project. Dreams of the road and my love of tea coalesced into one idea: a tea tour through Africa on a motorbike, stopping for tea with people I meet along the way and collecting the used tea bags – each one hopefully with a story to tell. If tea is the ultimate democratic drink, is there such a thing as the perfect cup of tea, that elusive, definitive cup? It must exist out there somewhere...

I had just been inspired by a quest. The flame had been lit to search for the ultimate cuppa.

Next morning I continue through the Rif Mountains as far as Ketama and turn right down a spectacular and little-used road towards Fez. Accompanied most of the way by the sight of the 2,448-metre peak of Jabal Tidiquin, I travel by breathtaking mountains and cliffs, fir forests and perilously placed villages served by sparkling springs and waterfalls. There is hardly a straight piece of tarmac in the entire 150-kilometre ride into the ancient city. For the first time I feel the pulse of the journey as I make my way south towards the Sahara, Senegal, The Gambia, Mali, then a yet-to-be-determined route to Cameroon, Congo and down the west coast to my final destination of Cape Town, South Africa.

The journey to Fez is also memorable for the lengths to which the infamous hashish sellers of the Rif will go to make a deal: I am waved down, chased both on foot and on bicycle, stared down in a high-speed game of 'chicken', flashed at by every other approaching vehicle, overtaken and yelled at from a car window – three times – and approached directly on a water stop at the side of the road by twelve guys amiably expressing a long-held desire to brew tea for a guy on a Triumph Tiger '... and maybe some time for kif?'

Fez lives up to expectations: very hot, noisy and enjoyably cramped. It is children's day for Ramadan and in tiny school rooms throughout the medina all the little ones are dressed in gay costumes singing festive songs. There are craftsmen whose techniques cannot have changed much in hundreds of years, using open fires and bellows, primitive tools and inherited skills. I stumble across a windowless workshop with a fellow making teapots – tiny, silver vessels with beautiful inlaid decoration, just big enough for one decent cup. The heat from his torch is fierce and the seating position in the tight corner must give him day-long cramp. I want to buy a teapot but there is not a square centimetre left in my panniers. I know I will regret it, but I have to leave empty-handed.

The next day I make Rabat on the Atlantic coast after 200 kilometres on a dusty highway and hole up in a hostel filled with other European travellers. My ill-timed Tea Encounter with Mohammed in Chaouen was my first experience of Ramadan, but here in Rabat, while it is clearly a prayerful time, I see also a joyous festival with whole families on the street in the evenings in their finest clothes taking time to chat with neighbours while grazing on food from rickety stalls. During the day cafés are closed, so hungry Europeans have to buy food from grocery stores or stay in their hotels.

Early on the second morning the first sung note of the *adhan* wakes me. The whole tones of the call to prayer rise slowly up the scale. The voice pauses and repeats, but the second time it ends on a discordant, mournful note. I sense the *mu'adh-dhin*, who calls the faithful to prayer, is not too far across the city of Rabat, in a mosque, down an alley, sitting in front of a microphone, eyes closed. Languidly, the voice, middle-aged, clear and earnest, returns to the beginning of the phrase and repeats the call. It is still dark, too early to see the hands of my watch, but I guess it must be around five o'clock. Many of the faithful are already making their way to prayer, the first of five daily devotions on this, one of the final days of Ramadan. Traditionally during this month Muslims ask for forgiveness for past sins (and guidance to avoid future ones) and pray for patience, spirituality and modesty – three virtues I could benefit from on this trip.

The voice over the loudspeaker continues its pleading, melancholic motif, but now it is joined by a louder and more insistent call from a closer mosque that seems to say, 'those of you who were not moved by the first call cannot ignore mine'. If more convincing were needed for the stragglers, a third plaintive voice fights for attention across the rooftops. I look out through the stained glass window of the dorm to the first bluish hints of daylight and wonder if it calls to me. The sounds build, until it seems the three voices have me located like a GPS. Finally, two sirens signifying the start of the day's fasting rev up and fill any empty space in the atmosphere and any thinking space in my brain. It is a sound that calls everyone, excludes no one, so long as you are a believer. As the three voices and the sirens reach a powerful crescendo they all stop as one, leaving the ears bereft and hurting. The only remaining sound in the atmosphere is gentle birdsong, which brings me back down to earthly concerns. I step out into the open courtyard in my boxers and look to the dark sky, which now has tints of deep blue, light enough to see it is half past five. There is a slight chill and I dress. Rabat is ready for another day's fasting; I am looking forward to tea and breakfast.

This large city is easygoing, and an aimless stroll through its streets can be enjoyed without the annoyances of the leech-like shopkeepers and guides of Fez. Rabat became the capital of Morocco – stealing that honour from Fez – after France invaded in 1912, and to this day the layout of the streets, the grand buildings and relaxed nature of the city reflect the influence of its old colonial master. Although on the surface Rabat appears to straddle the fence that divides Eastern from Western values – modern office blocks are filled with men wearing djellabas and slippers who are called to prayer five times a day while BMWs ferry around burqa-clad women who scutter into beauty salons – the early call to prayer is the defining introduction for me to Muslim North Africa.

I spend much of the next day at the Mauritanian embassy applying for a visa. Still finding it difficult to judge the width of the panniers on the bike, I leave a deep scratch and dent in the side of the ambassador's Mercedes, which is parked outside. The incident is spotted by some sharp-eyed villains lounging on the bonnets of three Mercedes waiting for their own visas. They say they won't tell anyone as their Italian-plated stolen cars are in transit to Mauritania. I am a little uneasy that they treat me as one of their own.

With the visa stamped in my passport, I make Casablanca in an hour – and spend another hour fighting my way through the city's traffic to my next Tea Encounter.

'You'll have no problem with me; I love the British.'

Such is my welcome from Mehdi Benslimane, a good-looking, twentysomething who somehow befits the archaic description 'dapper': close-cropped hair, crisp white shirt, black trousers, European shoes, designer horn-rimmed spectacles and precise gestures.

Mehdi, who was introduced to me by a contact in Britain, brings me to the family home, a very comfortable one-storey house with a small garden but still large enough for some gorgeous flowering plants and bushes and a palm tree or two. I park the bike inside the gate and follow him into the house. The large main living room is immaculately clean with three distinct seating areas, two with large couches and chairs and one with a chaise longue. The kitchen is occupied by a maid, Fatima, who is busy preparing food for the following day's festival of Eid, which marks the end of Ramadan and is the nearest thing to the end of Lent and Christmas Day rolled into one.

Mehdi says, 'Welcome to Casablanca, will you have something to drink?'

'Before sundown?'

'We don't worry about things like that as long as we eat and drink behind closed doors! Our neighbours are probably doing the same. In any case I'm not very religious, although it is a crime in Morocco to break the fast before sundown during Ramadan. That means no food, no drinks, *no smoking*,' Mehdi says with some vexation. 'So I have a coffee and my first two cigarettes of the day at home before I go to work, then I shower to get rid of the smell. I observe the rest of the fasting at work in front of colleagues.'

He rolls his eyes.

'For me, Islam and religion as a whole is all about coherence. You can't be praying at the mosque in the afternoon and gambling at the casino at night. I'm an all or nothing person, and for now it's nothing. Right, let's have tea.'

The maid brings a tray with two small glasses and tea in an extravagantly inlaid silver teapot. The mint tea is poured; it is mild and clean tasting.

Mehdi is an exceptionally enthusiastic host, calling for the maid to bring this or that, putting on music, making sure I am comfortable, and all the while giving me an entertaining history of Moroccan politics and the legacy of French colonial rule. During the course of the afternoon the rest of the family arrives. Driss, Mehdi's father, is involved in property, facilitating European developers' move into Morocco and away from the collapsing Spanish market. He is agreeably dishevelled, bald on top with greying unkempt hair to the sides, and wears ill-fitting trousers and an unironed shirt. He rarely makes a comment in English without ending it with a charming crooked-toothed smile. He has the most smiling eyes I think I have ever seen.

The first time I meet Mehdi's mother, an elegant, slightly built woman, she is bringing food from the car for the celebrations, and almost every other time I see her during the following twenty-four hours she is carrying food; it is a measure of the easy, warm reception to her home that the only word of English she utters is 'welcome'.

Nightfall signals the official end of fasting for the day and the end of Ramadan for another year. We sit at a large round table laden with enough food to feed twenty ravenous navvies although there are just eight of us: Mehdi and his brother Bashir, father Driss, mother and sister, and the three strangers to the house – Bashir's new Dutch girlfriend with film star looks, Daniel, a Jewish property developer from London who is in town on business, and myself.

The plates on the table are piled high with hard-boiled eggs, dates, croissants and sugar pastries, chickpea and chicken soup, fresh soft cheese, tiny meat pancakes, latkas and water or espresso coffee. It's a suitably indulgent spread with which to celebrate the end of a month's daytime fasting. There doesn't seem to be any accepted order in which to taste the carefully presented food so I just dig in hungrily.

Daniel, the developer, cheerfully puts his cards on the table describing how racist his mother is and how she worries for him, as a Jew, doing business with Muslims. The Benslimanes laugh good-naturedly and insist he would not be eating at their table if he was not welcome. Daniel is a jovially open man who is fascinated by my trip, but when I tell him my proposed route his head sinks into his hands, and as I reel off the countries I will be riding through he starts groaning with incredulity. He looks up with arched eyebrows as if to ask the question 'you're not serious?'

'Do you want some advice about the DR Congo?' He asks.

I nod my head.

'Don't go.'

I wait for the punchline...

'Don't go,' he repeats. He is serious, still in a state of amazement.

'Well...' I begin.

'Don't go.'

'Yes, but...'

'*Don't! Bloody! Go!* The place is totally lawless. If you get into any sort of diffi...'

'But I have no choice!' I manage to blurt out. 'There's no other way down the west coast.'

He thinks for a few seconds while he tries to weigh me up.

'Well, if you absolutely bloody have to... don't stop. Don't stop for *anything*. If they try to stop you at a checkpoint or anywhere else just throw dollars at them and *get the hell out of there*.'

As he is the only person around the table who has actually been to the Democratic Republic of Congo, nobody has anything to add. They all silently ponder my slim chances in the heart of Africa.

'This is civilisation, Morocco,' says Driss. 'But Africa...' He shrugs.

After breaking the fast the family tell a string of awful jokes. Driss tells only gags that begin 'There was a priest, a rabbi and an imam...' He struggles a little with the English so Mehdi has to translate the occasional word, but he never misses a beat and finds every well-worn joke deliriously funny. We're all in fits.

The family switches between Arabic, which is always spoken for family matters, French and English for the Brits' benefit. The Arabic sounds like a disagreement in a carpet shop, and in the middle of one animated discussion Mehdi stops the conversation dead and says, 'We'd better talk in English or Alan will think we're arguing!'

The Benslimanes all rise as one from the table and either help to clear the dishes or make their way out into the garden to have a smoke in the cool night air. Driss lies flat out under a light blanket on one of the couches in the living room and takes a nap. He is soon snoring gently while the bustle of family life continues around him. As the maid brings tea to the lounge, Bashir's girlfriend and I are left momentarily alone at the table. We look at each other and mouth simultaneously, 'What a family!'

Later, after inviting me to stay the night, Mehdi takes me to a sidewalk café in the glitzy city centre to meet a friend. At eleven o'clock, as I am looking forward to returning to the house to sleep, Mehdi looks at his watch and says, 'We have to go or we'll be late for dinner!'

I can barely believe we are going to eat again today, but we return home to the appetite-inducing smell of garlic roast lamb coming from the kitchen and the table being prepared for another feast. I go to bed replete, relaxed and happy.

In the morning while Driss is brewing up I tell him that I should quickly check on the bike, which has been left overnight in their front garden. I return relieved that all is well and he says, 'It's still there?' in a tone of mock surprise, followed by a private chuckle as he pours me tea to take the sting out of the teasing.

Later, the house is filled with friends and family who bring gifts of more food or sing songs and catch up on family news. Mehdi and I slip out to the only golf club in Casa, where there are a few less-than-devout locals in shorts and baseball caps ignoring the festival. At the swish club house Mehdi orders Lipton's tea 'the English way' so that I can take a tea bag with me.

The Benslimanes are among the first Tea Encounters in Africa but not the first on the Brew Ha-Ha, which started nine months earlier in Britain. I had tea with someone chosen at random, then asked for an introduction to someone else for tea and so on, hoping the ball would keep rolling. It did. I sketched out some criteria:

1. My host serves tea
2. I take a photograph
3. I get advice for the trip ahead
4. I collect the used tea bags
5. I ask for an introduction to another Tea Encounter

The memory of each Tea Encounter and the advice given by the hosts would come in useful on every step of the African journey.

The British Tea Encounters ended a few days before my departure for Africa on 1 October 2007. I had my own optimism and an open mind, and I had a mission statement – 'Never lose sight of the blinding light' – created with the help of tea drinker Mike Finnigan, who was one of the few people as enthusiastic as I was about the journey. The 'blinding light' was the dream, a visualisation of succeeding in the quest, which in my case was not only discovering the ultimate cuppa but also ending the trans-Africa trip by riding into the courtyard of the tea bag project. That was the goal, that's what was going to keep me going. I also had all the advice I could ever need to see me to Cape Town, which I printed and stuck all over the Triumph and panniers so I wouldn't forget it. Then I included one more piece of advice from myself that I picked up from real bikers who seemed to know about these things and that sounded sensible – 'Don't ride at night'. Africa was daunting enough without having to do it in the dark.

The weekend before I left, Olive and I went away for a couple of days, which may sound rash considering all the last-minute tasks that needed doing, but even the African Brew Ha-Ha had to pause for a landmark birthday celebration. It seemed at once oddly perverse and perfectly apt that the weekend before I go to Africa (perhaps to balance my growing concern about the ready availability of food on the continent) Olive should opt to go to the Fat Duck, a hysterically overpriced restaurant recently named the best in the world. I can remember finishing the fourteenth course thinking 'I'm going to Africa on Tuesday...' followed by a big empty space in my brain that needed filling. Now that the trip was only days away I had to admit to myself I knew little about Africa and less about the urge that was drawing me there. But there was only one way to find out.

Mehdi and I return to the house which is packed with more people preparing for yet another feast. They invite me to eat, but I don't want to outstay my welcome. I load up the bike and get on the road exactly twenty-four hours after my arrival.

During the journey south I find myself reflecting on the Benslimane family and their warm-hearted welcome to a stranger. I have struck tea gold in Morocco, the first African country I visit. If tea is social glue, the Benslimanes are well and truly bonded. Tea on arrival, tea after breakfast, tea with dinner, tea the following morning and tea at the golf club showed, if nothing else, that they had certainly cottoned on to the theme of the trip. And I left with yet more advice – from Mehdi: 'When in doubt, turn right,' and Bashir: 'If you hurry you will be late.'

The fight to get out of Casablanca is beset with some spectacularly absent-minded driving. The traffic gives me plenty of time to draft my own mini-guide to the Moroccan Road...

1. Indicators, like fairy lights on a Christmas tree, are for decoration only and come in a variety of

colours: red, amber and *au naturel* (i.e. with the glass missing).

2. Lit brake lights on the vehicle in front do not mean that it is stopping or turning, but probably that the driver is just making up his or her mind as to where to go – if you haven't gone into the back of the car already.

3. An especially large face-full of fumes indicates the driver in front has just changed gear and intends to take the next sixty seconds attempting to overtake the equally slow van ahead.

4. There is no need to drive between the white lines on a highway as you can easily get seven vehicles into four marked lanes.

5. Roundabouts are handy for:

   • Taxis to pick up a fare
   • Bikes to stop and ask for directions from polite policemen
   • Washing cars
   • Guessing if this particular town employs the 'give way from the right' rule or the 'give way from the left' rule.

6. If you're in front you're always in the right and the rules of the road do not apply.

The barren, red rust landscape on the road towards Marrakech 200 kilometres away is a shock to my eyes after the buzz of Casablanca. Occasional bedraggled sheep with knotted wool like white-haired Rastafarians dot the vast landscape, looking lost as they seem to tiptoe over the stony earth in search of nourishment. Along the route walled settlements, cloaked in mud, seem to rise up from the earth. I want to stop and find an excuse to stay the night with the people who live here, but I see no signs of life.

Marrakech is much further than I had anticipated and with dusk approaching the petrol gauge seems to be dropping like a stone. After a worrying half hour, I finally reach a village. No fuel.

'Prochain village?'

'Vingt-huit kilomètres.'

Oh shit. Twenty-eight kilometres to the next village and no guarantee there is any fuel there either. I open the fuel cap and give the tank a shake. I can hear a feeble slosh of petrol and decide to take a chance. I ride on at around 50 kph now to conserve the precious fuel as darkness falls with just the faint silhouette of the mountains for company. I reach the village and allow myself a small inward whoop of joy when I see the gaudy, battered sign of a gas station. There is no *sans plomb* but this is no time for having a crisis of conscience over CO_2 emissions, and I fill up with lead-rich Super. In fact, it is many thousands of kilometres before I use unleaded petrol again, and in any case the bike runs better on the more polluting fuel.

I get on the highway and realise I'm already breaking my own advice to myself, never to ride at night. The crosswind from the east is fierce, so bad that I have to lean at an angle, bracing myself into the force of the storm, and when large trucks pass me they draw the air out of my lane creating violent turbulence. It is as if I am being sucked into the wide empty space of Africa.

Then the rain starts and epic lightning illuminates the outline of the mountains like the backdrop to a cheap film:

The Road to Marrakech
starring
The Triumph
as himself

2
DESERT DRIFT AND THE ROAD THAT'S ON FIRE

If you hurry you will be late.
Bashir Benslimane

Marrakech is a blur, full of tea-drinking men with impressive moustaches like extras in a Mexican bandit movie and noisy teenagers celebrating the festival of Eid in less-than-traditional style – cruising to McDonald's in open-top cars. Mehdi has arranged for me a Tea Encounter with Constance Thiollier, a French journalist living in the city, who I meet on the Djemaa el Fna, a huge gathering place of food stalls, snake charmers, fortune tellers, hustlers, touts, tourists and lookers-on.

She arrives on a tiny motorcycle and negotiates with some locals about guarding my bike while we go for tea. She is unhappy with the first two stands but at the third she is sure that the bike will be there when we return. It is very dark in the alley and there are thousands of people on the streets; it wouldn't have been my third choice (or thirtieth) but I trust her judgment. The China tea is crammed with fresh mint with optional sugar on the side, and it's such a spectacle from our ringside table that we order another pot.

After spending the night on Constance's couch, I push on to Agadir, a flashy coastal resort about 300 spectacular kilometres through the High Atlas mountains. I call the number I have been given for a Tea Encounter but nobody in the household speaks English (or should I say nobody on the Brew Ha-Ha speaks Arabic) and then I run out of coins for the phone. It's not going to happen.

The following day the road south to Tan Tan 300 kilometres away takes me through the first real stretch of desert of the trip and it's a breathtaking experience. The heat is searing. The sun reflects off the crumbling tarmac, and the bike soon becomes too hot to touch with my bare hands as I ride through the featureless landscape – but I guess that's the point of a desert. The closer I get to Tan Tan, the more men wear folded robes hanging heavy from the shoulders, some with turbans and neck scarves, Tuareg style, while women drape themselves in what looks more like a sari than a djellaba, the thin material scooped up over their heads. Their skins are darker than those of women further north and their eyes more slanted against the sun, the wind and the swirling dust.

I see a sign: 'Dakhla 1152'. Could this place possibly be in the same country? I thought I was already *in* southern Morocco. I unfold the map and for the first time get the red squiggly line towards Mauritania and down the west coast into some kind of geographical perspective. Christ, Africa's big.

I can remember vividly the day the three Africa maps arrived by post three months ago. I immediately spread them out on the living room floor, eight feet square. I thought, that's going to be difficult to hold still on the bike! This was the most excited I had yet felt about the trip, and being able to trace a route made it ever more real. I had spent most of the previous year bringing Olive around to the whole idea of me disappearing for a few months, so the arrival of the maps was a no-turning-back act of intent. I pointed to the open maps.

'Choose a place where we can spend Christmas together,' I said magnanimously.

'I'm not going to spend my Christmas in a mud hut, thank you very much,' Olive said. Then after a pause, 'Zanzibar's supposed to be nice.'

I looked at the map again. Crikey, she couldn't have chosen a less convenient halfway point: an archipelago of islands off the mainland of Tanzania, on Africa's east coast thousands of miles off my route.

With the trade-off out of the way (and, it has to be said, Olive's steadfast belief that I would be successful in the quest), the following morning I called Jill in Cape Town and told her my progress 'planning' the trip, making Original Tea Bag Designs the final destination.

'That's great. How long's that going to take you, then?'

That was a very good question.

'Err, about five months... or so.'

'And you're leaving when?'

'October first.'

'So, you should arrive towards the end of February?'

I got out next year's diary.

For no good reason I said, 'February the twenty-second.'

'Right. I'll expect you then. Shall we say two-thirty? We'll have a little tea party on your arrival. I'll have the kettle on.'

The milky light of the late afternoon disappears as dusk approaches. It's been a hot day, and although the coolness coming off the Atlantic is welcome, the westerly wind is fierce and unpredictable. I flip up my visor to cool off, but a doodlebug of an insect smacks into my forehead. I have to stop and draw part of its splattered body out from under my skin; the sting makes me wince. I shut the visor and continue on with a mild headache.

Towards the end of day the clouds clear, revealing an indistinct horizon off to the west as the sun sets here in Africa and heads for the skyscrapers of America. The sky is soon scarred with layers of burnt orange and a deep twilight blue; to the east it is nearly black. I reach the crest of a rise I've been climbing for ten minutes and see the yellow lights of Tan Tan around thirty kilometres away. The road ahead can be picked out by the lights of the oncoming vehicles stretching into the distance. They start to mesmerise a little, and as I feel the tiredness of the day catch up with me I turn all my thoughts to the patch of tarmac immediately ahead to prevent drifting over the white line or into the ditch.

At the first sign of artificial light in Tan Tan I pull in to a hotel that has its entrance, rather uniquely, in the forecourt of a petrol station with a string of small kiosks that acts much like a town square. The tiny man who is standing on a box at reception writes down the price of a room. I agree to take it, and he asks, *'Et pour moi?'*

'Pourquoi?' I ask, thinking he hasn't even done anything for me yet except write down a number on a scrap of paper.

He says something that I suppose is intended to mean that it would not be worth my while to get on the wrong side of him, so I give the little fellow fifteen dirhams (about £2) and he jumps down off the box. I now see he is the smallest man I have ever set eyes on who is not a dwarf. He has the appearance of a fifty-year-old child; as we walk to a lock-up for the bike I look down at the top of his head and have to resist the urge to pat it. Then he grabs all my stuff at once and carries every last item upstairs to the room. This guy should be in a circus.

There is no menu, but he asks, *'Côtelette ou tajine?'*

'Cutlet, *s'il vous plaît.'*

'Kilo ou demi-kilo?'

'Demi... avec frites.'

'À boire?'

'Thé.'

Later, I sit at a wicker table with a panoramic view of the oily forecourt as a truck pulls in for a full tank of diesel. The food arrives; I can't complain because I get exactly what I asked for: half a kilogram of lamb chops, a mound of chips and a pot of tea.

I am beginning to look and feel road-weary, not only from the rigours of riding in the fierce heat, but also because after conscientiously doing my laundry in the Rabat dorm's sink a couple of days ago I left all my underwear and T-shirts drying on a courtyard bush. Good underwear should not be noticeable – no underwear is extremely noticeable.

At least the T-shirts were free. For my last British Tea Encounter I rode to Philip Youles Motorcycles in Blackburn, Lancashire (the town Beatles fans will know as the place with the four thousand holes) for tea with around a hundred

Triumph bikers who gave me an appropriate send-off by stuffing themselves with tea and cake at a Mad Hatter's Tea Party. I stood beside the bike gleaming with the new metal panniers feeling very self-conscious in my pristine all-weather gear. The ignominious episode that heralded my motorcycle career returned in my mind – the one when I ran out of petrol during my bike test – and reminded me that sometimes my biking aptitude isn't always up to the job. 'Ride around the block and return to this spot and when I step into the road with my hand up, I want you to do an emergency stop.' The tester had a long wait. The bike spluttered to a halt the second I turned the corner.

Was I really up to this trip? People fired the same questions at me all evening: 'Are you *sure* you know what you're doing?' 'What? *No phone*?' 'You do know that's got to be at least 15,000 miles?' 'Of course, you must have done a lot of off-roading...' 'You're going to ride all that way in *five months*?'

The longer the evening went on, the more I considered that maybe the rashly proposed arrival date of 22 February was too ambitious, but I didn't air my thoughts.

For weeks before the send-off I would show up at the dealership and pump Philip for some much-needed spare parts and supplies, or ask him to show me how to change a tyre or adjust the chain tension. In return I said I would arrange some puff for him through local media interviews, for which I was to wear his branded T-shirt for photo shoots.

I asked him if he thought the bike, now fitted with an impressive collection of mostly free off-road extras – making it *even heavier* – would successfully complete the trip.

Without a moment's thought, he said, 'It'll be reet' (that's Lancashire for 'don't worry about it').

He then braced himself for yet another request for bike extras, but instead I asked, 'Do you have any advice, Philip?'

He asked, 'Are you going to Nigeria?'

'Yes.'

'Well, if you get kidnapped by some crazy militant group and they force you to make one of those hostage videos... just make sure you're wearing my bloody T-shirt!'

The following day I reach Laayoune in the Western Sahara, a disputed territory largely administered by Morocco. The non-descript desert town 350 burning kilometres south of Tan Tan, strangely, has three Western-style hotels. I wonder why anyone would bother to build them in such a remote place, but all becomes clear when I spot a rash of UN vehicles – white TLCs (Toyota Land Cruisers) gliding past like so many kerb crawlers. The town is also home to a Moroccan military garrison, the caged windows of their vehicles austere reminders of tensions in the area. The UN is here to oversee the ceasefire between Moroccan troops and the Polisario, the political movement that represents the Sahrawis who have campaigned and fought for independence for the Western Sahara since the Spanish left in 1975. On the Spanish retreat, King Hassan quickly sent 350,000 civilians on what became known as *La Marche Verte*, The Green March, to populate this part of the Sahara with Moroccans. But they underestimated the determination of the Sahrawis to fight for an independent Saharan state. Nevertheless, nearly 40,000 fled to neighbouring Mauritania and Algeria to live in remote refugee camps, which to this day house thousands of these stateless people.

Despite the military presence, the town is superficially quite sleepy. Copper-brown men wear embroidered robes of khaki or light blue with sandals and turbans and full face scarves to protect against the sun and the permanently airborne sand. They shuffle through the streets, drive the taxis or sit smoking as if in a trance at café tables, cupping their chins in their palms and squinting into the sun.

In the early evening a man walks up to me while I am considering eating at a hugely unappetising buffet and says, 'Hello, where are you from? My name's Fergus. I'm from Ireland.'

I give him the gist of my trip, ask him to meet me for tea, and a little later I am sitting with Lieutenant Colonel Fergus Hannan, who is having his shoes shined at a pavement café. He could easily pass for a tourist in his chinos and short-sleeved shirt, but of course none come to this featureless town. He has cappuccino, I have tea from a tiny pot and saucered glass. The glass is stuffed with fresh mint leaves onto which I pour the steaming tea. The drink is especially sour, it being towards the end of the day with all the taste now brewed out of the barely distinct leaves. No combination of fresh mint or sugar can bring this brew back to life. I swallow a couple of sips and try not to wince.

'I've been posted here as a UN observer overseeing the ceasefire between the Sahrawis and the Moroccans,' says Fergus. 'There's a demilitarised zone along the berm, a kind of sand wall, that divides the country in two – it's a couple of metres high and over 2,000 kilometres long. Our job is to make sure the ceasefire sticks, although it's generally very quiet. There are over 500 of us in the armed force made up of twenty-six different nationalities based here and in encampments throughout the country.'

Fergus goes on to tell me some of the background to the UN mission on the Moroccan side of the berm. I am surprised at the relaxed nature of the operation and Fergus's easy-going character, but that's the Irish for you. He lifts his feet admiringly from the wooden box and hands the shoeshine a few coins.

'Don't go quoting me on any politically sensitive stuff now, will yeh?' he advises pointedly as he strides off down the sandy street in his newly polished brogues.

I reflect on our conversation but cannot recall anything that might compromise him. I wait until he is lost in the crowd, then walk among families out for an evening stroll now that the temperature has cooled; they stop and talk at length with friends and neighbours in a desert version of the *passeggio*. Men greet one another by patting each other rhythmically on the back with chests together followed by a handshake and a kiss on the cheek. Some touch each other's heart, then kiss and shake hands. The greeting is ritualistic, never rushed, and much enjoyed and appreciated.

I find a café, and as I wait at an outside table for my order a young guy walks up to me with a friendly smile and shakes my hand.

'Five dirhams, *'ote' Ca'ifornee*,' he says.

Is he a tout for a local flophouse? Perhaps he's a guide. Then I notice he has a guitar on his back. He wants to sing to me. It seems like a good deal so I tell him to pull up a chair and give it his best shot. I take a bite out of the chocolate cake set down before me – my new vice – and wash it down with a swig of fresh tea – an old Irish one.

'*I am Omar!*' he announces by way of introduction and places the guitar on his knee with a flourish.

That was his finest moment, the flourish. It's tough when you peak too early, for he is spectacularly and ear-abusingly awful. The guitar is so out of tune he doesn't know which of the notes in each tortured chord to latch onto, drifting up and down the scale in search of a tuneful one. Just one would be nice.

The sound emanating from his throat is a bizarre falsetto trilling phonetically learned English. '*Weh-corm to 'ote' Ca'ifornee-ee… is a wuvvy pace… is a wuvvy pace.*'

He struggles through an amazingly disjointed version of 'Hotel California' – thankfully without the guitar solo – then goes into a Tracy Chapman number.

'*Sor-wee… is aw dat ooo can say-eee…*'

It is rather like indulging a very keen young nephew at a family party: you want to applaud the effort but at the same time the adults can't wait for the thing to finish. I decide to tune the ancient nylon strings for him before he goes any further, which he doesn't seem to mind; in fact he looks as if he has never seen it done before.

I hand the guitar back with a satisfied look: 'Now try it, slowhand.'

'*Arabia!*'

This'll be more like it; he'll be on home ground with a traditional song. But the tuning has done little to improve the situation. 'Arabia' cannot ever have been so tuneless. Passers-by stop their conversations to stare in horror, not at the singer but at me, for they know I'm paying him to perform. I show appreciation for his effort with a little solo applause and hand him ten dirhams, the price of a pot of tea.

I take myself off for a haircut in the local style at one of the many barber shops that stay open well into the night. It is very rare to see a Moroccan's hair beyond the collar, nor with much more than a hair out of place, the outline of the cut severe and clean. Self-consciously I walk out of the barbers with a newly-revealed band of white skin around the hairline on my neck and ears rimming the burst tomato features of my face, looking like a Neapolitan ice cream. The haircut emphasises even more the huge insect sting on my forehead I got a few days ago, so I immediately look for a pharmacy.

'England?' asks the pharmacist, in clear English. 'It is raining there now,' he says with a certainty that makes me think he might have just watched the BBC weather report.

'Here, it is always like this: a bit cool, a bit cloudy... a bit warm, a bit sunny, always the same. Manchester, *that's weather!*' he says with awe.

He stares at my ears and my sunburned nose in a look heavily suggestive of shame, then glances up at the ugly swelling on my forehead and, without request or explanation, places a packet of anti-histamines down on the counter between us.

'The sun, monsieur, is not a Manchester sun!'

The following day I make an early start and ride south through the desert on a road that's on fire. I am heading for Dakhla in Western Sahara (the coastal town that was 1,152 kilometres distant a couple of days ago), which is like aiming for the centre of the sun. My face is soon etched into a mask of anguish: my eyes are slits, lips sealed in a grimace, nostrils flaring yet not wanting to inhale too deeply the burning air.

The road is flat and featureless and I drift. My brain senses the balance of the bike and it knows the general direction it has to go; with the essentials taken care of that part of the mind that controls the bike relaxes. But as one synapse shuts down a dormant one re-emerges, as if the movement through space is shaking up the experiences in my head, regurgitating snippets of recent history: scraps of conversation, flashbacks of glances from veiled faces, encounters with shopkeepers and smiling policemen at the checkpoints as my weary mind tries to create order from the events of the past day, of the whole trip so far.

In my peripheral vision I am aware of the monochromatic beige of the landscape that does not change for hour after hour. Above, the blue is so oppressive I try not to look up. In front, the strip of black tarmac and the broken white line become as unreal as a video game. The vastness of the landscape forces me back inside my own mind. An occasional camel or black figure is not enough to return me to human-scaled certainty. The muscles in my limbs are so tired and locked in position and the drone of the engine so uniform that my mind plays strange games and I start to believe I can step off the bike whenever I choose. I overlook the fact that I'm actually travelling at 120 kilometres an hour. I am going to sleep. I gently float from side to side of the two-lane blacktop. There is some gravel and fine sand lining the road on both sides, a frail margin between me and the Sahara, between the unfolding journey and an abrupt halt. To be safe I do what most other drivers do – I hog the centre white line.

Approaching trucks, and it is mostly trucks, also straddle the line and we both leave it dangerously late to move to our own side of the road. The trucks emerge out of a thick heat haze that keeps me guessing (*Focus… focus*) until about ten seconds before they reach me. Many times I see a vehicle approaching, but my muscles won't let me move over. I see the thundering object looming larger, but I want to stay in the comforting centre of the road. I belong here. It becomes a monumental physical effort to swing the bike into the right-hand lane. Often the approaching truck driver does not see me because his mind is telling him the same thing – 'this tarmac is *mine*, I don't want to share it' – so he needs flashing and honking if he is to awaken from his own trance.

The thoughts in my mind, now living in a strange netherworld, are accompanied by a bizarre soundtrack: *'Fly me to the… Walking on the… Rocket man…'* Is there life on Mars? I think I've left the planet.

Another problem is stopping. After hours on the bike it becomes a titanic effort to bring my mental state to accept that I need water or to stretch my legs, which are screaming blue murder. My mind is telling me that I have to keep moving, every minute stopped is another mile I could be further through this burning hell. There is such little traffic – nothing has overtaken me for days – that I can lean forward while stretching my legs slightly and resting the chin of the helmet on the tank bag. Temporarily it's heaven as some fresh blood rushes into my limbs. Now all I need do is shut my eyes…

After twice skimming the edge of the road, I recall Bashir Benslimane's advice – 'If you hurry you will be late' – and finally pull into a rusting heap of a petrol station, unused for years. Probably couldn't get the staff. The pumps and offices are still there, but it has been sand-blasted to the point that the structure is unsafe. Great sheets of corrugated roofing lift in the wind and threaten to crown me; all the windows are missing and anything of value has been scavenged. The door to the jakes is kicked in and, amazingly, people are still using the shit hole. The bog has no roof, no plumbing, it's hundreds of kilometres from any kind of town, and people still go to the WC. Human nature. I do the same.

I step out into the searing heat and do a three-sixty. Dreamily, I face the shimmering horizon. The smudged line radiates its own energy; it is of this planet yet otherworldly, alluring yet untouchable, a metaphor for the trip maybe. It is the most beautiful thing I have ever seen.

My squinting vision alights on the bike, the only human-scaled object within sight. I give it a pat on the scalding tank and scare myself into wondering, 'What if the thing doesn't start?' Despite the soaring temperature, the thought gives me a shiver. I quickly lean over, turn the key to ignition, push the starter and am greeted by the greatest sound in my world – 955 cubic centimetres of British-made internal combustion.

I swing a leg over the bike like a rootless cowboy in a John Ford film and take a swig of water from the jerrycan but convulsively spew it all out. The sun has heated it to the temperature of bath water. If I had a tea bag at least I could make a cuppa. I put the helmet back on and continue riding south.

Shortly, I pass a sign in Arabic: '300 km Dakhla'.

Jesus.

3
THE BASTARD BEAST
BITES BACK

Make up your own mind.
Eric Hodge

Take a puncture repair kit.
Bill Beaumont

'If you are at one with the desert you hold the largest diamond of life.'

Carla sits back, lights up another cigarette, and allows me to digest that little nugget from the Sahara as she prepares the tea the waiter has set down on the table.

The sun is blinding after noon in Dakhla. A shared pot of tea in a petrol station on the edge of town is as good an excuse as any for not getting back on the scorching bike at this time of day. The welcome shade and the chance to speak some English is enough to convince me that Mauritania can wait.

After the 550 otherworldly kilometres through the desert this morning, it is startling to pass kite surfers in the bay and find a Mediterranean atmosphere in town. The tea is very sour when it first arrives, but that is soon corrected by Carla's ritualistic pouring and re-pouring of the butterscotch-coloured liquid.

'This can take hours sometimes,' she says. 'The process helps to brew the tea while mellowing the flavour.'

She pours two glasses.

'Slurp it through the froth.'

The tea is both salty from the high mineral content of the water and sweet from the huge amount of added sugar. I am surprised at how refreshing it is.

Carla stubs out the cigarette and after playing with the lighter for a couple of minutes lights up another. A petite woman of around thirty with lucid skin, she sports a number two shaved head and is wearing a man's shirt over her flat chest and jeans. At first glance she has the appearance of a teenage boy.

Scots-born Carla and her Bajan husband, Keith, used to enjoy a comfortable life in Germany. The day following his lavish fiftieth birthday celebrations in Monaco, he said, 'Let's sell up.' So they did. They sold the Porsche and bought a Land Rover expecting to drive to The Gambia but got no further than the Western Sahara.

'Three days turned into three weeks, then three months...' Carla explains.

Two and a half years later they are living in an encampment in the desert near the open sea, an hour from town.

Carla squeezes the last of the tea from the pot and calls to the waiter for a refill.

'You're welcome to stay,' she says, 'there's plenty of room. We sometimes take guests who pass through but we have nobody at the moment. In a few days we have some British charity fundraisers staying – if they can find us! The border to Mauritania closes at noon and re-opens at three, then you've got to get through immigration and over no-man's land, and ride on to Nouadhibou. It's best to do it in the morning. I'm stuck here until Keith comes to pick me up so let me show you how to get to the encampment.'

Carla sketches me a map to the camp and suggests I stop at a petrol station on the way to get the final directions from someone called Hamdi. She says she will also call a man who works for her, Bwedra, to keep a lookout for me on the dunes.

I take the directions and head out on the desert road. An hour later I find the petrol station with a rusting sign displaying '24/24', presumably indicating that it is open twenty-four hours a day, although from the road the place appears utterly deserted: a ghost station that has all but given up the ghost. As I approach, a man comes out of the ramshackle building.

'I am Hamdi,' he says with his hands in his pockets, his face and head covered by a full scarf and dark glasses, which he now removes. He gives me vague directions over some rough sand to the encampment he says is a couple of kilometres away.

'Follow the track. It is easy.'

I take the opportunity for a breather but the impression won't leave me that Hamdi is a shifty-looking bugger with a permanent smirk about whom I make a mental note never to trust. I recall the advice of Eric Hodge during an early British Tea Encounter in Poulton-le-Fylde: 'Never believe what anyone tells you; make up your own mind.'

I decide to wait.

'I'll hang on here for Carla and Keith,' I say.

He manages a broken-toothed sneer (I wish he wouldn't do that, it worries me) and says, 'There is but one track.'

He gestures that he couldn't care less what I do and walks back inside out of the wind. I follow.

The petrol station is a five-star dump. It stinks of shit and urine, there are flies on everything, and in one corner sit three sullen men at a table staring into space. Hamdi goes over to a back door, throws out an empty cigarette pack and leans against the door jamb. Outside is a rubbish tip. When these guys finish eating or drinking something, they throw the packaging and leftovers out the door. Eventually the wind picks it up and carries it... well, what do they care.

I go back out front and sit in the shade. No vehicle stops. I'm not sure the 24/24 has any petrol. I stare at the horizon and watch the occasional speeding truck whoosh by, inspired by an unhealthy dash of *insha'Allah*: if I die today it will be God's will.

My thoughts are interrupted by a dark figure. It is Hamdi who has crept up on me, his very presence filling the air like bad weather.

He looks down at me with a patronising smile: 'There is only one track, you must go.'

Another half hour goes by and, despite hating the fact that I'm giving Hamdi the satisfaction, I decide to ride out into the emptiness. I lose my way amongst a score of Land Rover tracks in the sand that head off in all directions. I follow the clearest track, which soon reaches the dead end of a steep sand dune. I try to retrace my own tracks but lose them and I am soon going round in circles. I then reach a sheer cliff about a thousand metres from the sea from which

I can see no obvious way down. I am struggling to keep the bike upright in the shifting sand, the weight I'm carrying not helping my non-existent off-road skills: two fully loaded metal panniers, a large waterproof hold-all, a tent, two spare tyres, and two full ten-litre jerrycans do not add up to stable, well-balanced riding.

I am sweating profusely now like a preposterous man lost in the desert, which I am. I stop the bike and look around. I spot some movement on a dune to the north. A man is walking towards me. His head and face are covered in a black scarf and he is wearing traditional knickerbocker pants with a short-sleeved shirt and sandals. Beside him trots a beautiful blonde dog.

As he approaches, he holds up a cellphone and says, 'Carla call. OK!'

Bwedra, for it is he, greets me warmly and, seeing that I am struggling to find my way, trots ahead with the dog. I follow but soon lose the front wheel and fall. Seeing me hit the ground brings Bwedra running back to help me right the bike and then wait for me to catch my breath before continuing on.

I try to keep up with him jogging across the dunes (I can't believe he is jogging anywhere in this searing heat), I drop the bike, he runs back, we pick it up, I pause to catch my breath, and so it goes on. The sand is now so deep and fine that it is difficult to get the bike moving at all, and when I do, I soon drop it again. This routine happens six times in quick succession, each time with longer rests in between. I am soaking, I'm gasping to draw a decent breath, and I'm so far out of my depth it's comical. I use a million excuses to Bwedra to cover my embarrassment but he speaks no

English, which is probably just as well. He keeps encouraging my futile efforts while indicating the encampment is not far away now, his expression never changing from cheerful optimism when he should be laughing at me. This carries on for forty tortuous minutes as I murder the clutch.

The slide down the precipitous drop to sea level is a triumph of ambition over physics, but once down I get encouraged by the sight of a boat in the bay and the encampment which is tucked under the ridge. I give in to hubris and increase the speed slightly, but instead of aiding progress I give the bike an ungainly balletic spin, which puts me on the deck with an awkward, grim finality. The bike is righted but will not move; the engine roars but the bastard beast beneath me refuses to budge like an ass that would rather die than take one more step.

I collapse next to the bike in the sand, exhausted, disgusted, disappointed. What's my next move? I don't think I have one.

But Bwedra does. He looks at me and utters two words: 'Du thé?'

Then we both hear a low rumble vibrating over the dunes; we look up and see a Land Rover approach with Carla and husband Keith in the front seats. Keith confidently diagnoses the problem as the clutch and predicts that once the oil redistributes evenly throughout the engine all will be tickety-boo in the morning. That's good enough for me. I stagger on foot to the camp and a welcome promise of a cup of tea. All the while I cannot get out of my head what Philip Youles will say if I can't get the bike running tomorrow and have to ring him for help. Our first meeting comes to mind.

'I'm going to Africa next year,' I said. 'On the Tiger.'

'O, aye?' said Philip. 'That's a fair clip.'

'I was wondering if you'd like to help in some way.'

'Which way?'

'Like, in a give-me-some-equipment kind of a way.'

I got a sceptical look.

'Depends what you need.'

'Well, not much... actually, everything. I've got the bike, though.'

'Not much of a start, but it's a start.'

Philip couldn't hide another sceptical look, and said, 'Who knows, anything's possible.'

I took this as a whole-hearted endorsement and, encouraged, stepped into the workshop to have a word with the head mechanic.

'I'm going to Cape Town on the Tiger.'

'Right.'

'Will it make it?' I asked, plainly.

We both looked over at the bike as if the black tank, wide sit-up-and-beg bars, high seat and spoked wheels would somehow give us the answer.

'Well, they're a good bike.' (Good news!) 'Do they have many Triumph dealers over there?'

'Aahh, no, not before Namibia...'

'In southern Africa? If you get there! It might be a bit heavy for off-road. You do know this is mainly a road bike, don't you?' (Bad news!)

I did know it would be a risk taking the Tiger, but it was the bike I had when I made the decision to go and, it being a British bike in the face of BMW's conquest of the 'adventure bike' market, I was stabbed by shards of loyalty and affection for the Triumph. The more people told me to invest in a

German über-machine, the more I resisted. I know, I didn't even convince myself.

'So African roadside make-do-and-mend outfits may be out of their depth if I show up with a sickly Tiger?' I asked tentatively.

'You could say that. Will you be doing much off-roading? Like, through the desert?'

An hour later I'm sitting cross-legged on the floor of the tent watching Bwedra brew up while two more Sahrawis and Carla and Keith all smoke like a fleet of Marrakech taxis. Bwedra is boiling up a pot of tea over hot coals and going to extraordinary lengths to blend, swirl and stir the dark liquid, adding copious amounts of sugar as he goes. He tastes and re-tastes at each pass, adding sugar broken from two misshapen lumps on the tray – each time, a swarm of gorging flies take flight. The ritual continues: pot to glass, glass to pot, pot to glass, glass to glass, glass to pot, taste, until there are six squat soldiers of rich caramel liquid with a deep head of foam on each lined up before him.

By the end of the second glass I am already struggling with the sickly sweet liquid and there's still another to go. The sweetness is making me gag, the tannin is puckering up my gums, and the sour caramel taste makes my eyes water. I am enjoying the ritual and the company but my taste buds cannot lie. Tea in the Sahara.

Carla translates from Bwedra: 'You must drink three glasses of tea: the first is young and strong; the second is not so strong and is beginning to mellow; the third glass is most mellow and is worth waiting for. If you don't drink the third glass it is regarded as extremely rude to your host.'

Actually, even though I put a brave face on it, the tea is getting no better.

The six of us, 77 kilometres from Dakhla in the Western Sahara, the last disputed remnant of Africa's colonial era, drink the tea in the largest of three full-height Sahrawi tents. The cooking tent is spread with overlapping carpets and cluttered with food and clothes. Unfortunately, the smell and grease has attracted a swarm of relentlessly bothersome flies which attach themselves to everything and everyone, although I seem to be the only person concerned by them. The encampment is about one kilometre from the shore, on a tight bay shadowed by a hill on one side with a small boat bobbing on the water. Two of our number are ex-members of the Polisario: Danny, a tacit handyman, and Sharif the fixer who spent six years in jail after falling out with the organisation's top brass. The third Sahrawi, Bwedra the tea maker, had his fingertips blown off when he discovered a landmine as a kid. The bomb was one of many inadvertently found in the cruellest way each year despite the Polisario and Moroccan forces agreeing to a series of disposal operations throughout the area. The problem is that no one knows where they are.

Bwedra deems the third pot of tea now ready. He lifts the pot to shoulder height and pours me the first glass without losing a drop. He hands it to me and I do what anyone in my situation would – I think of all that sand outside the tent and the hundreds of kilometres to the nearest town of any consequence, I sip the tea and politely lie, 'Excellent, the best yet!'

That evening Keith prepares some potent chilli chicken. It is a gesture I appreciate. With the bike crocked and my immediate plans a little uncertain, I could have done a lot worse than spending tonight here. But then again I wouldn't be here at all had I not ambitiously taken my first off-road riding lesson from a jogging man and his dog.

And now I am subjected to Keith's boorish personality – for he is king of the castle, titan of the tents. And don't you forget it. When he's not angrily administering orders around the encampment and has calmed down, he demands everyone's absolute attention when he speaks. He is in the middle of one of his interminable anecdotes when I feel stirrings in my gut. The chilli chicken has already found its way to my bowels and a sharp constriction down below tells me I have to leave the tent, anecdote or no anecdote.

'What do you do for toilets?' I ask.

'Take a long walk.'

I only manage a short walk before I have to squat down. Once I'm leaning over on the dark side of the dune my bowels decide to make the trip worth my while. But what I'd hoped would be a short shit and sharp return to the tent soon turns into a crap of major proportions. And very welcome it is too as for some reason I have not managed a bowel movement in some days. Now the aperient chilli chicken is living up to its name. The meagre supply of loo roll I have stuffed in my pocket is soon used and flutters down the dune as the liquid methane pours out of me. I am joined by the encampment dog standing at the top of the dune. Rather than bark furiously at me, as it has done throughout the evening, it stares at the recent insides of my bowels with an expression of some concern, then laps at it.

My physical relief is short-lived, however, as I look back with the light of my torch to see I have pebble-dashed my pale khaki trousers with the noxious substance. I can hardly breathe with the effort it takes to remain upright on the steep dune and in my annoyance I lose my footing and step back into what is now the dog's dinner. *O shit.*

I'm in a God-awful mess. The one pair of underwear I possess (already dirty after many days of wear) and my other trousers are back in the tent. What the fuck do I do now? I just want to step into a shower and throw away the shitty trousers and shoes, but I have to go back into the tent and make conversation with my new desert friends, who by all indications have settled in for a long night. But it's going to seem much longer to me.

The next morning, dehydrated and empty, with an arse on me I wouldn't wish on my worst enema, I prepare to head for Mauritania. Carla gives me her cellphone number and waves me goodbye. I let the tyres down to aid grip in the sand, then set off to the road which I manage in twenty minutes or so. On the Tea Encounter advice of Bill Beaumont in Lytham ('Take a puncture repair kit'), I have a small twelve-volt pump about which I feel very smug as I set about re-inflating the tyres. But now the first time I use it, it dies. What Bill meant to say was 'Take a puncture repair kit that works.' In any case, the clutch is fried – it is anything *but* tickety-boo. I can only manage 15 kph – downhill – so I swear some kind of generic revenge on the machine and after ten minutes pull in to a shambolic roadside settlement. I have travelled only two kilometres down the road.

El Garoub is the village equivalent of the 24/24: an almighty dump. But the string of down-at-heel dwellings in every stage of decay has some compensations, including a butcher who cooks me a demi-kilo of goat before joining me for tea. He pours direct from his own teapot sitting on the counter and, despite speaking no English, wants to start a one-way conversation. I imagine him saying, 'I can see you need a bit of help; here's a glass of tea'; 'You're not having the best day of your life, are you? Have a glass of tea'; 'Let me tell you where the nearest Triumph dealer is located – have some tea.'

Apart from the trickle of trucks that stop, there is a gang of orange Mercedes parked up, 1970s saloons, taxis all. Occasionally, one leaves and soon returns. Where did it go? There is no other life for many miles. The *adhan* calls at one o'clock and again at four, to which the faithful respond, scuffing along in sandals and flip-flops towards the breezeblock mosque to pray. For customers? For rain? For a lotto win?

I call Carla from one of the kiosks and she rescues me from El Garoub at five o'clock that evening. We leave the bike in a tiny kiosk shop and take the Landy back to the encampment.

After three days I am still looking for someone to repair the clutch and have to spend a lot of time with my hosts. Carla is sweet, but Keith, who has the personality of a small child – who chain smokes – will not leave me alone for more than a couple of minutes at a stretch. If I exit the tent, mostly to escape the smoke and the flies, he follows me, talking incessantly. Here is a classic Keith interaction:

Keith: What are your hobbies?
Me: I don't really have hobbies.
Keith: You do stuff; what kind of stuff do you do?

Me: Well…

Keith: Motorbikes, you like bikes, right?

Me: Yes, among other things.

Keith: Ask me what my hobby is.

(Smoking in people's faces and boring the pants off them?)

Me: What's your hobby, Keith?

Keith: Catching lizards.

(My head is spinning and I want to laugh.)

Me: And what do you do with them once you catch the lizards, Keith?

Keith: Carla photographs them. You've got to find their hole in the sand, position the Land Rover over the hole, put it in neutral and rev like fuck. They think it's an earthquake, poke their heads out of the hole and you grab the fuckers by the neck.

('Beat that' is engraved into his boyish expression of satisfaction.)

Eventually a truck is sent from Dakhla to pick up the Triumph. Helpfully, the whole community of El Garoub comes out to lift the bike onto the back, but maybe they are just pleased to see me go; after three days sitting and waiting and taking up space in the kiosk I've probably outstayed my welcome. Ropes are tied and we're off to repair the bike in Dakhla, what I whimsically hope will be the City of Bike Repair Shops.

The truck driver takes me to a strangely charismatic nephew of Sharif the fixer bedecked in gorgeous blue robes who takes it upon himself to find someone to work on the clutch. At the fourth tiny workshop we visit, the nephew deems himself satisfied. He explains the problem to the mechanic as if pronouncing a royal decree, then gets back in his Mercedes and disappears. I don't fully know what's going on. Sharif the fixer shows up and I ask him to translate, which doesn't shed an awful lot more light on the matter, so I use his phone to call Keith back at the encampment.

'Let him have a go at fixing it,' Keith says with certainty in his voice. 'You've got nothing to lose. If he can't manage it you can call for new parts from Britain on Monday.'

I turn back to the bike with Keith still holding on the line to see the Triumph's clutch cover on the floor of the workshop surrounded by all the bolts and springs and the oil draining away into a gutter.

'I guess he's got the job.'

I spend the following day with Sharif, who has a stonking hangover after staying up until the small hours helping some fishermen polish off three litres of rum and whiskey. These guys are professional drinkers, but Sharif is not used to alcohol and it shows this morning; he's still rat-arsed. Nobody at the camp has any credit in their phone so I cannot even call the Charismatic One in the blue robes for news about the bike in town. I feel helpless and more than a little concerned about my onward progress on the African Brew Ha-Ha. I'm only three weeks in, and although there has been a fair amount of brew, there's been precious little ha ha.

At four o'clock Sharif unexpectedly gets a call, which stirs him from his hurting hangover. He learns that the bike is waiting to be picked up. The bike is repaired? New clutch plates have been re-fashioned and replaced within twenty-four hours? I am so overjoyed I give Sharif an impulsive hug, but in return I get a look that says 'something more useful than a hug would be welcome' – like hard cash perhaps, or some Alka-Seltzer.

Keith takes me in the Landy to the workshop in Dakhla, where the mechanic asks for 700 dirhams, which, after working it out on my fingers a couple of times, equates to around forty-seven euros. I hand over the money gratefully, without negotiation. Happily mobile once more, I find a phone kiosk to call home, then look for something to eat. I'm so hungry I could eat a goat. Then I update the blog, which I started nine months ago to log all my Tea Encounters. I see it is getting plenty of hits and I open emails from people I have never met before wishing me luck.

The night is overcast and misty so I take it slowly on the tarmac road back towards camp. I unavoidably break my rule of not riding in the dark yet again and I nearly pay for my folly when I almost get wiped out by an oncoming truck that is overtaking a slower vehicle. Against every instinct in my body I stop at the 24/24 after midnight to park the bike until morning. I am curious to notice some vehicles on the forecourt with British number plates who appear to be on a Plymouth to Banjul fundraising run, a kind of old banger desert challenge. I'm sure Carla mentioned they are her paying guests due tomorrow. But the malevolent presence of Hamdi is there and after a silent acknowledgement of each other I trudge off into the blackness. I have a small torch which spreads an arc of light little better than useless, so I have to find my way by instinct. In the desert. At night. It's ridiculous. I trudge up and down dunes, over tracks and into deep sand and soon lose my way. After an hour of this I head for the beach and then walk south in the hope of spotting the storm lanterns at the encampment, but no chance. It is half past one when I stumble across the darkened, silent camp, soaked in sweat and with feet sopping from the incoming tide. I really must invest in a compass.

In the morning Carla takes me in the Landy up to the 24/24 to collect the bike. As we arrive the dozen fundraisers pull out after spending the night inside the shithouse petrol station. Hamdi looks as if he has just picked someone's pocket.

Carla sees red.

'Hamdi! I don't believe this! These were *our* guests. We needed that money and you knew they were coming to us! Wait until Keith finds out they spent the night here!'

My assessment of Hamdi's character has proved to be correct, but I don't get involved. I load up and get on my way to the frontier.

4
THE LAST MAN
ON EARTH

*There are more good people in the
world than there are bad.*
Hazel Harding

The first thing I do in Mauritania, or more accurately in no-man's land before I enter the country, is fall over. Rather too conveniently someone comes along as I'm trying to extricate my foot from under the beast and offers to guide me through to Mauritania for thirty euros. While I admire his entrepreneurial approach, not to mention his timing, I politely decline. At least he is good enough to lift the bike off me.

I spend a night in Nouadhibou, a busy port with a harbour like a ship's graveyard which is, rather incongruously, full of Korean crew darting in and out of Chinese restaurants, while every other local is squatting on the roadside brewing tea on a tiny stove, stirring and pouring, sipping and sharing.

Mauritania has endured more than its fair share of authoritarian rule since independence in 1960, before finally holding the first fully democratic presidential elections since that time just seven months before my arrival there. This poor desert nation, four times the size of Britain, is an unforgiving home to barely four million people scratching a living on the surface of the sun. Or so it seems.

I continue south towards the capital, Nouakchott, about 400 kilometres further on. The road is like a halogen hob, smooth and searing, the implausible heat reflecting off the tarmac. This is one of the hottest days yet. The drone of the engine and the blast of the wind have a hypnotic effect on me, and the constant squint into the sun is engraved so permanently on my face that my aching muscles scream for me to close my eyelids. I give in to the aberrant thought by testing how long I can shut my eyes without drifting to the edge of the road. Three seconds, OPEN. Four seconds, OPEN. Five, six seconds, OPEN. God, this has got to stop.

For mile after repetitive mile there is no shade, no life anywhere, not even a spiny tree to make it worth the stop, just the now-familiar mesmerising trio of blue sky, beige sand and black tarmac. I'm exhausted, my head is burning from the sulphurous atmosphere inside the helmet, and I'm shedding weight by the minute in vaporous sweat. After a passage of floating time, which could be twenty minutes or an hour and a half, I notice a small shack close to the road in the middle distance. As I get closer I see a raggedy tent nearby and some fish hanging absurdly on a washing line. The curious sight shakes me from my dreamlike state and I let go of the throttle.

I park up close to the shack and step inside. Within, there is a man and two children; the man, wearing calf-length trousers and a loose shirt tied at the front with a single button, barely nods at my arrival; the children, squatting on the ground in no more than rags, look up at me with watchful eyes. The sensation of being off the bike suddenly hits me in a wave of vertigo, and I become aware of the silence; silence except for the low hush of the gritty wind.

The primitive structure serves as a shop selling just five items: bottled water, dried fish, matches, torches and, rather bizarrely, three flavours of custard creams – orange, lemon and strawberry. The emptiness of the hundreds of kilometres of desert I have ridden through today catches up with me and the sight of the man almost makes me want to hug him. We look at each other as if we are the last two men on earth. What do you say to the last man on earth? There is nothing *to* say. I buy a bottle of water and offer to share the last of my food with him: an apple. He takes half and peels it clean, dropping the peel on the ground before eating the flesh noisily. I give the children a Fox's Glacier Mint each and have one myself, but for some reason their father takes the sweets off the kids and hands them back to me silently. Maybe they're not halal.

I squat down on my haunches. It is just me and him and the two silent children in the tiny shack with not another soul for miles, seemingly fighting against insignificance. I step outside the shack, careful to stay in the shade, and squint to the dazzling horizon full of emptiness, then look back inside and try to calibrate the vastness of the Sahara with life in the shack. It is an impossibly breathtaking moment. I instantly feel I have taken a great step away from my life back home. Tethers are being cut. At this moment in time, at this juncture of my own personal history on this earth, there is nothing more than this. This is my entire life, my life on the road, and it is wonderful.

I try to imagine what the life of this silent, suspicious man must be like, the constant gusting an immutable companion while the occasional trucker, I guess, stops by for a packet of custard creams to make his day. But what are this man's ambitions, his hopes, dreams? What does his family think of living this close to the edge of nothing? Where the hell is the nearest cash and carry? But we all make big lives out of small lives. This man has a life. He has loved ones; what more is there to strive for?

I leave the family in their stillness and drink the water up against the side of the shack. I'm thankful for the shade, a tangible thing here; it is not a negative – 'out of the sun' – but a positive life-saving condition, something to celebrate.

This brief stop is too extraordinary to comprehend, so much so that my brain does not have a folder to file the information. So the hard drive deals with it the best way it knows how. It closes down. Reboot. I have to get back on the bike.

'*Merci beaucoup. Au revoir*,' I say softly.

The father nods almost imperceptibly and follows me out of the shop. I think he'll be happier with me off the premises. The family allow themselves a shy gaze at the bike as I put on my jacket and helmet and fire the ignition. I get a mind's-eye glimpse of how I must look to them: who the hell would go out in this heat in the middle of the day? The man in the black suit. The fifteen-minute stop is disorienting and I leave knowing I have to focus on something beyond this nothingness to pull me out of here. I put all my hopes of the future in Nouakchott, City of Light. Well, it's worth a shot.

Nouakchott is a mess. It is my first impression as I arrive at day's end and it is my last. After the dreamlike ride through the desert, the town is a blast of dirty realism – shops spilling out onto sandy streets, ramshackle bars and restaurants, barely drivable cars, decrepit vans with the sides punched out used as taxis, reluctant donkeys used for everything else and indiscriminately beaten with pieces of timber. There seems to be no order to the traffic; if a space exists which offers a route past the vehicle in front, it will be taken – down alleys, between stalls, alongside parked cars, past men squatting next to their tea. And all the time people mingle amongst the traffic in folded robes and turbans, masked against the blasting sand.

Since arriving on the continent a few weeks ago, I have been curious to discover where the Arab lands end and black Africa begins. I think I have found it in Nouakchott, a capital city I had not heard of before this trip. Although the first few days in Morocco were heady with the excitement of having arrived in Africa, no Moroccans I spoke to regarded themselves as 'African' at all. 'I am not African, I am Arab,' they would declare, 'look at my skin.' Things are not so clear-cut in Nouakchott, with a mixture of skin colours and textures, an assortment of costumes and colours, and local versions of Islam, Christianity and animism.

I have always thought of Africa as the whole continent, that sensuous atlas-bound silhouette, a place of mystery – containable and a place apart. But the idea that Africa is one culture, one notion, is a Western concept that lumps the hundreds of languages and cultures into one catch-all term: African.

I go to a welcoming hotel filled with other Europeans, air conditioning – a first – and some English spoken. In the evening I go into town for a ludicrously expensive beer surreptitiously served from beneath the counter – Mauritania, ostensibly, is dry. I stumble upon a Rotary Club whose members tell me about their charitable efforts to alleviate the overwhelming social needs of the country. Poverty, disease, poor health and homelessness head the distressing list of projects they support. After an hour, I return to my hotel with an invitation to tea and dinner tomorrow. It's a friendly place, Mauritania.

Next day, on the way to tea, I pull up at a roadside repair shop that opens directly onto a fearsomely congested roundabout, which if nothing else must be good for passing trade, it being permanently gridlocked with donkeys and carts and whacked-out taxis. How they don't all smack into each other seems curious. I have come here to repair a niggling problem on the bike but there's no way they can sort the fault; I've got more tools under the pillion seat than in the whole workshop.

The onslaught of traffic is squeezing me into a corner and I sense this is going to end badly. I sit on the bike and roll it backwards onto the roadway and am suddenly engulfed by donkeys and carts racing for my tiny piece of ground. Most handlers convince their animals to make a last-minute swerve ('Heh! Heh! Heh! Heh!') except for one. I am still stationary, I haven't even moved away from the kerb yet, then *OOOMPH*: I find myself on the ground under the bike. The cart doesn't stop but pushes its way directly over the back tyre. My leg is trapped and I'm yelling to get the bike the fuck off me as the donkey works its way over my machine. I somehow manage to wriggle my boot out, which is twisted horribly.

I'm now hopping around on one foot in agony, waving my arms in the air. Six people immediately try to help by dragging the bike along the roadway for some reason. Yelling at the top of my voice at this point will, I feel, not only calm the situation but also make me feel an awful lot better.

'SHIT, MY FOOT! LEAVE MY BIKE ALONE!!!'

Everyone in the crowd, which has instantly swelled to around thirty onlookers, takes a big step back. Limping around, I decide now is the time to swear at the donkey handler and his bemused family sitting alongside. He looks at me with absolutely no expression on his face whatsoever. He respectfully waits for me to finish my rant, then turns around, whips the donkey into motion and disappears into the dust and fumes.

When I get enough movement back in my foot to change gear, I ride to the Cabinet Dentaire Ramadan for my Tea Encounter arranged yesterday at the Rotary Club. My search to find the cusp of black Africa has ended with my arrival at the dental surgery of Dr Doudou Yahya.

'My father is black, my mother white,' Dr Yahya says. 'I am mix. I speak Wolof for my father and Arabic for my mother. There are many languages here in Nouakchott; many white people [Arabs] come from the north and blacks come from the south. It is good mix; my wife is from Côte d'Ivoire and is Catholic, so I see both sides. There is a Hassaniyan proverb: 'The more languages you speak the more people you are.'

Dr Yahya calls for an employee to bring tea, which arrives sharply. It is sour and served in tiny shot glasses. We are soon brought a second pot and Dr Yahya jokes that if I don't drink the third I will have to pay ('It is custom!'). But as the saying goes, 'The tea cannot be bad where the company is agreeable,' and so it is with Dr Yahya; he is a terrific host.

To supplement his Wolof and Arabic, Dr Yahya also speaks Fula, French, English and Russian, this last because as a student he benefited from a medical scholarship in Moscow.

'After training I went to Paris and then I return to Mauritania because it is easier to make contact with people here. It is too difficult in Europe to make easy contact, you understand?'

Yes, I do.

He gathers up his *boubou*, or blue robes, and takes me on a tour of his surgery, which is remarkable only for two things: for the tiny prayer room just large enough for one person, and for how similar it is to my own dentist's in Lancashire.

With his robes billowing like a sail, we stand on the first-floor balcony that overlooks the city (which doesn't look any better from up here).

'This is Nouakchott,' he says, looking out over the rusting corrugated rooftops, 'I have come home, yes.'

I guess it's a place that grows on you.

Dr Yahya arranges to meet me later in the evening and returns to his appointments. I take advantage of the free afternoon to browse a street market for some new underwear but the best I can find is a three-pack of posing briefs. They're so petite they would embarrass a transvestite on a Gay Pride float. I feel self-conscious just wearing them under my trousers.

That evening Dr Yahya picks me up from my hotel in his battered Toyota.

'You are a guest in my home tonight – do not worry I will return you!'

I am introduced to Mrs Yahya, an attractive, light-skinned woman who shyly bustles in the kitchen with her mother. She has recently had twins who doze on the table beside her.

Dr Yahya and I sit in his backyard under a flowering tree at a table set for two.

'We are strange people in Mauritania,' he says, 'Although we have the houses we like to live outside, so we have a tent in the garden to remind us of what it is like in the open.'

'Would you like beer? We buy it from the French embassy. We are not supposed to drink alcohol but people do. Tea will come; don't worry, you will have your tea. Do you know we drink so much tea in Mauritania? All the time we have the tea. Do you drink tea in England?'

'I thought the British drank a lot of tea but maybe not as much as Mauritanians,' I say.

It is true. I have never seen a country so dependent on the ritual. Tea here is served in tiny glasses with a frothy head, and it is a common sight to see men hunkered down on the street brewing their tea on hot coals all day, every day.

With a European at his table, Dr Yahya is keen to talk about the big issues.

'Things are very difficult here now,' he says. 'Many peoples are coming from the south and there is no jobs. Many peoples they leave when we have the coup, for Mali or Senegal or Algeria. They come back now, but to where? To what? There will be a big explosion, I think. Soon, in one year or two years, I think, another coup. This is a very rich country. Now we have the oil, the gold, the fish, but where is it, the money? The government take it. Also we have much money from the

EU which is to help the people but they see none of it. The military are very rich. They all have villas in *España*, it is true.'

One of Dr Yahya's sons brings two plates of chicken and couscous to the table.

'We have elections, it is true,' he continues, tearing at a chicken leg, 'but we have not democracy like you have in England. There is black and white here but only two blacks in the government. There will be a big explosion, I think. But we cannot have people disappear now with the Internet, I think. There are no secrets, nothing can be hidden. It is not like before.'

Dr Yahya is very well informed about world events and paints an engaging picture of life in Nouakchott. Maybe I have judged it too harshly. But his prognosis on the political health of the country is quite pessimistic, and I sense he is only talking so frankly because I am European. To speak so openly with other Mauritanians would be unwise.

After he recites to me a poem which compares a glass of tea to a beautiful woman, we end the evening with a pot of our own – sweet, dark and persuasive.

'I will translate the poem to English and send to you. It will take me some time but you will appreciate it.'

Dr Yahya has been a model host and his welcome a reminder of the power of the tea ritual. I finish the glass and gratefully accept his advice about the road ahead towards Senegal. Before I leave, he makes a telephone call to someone who he says should ease my passage through the border control.

'Be watchful. The frontier is full of trouble!'

On the third day in Mauritania I ride the 200 kilometres or so to the Senegal border. It is an uneventful stretch of road, apart from being searched at gunpoint by two overexcited teenagers in fatigues and reflective shades who take a close interest in my shortwave radio and shoes. I'm not sure the tan Timberlands would have coordinated with the military look.

As if to signal a new country, the landscape changes dramatically about fifty kilometres before the frontier; now luxuriant greens line the road, a visual delight after the days spent in the desert. The sight of a flowering tree for the first time in an age is a thrill.

At PK5, the five-kilometre checkpoint before the frontier at Rosso, an older police officer who employs an intimidating tactic of nose-to-nose interrogation insists I tell him my Christian name rather than the usual *'nationalité, profession, destination?'* The question throws me.

It takes a while before he asks, 'Mister Alan?'

'Yes.'

He takes my hand and beams a knowing smile.

'Doctor Yahya is my friend, yes. He call the phone. You take ferry over river, yes?'

I feel relieved enough to get off the bike, remove my helmet and readjust the straps and bungees on my gear, which is looking more like the chattels of a refugee with each passing mile. He takes my passport, driver's licence and bike documentation as a car screeches to a halt beside him.

'I go now,' he says and leaps into the Mercedes, which speeds off with him and all my papers. I gather my things and give chase.

Rosso is in chaos. There's a crush of hundreds of people arriving or preparing to leave with their meagre belongings on their heads or in sheets and plastic bags over their shoulders. The police chief is already deep in the throng waving my papers above his head indicating for me to follow. I push my way through, nudging the crowd gently with the front wheel and the panniers on either side. Nobody wants to give up their place, but they have little choice, and when I get an earful of abuse I point to the police chief apologetically. The chief tells me to park at a precise spot while he goes into the *poste de contrôle*. I get off the bike and head for some shade. One of the many touts and hustlers attaches himself to me, but I'm not sure if he is here on the instructions of the police chief who is now signalling from a first-floor balcony.

'Mister Alan, here!'

I have to trust the tout to watch my gear, which is rather conspicuous among the rag-tag crowd, while I go up to the office, jumping a queue of people stretching down the stairs. A senior officer hands me a two-page form. There is not a word of English on it, but my chief puckers his lips and nods reassuringly. I sign the bottom.

On the way back down the stairs the chief itemises for me all the charges for the police, the *douanes*, the ferry and border post and says, 'I pay to save time.'

But I'm not sure about this; I feel as though my fears about border post bribery are about to be realised. When I return to the bike it is deluged in a sea of people who are all rather too interested in my gear. I get back on the bike and nudge my way up to the ferry ramp.

I am through all border formalities in twenty minutes and the receipts I have thrust into my hand show it has cost me 9,500 ouguiya – exactly what the police chief paid. My suspicions prove to be groundless.

'Doctor Yahya, he ask me look after you. Everything is good for you?'

'Brilliant. Thanks.'

And I mean it. 'There are more good people in the world than there are bad,' as Hazel Harding advised in Preston on an early Tea Encounter. And a lot of them are in Mauritania.

I ride on to the ferry with the tout who has now become my minder in tow to the Senegalese formalities on the other side of the river.

The ferry is thirty minutes of relative calm, and I'm pleased to be leaving the grim environment of the Mauritanian border behind. But as soon as I disembark I realise I had it easy on the other side. There are hundreds of people moving in all directions, touts, hangers-on, mendicants and money-changers in a locked, dusty compound with a chain of dilapidated buildings that I suppose must be the border control. As soon as I get rid of one parasitic chancer another attaches himself to me. The temperature reaches oppressive levels as it approaches midday; the sun burns me up as I fight my way to the front of every queue. It's every man for himself. My minder tries to yell louder than the other thirty people pushing and shoving their way to the first barred window and waving some piece of documentation that needs stamping as if it was the one great necessity of their lives. It's mayhem. In comparison to the pandemonium, the attitude of the officials is one of complete and utter apathy. The man at the window takes my passport, throws it onto a pile of others on his desk and wanders off aimlessly. I manage to grab it back through the grill and find a door into the office, which we enter to engage somebody on a more personal level. The British passport raises a certain amount of interest in one of the uniformed men who is stretched out with his feet on the desk.

I tell my minder, 'Watch where he takes my passport. *Don't lose sight of him.*'

He gets the message that I'm rattled and don't want any cock-ups. While we wait, I change some dollars into local currency from a sinister-looking money-changer with a greasy, Fagin-like demeanour and tiny piercing eyes. Despite my own unwashed condition, I barely want to handle the money that his fingers have touched.

Fifteen minutes later my passport is handed back over the heads of the crowd at the grill. I check to make sure there is a stamp of some kind in it and we rush to another building.

A small man behind a big desk (a heart-sinking combination in a uniformed official) reacts like I'm bringing a birthday present when he sees his prey enter his office.

'*Assurance!*' he says to me.

'I don't want *assurance*. I don't need it.'

I show him my British motor insurance certificate in the vain hope that he will waive me through.

'*Assurance!*' he repeats with some finality.

'*Combien?*' I ask (the most disheartening word in the French language), with growing frustration.

I can almost see the floating dollar bills in his eyes. He takes out a calculator on which he does some meaningless calculations and pushes it across the desk: the read-out shows 70.

'Dollars,' he says, 'YOO-ESS,' in case there's any misunderstanding. Well, it would be, wouldn't it?

'No way. I don't have it, and anyway I don't need it,' I say, exasperated.

I wonder if he's taken into consideration my no-claims discount?

'Assurance est obligatoire!'

I've met my match in this guy. I dig into my pocket and pull out a fifty-dollar bill with some Mauritanian coins.

'Is OK!' he says once he sees the colour of my money, and snatches it out of my hand. He gives me the hand-written insurance document and I leave the office with the sensation that I've just been mugged.

Outside I am besieged by more money-changers and touts and people trying to sell me indispensable items such as groundnuts or cellphone cards, or standing in my way until I have to raise my voice to get rid of them. The inconceivable heat added to the friction of hundreds of people rubbing up against each other in the tight compound brings the atmosphere to a steady boil.

'Where to next?' I ask my minder.

'Douanes.'

The relatively calm environment of the customs office is so tranquil somebody in uniform is taking a nap on a mattress in the middle of the floor. The only sound is the clack-clack of worried-looking men tapping at battered typewriters or scratching at carbon-papered forms. It is like stepping back in time. I'm in and out quick enough.

Thinking I must be finished with the formalities, I prepare to leave for St Louis.

But then I am approached by a young man who holds out his palm and says, 'Three thousand!'

'And what's that for?' I ask.

'I open gate.'

I want to laugh in his face. I glance over to the huge battered and bolted metal exit gate with a large rock leaning against it that is my road to freedom. My minder doesn't want to tackle this one, so he takes a meaningful step back with a look on his face that I interpret as 'I don't think you have much choice.'

'I open gate but gate lock in ten *minoots*,' the guy says triumphantly.

I look at my watch, which shows ten to twelve. 'And what time does it open again?'

'*Quinze heures.*'

So the choice is clear: pay the three thousand – about £3 – for someone to slide the bolt on the gate and kick away the rock or stay in this dump for another three hours. And what is it worth not to have to do that? A lot more than three thousand, and all three of us know it.

Everything inside me wants to get this place behind me, so I pay up. I finally prepare to leave when another young man walks up to me and insists on a further three thousand to open the gate. I lose it. Be polite to the locals, I think, my arse.

'I DON'T HAVE ANY MORE MONEY!' I scream at the top of my voice so that as many people in the compound as possible can hear me.

'CAN EVERYBODY HEAR ME? CAN *YOU* HEAR ME?' I shout in the guy's face. 'I'm not paying you a penny, just open the fucking gate and *let me out of here!*'

He remonstrates with me and says if I don't pay the gate stays closed.

I employ the jabbing finger technique: 'THE OTHER GUY IS OPENING THE GATE, *YOU CAN FUCK OFF!*'

I don't have anything more cogent to say than that. I realise my diplomatic skills are deserting me, but my mind is frazzled. I look around, but the first gatekeeper has disappeared with my three thousand francs. I feel ridiculous.

There is a stand-off until, nine *minoots* later, the original gate man returns and hurries me out as the compound is about to be locked.

'Which way to St Louis?' I ask.

It sounds absurd once the words are out of my mouth and my question is met with a large slice of derision: 'There is only one road, *mon ami*. Follow it!'

I'm out, and hear the bolt slide shut behind me. It's cost me a small fortune and a hell of a lot of sweat and aggravation, but I'm finally in Senegal. But officialdom is not through with me yet. A mile up the road I am stopped by drugs officers who rifle through all my things and rather unsubtly ask for 'something for us, something for your security'. But all they get is my best look of disdain; I pack up all my gear that is now strewn over the road and leave for St Louis, a hundred kilometres south.

Having moved out of the tea-addicted Mauritania, I pull up in a village after an hour to buy what is fast becoming the alternative taste of Africa – a bottle of Fanta – and the only edible thing in a larder-sized shop, a packet of coconut biscuits. A group of children follow me in to the shop and then out again asking a blizzard of franglais questions about the bike, my clothing, my sunburn, my home, the position of Arsenal in the league. Adults are a little less effusive, but not much. Self-assured women dressed in Western clothes or colourful West African costumes create hubbub amongst idle men. A simple returned gaze tells me the culture has changed.

Sitting on a bench outside the shop, I congratulate myself on reaching black Africa from Lancashire in less than four weeks. As if to emphasise the fact, the children chant 'white man, white man' in an improvised dedication. I suppose this little scene is what I had in mind when I left Britain. Place names in Africa ahead of me – Tombouctou (or Timbuktu, as I've always known it), Ouagadougou, Congo – now seem to radiate off the map.

As I was planning the trip, people gasped at the proposed mileage but my hunch at the time was that the riding was going to be easier than dealing with officialdom – arranging visas, the *carnet de passage* (the temporary import licence, a kind of passport for the bike) and negotiating borders being the most important. Remaining confident about my own abilities was another concern, as talking about the trip to others rarely left me more optimistic about the task ahead. Almost everybody I met questioned the wisdom of riding solo through Africa: 'Fifteen thousand miles – on your own?' 'Are you bringing a gun?' 'I hope you have a comfy seat!'

But sitting here in this friendly village with a Fanta in one hand and a stale biscuit in the other, I don't have any misgivings about coming to this place, nor a single doubt in the world about finishing this quest.

5
THE BEATING HEART OF WEST AFRICA

The smallest things can make the biggest difference to people's lives.
George Bokari

The following day I ride about 250 kilometres to Dakar, the capital of Senegal, to apply for an onward visa. The air in the dusty, smoggy city is charged with tension. At night, the streets turn sinister. When I leave the hotel after dark, the jumpy guard checks the first corner for muggers before he quickly waves me on. Later, afraid to walk the 500 metres back to the hotel, I get into a taxi with a 'minder' who insists on taking me anywhere but where I want to go. After some yelling and edgy negotiation for a fee I am released back into the night.

Since arriving in Africa, I have been sober. In fact, disgustingly so. But that all changes in Dakar. Despite the nocturnal anxiety, on the second night I pal up with Chris, another motorcycling Brit and a welcome drinking partner for the night. We find a heaving club and look forward to a night off. Chris, half my age and with eyes agog, shouts above the sound of the band, 'I don't know what to make of this music. It's weird!'

I shout, '*Deux bières*' to a passing waitress.

Regally, the singer sits erect with his sleepy eyes surveying the crowd as he sings his stories in Wolof, the most popular African language in Senegal. The sounds of the instruments are foreign but seductive to my ears. The multi-rhythms of the band weave through the crowd while the singer's voice, authoritative and knowing, mesmerises us all. Occasionally he is amused by his own inventiveness and that of the respectful musicians behind, who play a mixture of modern and traditional instruments. He purposefully rearranges his heavy blue robes which must be hot under the glare of the lights; he moves little, sitting on a hard high-backed chair. We are in his grasp and he knows it, this charismatic man of pensionable age. He invites a younger singer to join him, one twice the older man's size and half his age. The singer's voice soars, and the effortless sound coming from his throat is powerful and startling. The new pretender, probably an acolyte of the older man, is now coming into his own and will soon perhaps assume his teacher's mantle, but for now he leans protectively over the chair, careful not to steal too much of the limelight.

The beer and the music hit those places in me that have been neglected over the past few weeks: that part that does not want to reason, justify or rationalise, that does not want to move or make a decision of any kind. It is enough that my capacity for enjoyment is being met by booze and this gorgeous rhythm.

'Deux bières...'

The club is crowded with attractive young Dakarites, young women with exotic hairstyles and shop-new costumes, the vibrant colours radiant against their glossy black skin. The revelation of seeing women dressing to please the eye after the anonymity of North Africa is visceral. The women are fragrant and are not afraid of men. They gaze at men, and allow their curvaceous and perfect bodies to be gazed upon. The men wear tight new T-shirts to emphasise their physique or baggy shirts to disguise it; there are elaborate belts designed to focus attention below the waist, sunglasses wedged on heads and shiny cellphones glued to bejewelled ears.

The few Europeans in the club look awkward, underdressed and in awe. We want to emulate them, to be African for tonight, to assimilate and feel the rhythm, and become intoxicated by the atmosphere as they are.

The waitresses, all dressed identically in white T-shirts and black trousers, have their hair brushed back, revealing the high forehead characteristic of this part of West Africa. But each has distinguished herself with a unique hairstyle, an intricate crowning creation. At each pass the waitresses observe the amazement in my face; they smile and throw a knowing look that says, 'This is how we play here, stranger, but you are welcome.'

'Deux bières...'

The singer ends his set with a beguiling smile and modestly acknowledges appreciative applause from other musicians sitting at the bar. He stands, rearranges his robes one last time and exits stage right.

Stage left there is a large group of men in a variety of outfits from business suits to Cuban shirts, robes to Rastafarian.

With a combined age that must be approaching 800, and with no discernible leader amongst them, they take their places on the stage in ones and twos without any apparent sense of purpose. They pick up their instruments casually and within a single backbeat music emanates from them effortlessly, gathering steam, building into a rhythmic train onto which each musician soon finds his way.

The players join and leave the stage as their mood takes them. One, the tenor sax player, cannot find room on the low dais so remains on the dance floor blowing and dancing with the crowd, egging them on. He is not fully mic'd so the crowd either gets an earful close up or can barely hear him at all. But we all see him with his hat pulled down over his ears, mugging for imaginary cameras; he is a star.

'*Deux bières...*'

The band is moving in all directions now – their actions take over the club: the guitar player wants to take a cigarette break so the bass player from the previous band takes over mid-song; one leaves his guitar and visits the toilet behind the stage, returns, lights up and continues in the fray; the sax player wants another drink and, without interrupting his solo, walks to the bar and orders a cocktail; the singer jumps off the stage to welcome some friends who have entered the club and returns to finish the song before he is missed. There are twelve people on the stage now creating a joyous sound, some playing, some not, some clearly learning the song as they go, some with eyes closed, captivated by their own music.

A vocalist who has been loudly entertaining a large group at the bar uses the commotion to make an entrance. His appearance prompts a new groove which fills the floor;

waitresses now have to dance their way through the crowd to reach their customers at the far side of the club.

Dance? I would if I could stand up and make some sense of these two feet. I ignore the voice of reason in my head and stagger across the floor which by now feels like the deck of a moving ship and ask a beautiful woman to join me on the floor. I have a second in which I imagine she says 'What kept you?' but instead she snubs me with such precision that I almost enjoy it. I remain swaying in front of her for a second or two to give her a chance to change her mind before I admit defeat and weave my way back to my seat holding on to the backs of chairs.

'Fuck it… *Deux bières…*'

The older singer from the previous band is invited up to accompany the groovers on a traditional Senegalese tune and proudly enjoys the power of the big band now backing him. The four singers and each musician have found their own rhythmic pocket as they hit an irresistible groove, and the gorgeous, muscular sound is soaked up by the dancers and drifts sweating out into the sweltering Dakar night. We are all lost in the sublime moment; it is three o'clock and the club has become one writhing body. Stay for a little longer, put off the inevitable, stretch the night and the music to breaking point. The time is now. I have found the beating heart of West Africa, and I don't want to be anywhere else.

In apparent sympathy with my delicious hangover the next day, the Senegal/Gambia frontier, compared to the Rosso border, is fairly stress free. Mind you, the entrance to the gates of hell would be stress free compared to Rosso. After fending off customs officers who want my radio and the drug search squad insisting on the usual 'gift for your security', I ride the dirt road through bush lands to the river Gambia and buy a 30p ticket for the crowded ferry to Banjul, the capital of The Gambia.

It's 1 November 2007, the African Brew Ha-Ha's one-month anniversary, and what a month: the excitement of arriving in Africa, the splendour of Morocco, my first profound experiences in the desert, a fried clutch in the Western Sahara, my passage through the gates of hell, the fizzing voltage of Dakar, being run over by a donkey (... that one's not really a highlight). And already some memorable Tea Encounters, and hopefully more to come.

Sitting at a pavement café in Banjul I am greeted by almost everyone who walks by, many stopping to pass the time of day, enquire after my well-being, share a joke or try out some English colloquialisms. Here comes an elegantly robed middle-aged man – 'Having tea?' – and two older men who cross the road to see me – 'Very nice to meet you' – and now a young man, who bows politely, in Western clothing sitting at another table – 'It's a lovely day.'

On the second evening in Banjul it is hot and humid enough to bring on a sweat without doing too much, so I order some tea and enjoy the comings and goings on the wide boulevard. The avenue has raised pavements on either side with the 'Arch 22' at the bottom acting as the full stop to the exclamation mark of Independence Drive. As traffic is prevented from driving underneath the arch, all the vehicles heading for Serekunda have to negotiate a tricky unmade road which is barely wide enough for two cars to pass. It is an ignominious end to the grand avenue lined with trees weighed down by purple, cerise and orange blossom.

The scene from the café table is a tableau of African idiosyncrasies: men in ragged robes who speak perfect English ask for a few coins so they can eat today; three young children walk past in single file, each taking a swig from the glass of water on my table; another group of children in school uniforms stop one by one to shake my hand and solemnly walk on. Groups, mainly men on the kerb or on low walls and in loose circles of chairs, congregate on the thoroughfare – by day to make themselves available for work, by night because it's cooler than going home. Women sell coconuts and peanuts from oversized bowls balanced on their heads.

Two attractive young female road sweepers, neither more than sixteen years of age, brush past, one in flip-flops, a pink halter dress and matching plastic earrings, the other with heavy make-up wearing a maxi-length denim skirt, a revealing blue top and carefully brushed hair. They do their best to clear the pavements of leaves and litter, but there is so much sand they must wonder if it's worth it. But they waft past, disregarding my curiosity and trailing perfume in their wake, engrossed in their task.

After all the restaurant orders are filled and people start drifting away from the outside tables, the kitchen staff sit out on the pavement and eat a few scraps of leftovers. My waitress takes a half-finished bottle of water to an old woman sitting in the gutter on the other side of the road who hugs the bottle like an old friend before putting it to her lips to take a swallow.

I take the cue that the evening is nearly over at the café, leave my seat and step past the woman on the kerb towards my hotel. On the street outside the Carlton, the hotel cook has just finished his shift and begins brewing up a pot of tea over four or five tiny pieces of charcoal. He uses the tea as a greeting – he is not going to brew up without offering me a glass of the precious foamy liquid. We are joined by two kitchen porters who take a seat on either side of the stoop as he performs the ritual with care and lots of dramatic humour. Potent 'gunpowder' China tea is used so it will need thorough brewing and blending with sugar to be made palatable.

A full forty minutes after the water and tea hit the pot on the coals, the cook lifts it and pours from a height of four feet into a small shot glass. He lifts the lid of the pot and returns the liquid from whence it came. He pours again, into a different glass, then lifts it up to the light and pronounces it nearly ready. He pours the tea into a third glass, then a fourth. From the last glass he spills it into the third, then second then back into the first. All the while the head gets foamier and darker, looking more like a miniature Guinness at every pour. Finally, he offers the first glass to me. I am touched. All three men anticipate my reaction after the first sip; in mock sympathy they impersonate the pucker of my face and screwed-up eyes with howls of laughter.

The cook stretches the tiny quantity of tea to satisfy the four of us just enjoying being here on the pavement on this balmy evening, sitting and sipping and greeting everybody who passes. Sometimes the unexpected Tea Encounters can be the most fun.

Open criticism of the president of The Gambia is not expressed lightly in the country; in fact, it's rarely done at all. My next Tea Encounter (arranged through an introduction in Lancashire) is scathing about the current regime under President Yahya Jammeh. Jammeh, for his part, is doing his best to develop a personality cult, with huge banners of himself proclaiming all the apparent successes since he came to power in 1994: 13 Years of Peace and Prosperity, Healthcare Our Priority, Vote for Peace and Prosperity, etc.

A tourist guidebook refers to The Gambia as 'Africa for beginners' but the benign exterior of the population and the international holiday resorts conceal a different story – one of repression and autocracy. Many people who criticise the regime find themselves arrested on trumped-up charges and spend long periods in prison, while others 'disappear' for their dissenting views. For this reason my Tea Encounter cannot be identified; I'll refer to him as George Bokari.

'A little learning is a very dangerous thing,' George says. 'When you have a high school graduate for a president running the country, it's going to be a disaster. The whole country is corrupt, from the government to the hospitals to the policemen at the checkpoints. Nepotism and tribalism are killing Africa. A very few have a lot, while most of the people live in poverty.'

We have come for tea at an outdoor restaurant crowded with Europeans in the tourist resort of Serekunda, a few kilometres along the coast from Banjul. We are in the heart of the resort's fleshspots, a feature of which is the striking number of white, middle-aged women with lithe, young black men on their arms. The couples look like they are Olympic athletes having a day out with their adopted mothers. The men spend their time driving the women around, accompanying them to restaurants, or carrying shopping. But their main use is for sex. The flabby skin and bulging flesh of the women is exposed in shorts and sarongs. Exposed too are hints of embarrassment when they catch another westerner's eye; some ignore critical gazes with unabashed looks of guilty contentment. To a lesser extent, Western men drag around shapely Gambian girls in the sunshine or sit with them in post-coital boredom at pavement cafés.

I order tea and it arrives Western-style – a mug and a stringed tea bag. But our tea together is cut short when George receives a phone call telling him that his cousin has been arrested.

On the way to the police station George explains, 'These charges are false. He told me he discovered some government corruption. But now he is arrested!' We pass Arch 22 and George fills me in on political and civic life in the Gambian capital.

'Have you seen this arch? It's a joke. Jammeh built it as a monument to himself and his so-called achievements but now they won't let cars drive under it because bits keep falling off! Typical. This is a man who believes he can cure AIDS with his own three-day herbal remedy. Madness!'

We drive through shabby potholed streets lined with crumbling buildings.

'Why aren't the street lights working?' George continues. 'Because the mayor is corrupt and illiterate. Illiterate! Maybe the energy company has not been paid. It's as simple as that. But where is the money?'

We drive past another presidential poster – Leading The Gambia into the Future.

'If he was such a good president he wouldn't need to keep reminding us what a good president he was,' George snorts.

We park up outside a once-grand but now abandoned building.

'Evidence of corruption is all around us. But nobody condemns it publicly, or criticises the mayor, or the blacked-out street lighting, or the beautiful old buildings decaying around us, or the human rights, just in case.'

George goes into the police station to check on his cousin in custody but suggests I stay in the car; 'otherwise the police will think you are a journalist and get jittery, it will only make matters worse.' He posts bail and returns to the car optimistic of an early release.

'It's crazy. The minister was found selling diplomatic passports, and my cousin, who discovered the deception, is arrested! There is no due process, no real democracy.'

On the way back to his home, George says, 'What The Gambia, and Africa, needs more than anything is principle-centred leadership. Without it, things will continue as they are.'

He gives me a look of resignation and a sad, knowing smile. 'We do what we can,' he says.

His advice for the trip? 'The smallest things can make the biggest difference to people's lives.'

I ride back to Banjul and check my emails. I have a number of messages from strangers who are enjoying the blog, including a very concerned communication from someone called Simon Milnerton who is a security officer at the British High Commission in Lagos, Nigeria. It is easier if I include it whole, as I still can't make head or tail of some of it:

You must be receiving a great deal of emails so I'll keep this short: Ghana, Togo & Benin are lovely countries and well worth the visit, however, I would be surprised if you are not delayed by as many as 7–15 'checkpoints' as you cross into Nigeria. Not all police, some will be 'area boys' but a certain amount of 'dashing' may be required (£1 = $2 = 250 Naira being the cost of a 'Roger').

My real concern for you is the Niger Delta – Eastern Nigeria. Please read the following page [he provides a link to the current situation vis-à-vis security].

May I suggest that you 'go North/Central' in Nigeria and circumnavigate the Delta, Bayelsa, Rivers, Aqua Ibom, Abia, Edo States of the Niger Delta area? Should you require a more detailed route, I will see what I can obtain as there are several 'bikers' out here who have ridden Lagos–Calabar in the past.

I am told that Cross River State (Calabar) which borders Cameroon has some of the most beautiful countryside in Nigeria – and has been incident-free to date. It is just the greed/kidnapping/armed robberies of the Oil & Gas States that raises my worries about your 'Nigeria leg'.

Anyway, the support (if I can) is here and I'll log on to watch your progress with great jealousy!

Yours in the cause,

Simon

Nigeria sounds a barrel of laughs. If nothing else, Simon has managed to add another layer of excitement to the journey ahead, and I consider printing the email to keep handy (next to my Philip Youles T-shirt) in case I'm kidnapped.

I meet up with a woman called Sara Pownall from the British High Commission here in Banjul who has also been following the blog. While we are having lunch, she asks if I would like any help applying for my visa for Nigeria, a few weeks further down the road. She makes a quick telephone call to the consul at the Nigerian High Commission. It sounds like good news.

'He's expecting you tomorrow. Go early,' she advises.

As suggested, I show up first thing the following morning at the Nigerian High Commission. The man at the gate doesn't acknowledge me and, without breaking off from reading the Quran, points to a door. I enter. Under sickly fluorescent lights, the room is the interior design equivalent of despair: soiled curtains pulled halfway across the windows, dirty, barely serviceable furniture and the whole sorry place needing reacquaintance with a paint brush. There is a magazine on the table from 1991.

A middle-aged woman behind a desk is chewing gum so loudly I think she might be trying to attract somebody's attention, but there is only me here. She hands me two forms. I fill in only one as they are identical and hand them back. She clicks her fingers at me and points at the blank form.

'But it's the same form,' I say.

'Yes,' she says expressionlessly.

I fill in the second form. She tuts, she chews, she clicks her tongue. A young secretary comes out to join us.

'When will the visa be ready?' I ask.

'Tuesday.'

It is Thursday today.

'I can't wait until Tuesday. I have to leave today,' I lie.

'No. You apply Tuesday, you pick up Thursday. You apply Thursday, you pick up Tuesday.'

'Is there any way I can get it today? The ambassador is expecting me.'

Now there's a line you don't use every day.

'Sara from the British High Commission rang Mr Dunladi yesterday. I really need it today,' I say, softening my voice and trying to get a little eye contact going.

The secretary responds for both of them, 'And when we want a visa to go to England they ask us a million questions and make us wait and wait. Why not the same for you?'

They've got me in a corner, so I apply a bit of emotional top spin, 'I know, I heard about that and it's terrible. I think you should be able to come to Britain whenever you like. I had the same trouble when I applied to go to America; they asked me a million questions. It's not right.'

She looks at me doubtfully, clicks her fingers, points at the forms on the table and says, 'Pay.'

'Only if I can have it today. My other visas will expire if I don't get to Nigeria quickly,' I babble.

The receptionist reluctantly picks up the phone and after a short inaudible conversation says, 'You can explain it to the ambassador.'

I'm in. I am shown upstairs to a darkened office except for the light of a TV screen showing a soap opera.

'Mister Dunladi,' I try to muster some bonhomie, 'a pleasure to meet you, I believe Sara from the British High Commission called you yesterday about me.'

'Yes, yes, how are you? Welcome-welcome,' he ushers me in and gestures for me to sit down.

'You want to come to my country, and you have come from where?'

I give him the outline features of my trip. We chat about Africa and some of my experiences so far, although he is not too interested in the details. I am sitting in a low armchair facing his desk but for some reason he stands next to me at my right side facing the wall at my left. It is impossible to look him in the face at such an angle. If I look up all I can see is the underside of his chin. I soon realise Mr Dunladi is talking to his own reflection in the sliding glass door of the bookcase on my left. He launches into what sounds like an address to a large audience.

'You are from a developed nation and travelling through this continent,' he begins in earnest. 'You are undergoing the harsh climate, the terrible terrain, the crumbling infrastructure and the strange people for this selfless act! Maybe you are a humanitarian, and if you are you must find a way to share the goodness of what you are doing with as many people as possible.'

His eyebrows are going and he gives his reflection the occasional smile. He opens his arms.

'When you go to Lagos' (who said I was going to Lagos?) 'you will go to the NTA, there it is on the telly,' he points at the scratchy picture on the screen, 'our national television channel, so you can share what you are doing with the world. NTA is on satellite now, the people in America and your home country will see that you are well looked after, O yes! And when you arrive at those many, many checkpoints in my country, they will see you and they will say "O, he is the one on the telly, he is famous" and they will want to help you. They will not rob you!'

(Any chance of a visa?)

'Maybe you do this for your own interest but it is also of interest to others and it is your duty to share it with as many people as possible. My uncle used to say that the white man is so rich that he now looks for new ways to die! Black Africans do not have the food or the shelter or the basic necessities, they laugh at the white man who drives a car around a race track to put himself in danger.'

He finally looks down at me. It is rare that I am totally dumbstruck, but bloody hell...

Again, he addresses the book case, 'You understand?'

I look up at his chin and nod.

'So! I am going to find a way to tell the Nigeria Television Authority to expect you and you can tell your story. This selfless act is an example to us all and... and...' (I think he's running out of steam) 'this visa will be ready this afternoon so that you can leave today. Your mission is very important. Come back at four o'clock. No problem.'

The abrupt ending to the speech takes me by surprise. Will I have to undergo this for every visa in Africa? He walks me downstairs and tells the receptionist to process my application immediately. He shakes my hand for a little too long and returns to his office. What a great guy.

The chewing receptionist smiles conspiratorially and gives me two thumbs up. What's got into her, all of a sudden?

'Where is madame?'

I presume she means my wife.

'At home. In England.'

'Is she not scared you will be kidnapped?'

'But Nigeria isn't really a dangerous country full of bandits, is it?'

'Kidnapped not by bandits but by another woman!' she says as she pats me significantly on the arm.

'This eighteen hundred dalasi is a lot of money,' she says. 'Maybe you should stay in Banjul more days. I think maybe you should wait until Tuesday for your visa to see more of the city. I can show you; why not, hey? Do you like to eat out, to dance, to go to nightclubs?'

'Ye-e-s,' I answer, thinking, where the hell is this going?

'So do I. We could do all these things with this money you pay for visa. If you leave today I will be sad.'

I hand over the cash.

'This money could pay for dinner, a night out... and for our breakfast.'

All right, lady, this has gone far enough, thank you very much. I try to muster a combination of looks on my face that is supposed to mean, 'You're a nice lady and all that, a bit pushy (well, desperate actually), but all I came in here for was a visa, so if you could just process that I'll be on my way. And no funny business.' But what I probably do is just smile sickly with raised eyebrows.

She lays her cards on the table (thankfully that's all she lays on the table): 'I am widow, my husband die and leave me with two little ones. It is difficult.' And then by way of an afterthought she asks, 'Do you have email?'

She writes her name, address, telephone number and email so fast it makes me think she may have done this before.

'Why not stay longer?'

I edge closer to the door.

'I'll be back at four for the visa,' I call as I exit the premises. 'Bye!'

I return at four o'clock and after five minutes of cat and mouse in reception (you can guess who plays mouse) Mr Dunladi picks up from where he left off this morning: 'You have a duty to share with the world the purpose of your visit and tell them you want to get to know Africans and that you want to explore the continent.'

He reminds me of an overeager young priest; I half expect him to end each sentence with 'my child'.

'You will go to the NTA to tell the satellite what it is you are doing because we are all the same in the eyes of God [my child]. Because the Africans will see you and will want to meet the "crazy Englishman". They will be amazed at what you are doing, this "crazy Englishman".'

As I turn to go back downstairs he says, 'Do you have business card? Here is mine. It is good to have friends in different places; I never know where I will be posted next [my child].'

I'm not sure why, but it is a faintly sad end to the transaction. I like Mr Dunladi, and I vow to go to the NTA studios if I get to Lagos.

The receptionist adopts a gloomy visage when I come downstairs clutching my precious visa-stamped passport.

'I have had bad day,' she begins.

My skin starts to prickle as the outer door swings open and Sara Pownall walks in. Saved by the British High Commission – and that doesn't happen every day. I use the interruption to stride towards freedom. I call to the receptionist, 'Stay in touch' and sidestep out the door.

6

'FIVE HUNDRED WILL BUY TEA AND BREAD'

You can't walk away from Africa, can you?
You've got to keep trying.
Dr Alex McMinn

Looking forward to making progress towards Tombouctou or Timbuktu (a place name that has weaved its spell over me like many Europeans before) in Mali, I take the ferry back over the river Gambia, ride to Kaolack in Senegal and then head east. I really can't justify the extra days riding in the opposite direction to my destination after the four days with no clutch in the desert, but I'm unlikely to have the opportunity again.

My aim is to reach Tambacounda in Senegal that night, but the more this trip goes on the less I trust my own daily mileage estimates. The greatest influence on pace is not distance but the road surface, and this one is a shocker. It's a mostly tarmac road, but it has huge potholes like giants' footprints. The bike is getting a bashing and my gear on the back is bouncing around with every jolt. Occasionally there is a short unbroken stretch, but as soon as I increase speed I get caught out by a shuddering bump as the bike dives into another gaping hole.

The road through low bush and waist-height golden grass is a truck graveyard. Many have been abandoned after overturning – there is no vehicle recovery service out here – and other stranded vehicles have broken axles, flat tyres, twisted wheels, shot gearboxes. If catastrophe befalls them, drivers take out their prayer mats, find a shady spot under the truck and go to sleep until someone arrives with a spare part; sometimes they wait for days. The villagers along the route take it upon themselves to repair the road surface through their village with soil, sometimes by the handful. It's a thankless task with trucks churning up the ground with every pass. The villages are amongst the poorest I have seen yet: mothers pound manioc in tubs, old men's faces are creased with looks of despair, and pitiful children and dogs chase the bike down the road.

About 300 kilometres out of Banjul I arrive at the dilapidated roadside settlement of Koussanar hoping to find a hotel in which to rest up after the slalom ride around, and through, the potholes. People in the last village told me there would be accommodation here, but I got the same story on the two previous stops. Maybe they just didn't like the look of me and thought it best I move along. Night is falling and I decide it's too risky to continue to Tambacounda because of the state of the road so I wait for someone to come up with an idea. They're never short of ideas in Africa.

Once the crowd around me accepts that I'm not moving on, a small boy gets on a bicycle and indicates for me to follow.

He leads me a kilometre off the road to a small compound with women cooking outside, dressed in multicoloured, loose-fitting robes and high headdresses. One woman speaks a little English and says the centre is full 'because the French, because the French', but adds that I can stay the night if I sleep outside and she will feed me, which is exactly what I was hoping she'd say.

The compound has a dorm, an outhouse, an external kitchen and a separate building with some dormant first-generation computers. Soon, around a dozen visitors from Saint-Cyr-sur-Loire in France join us and explain that their town has a twinning arrangement with Koussanar.

Julian, a blonde-haired student who looks like a whippet with a fringe, says, 'We built the compound some years ago for our visits. The first year we bring computers; this year we are here to unload a container we have sent from France with medical supplies for a children's clinic. But the container is delayed in Dakar because the local prefect will not – how you say – sign documentation until we leave.'

'Why won't he release it?'

'Perhaps he would have all the glory for the clinic. After we leave, they will believe the clinic is from him. Or perhaps they do not get… *all* the supplies. You know?'

Yes, I get the picture. Needless to say, the French are frustrated and there is a heavy air of disappointment and incredulity, and even though I want to know the deeper story their bitterness won't allow them to talk about it. They have all taken a week off to come to this godforsaken place and there's no container, no supplies, no clinic. The friendly group of teachers and students do not seem to have an agenda of their own – they are not missionaries and do not represent a formal charity – they are merely people who want to help some other people in need, a joy that has been denied them.

The following morning I join them for tea and breakfast. Now that their plans appear to have come to naught, they are aimless and a little embarrassed.

Still aghast at the turn of events, Julian says, 'We can do nothing. We cannot even get angry. They say we do not understand how Africa works. That is true. But these people waiting for the clinic do not understand either.'

We drink our tea and munch on the stale bread and jam.

'Ah, Africa,' he sighs.

I want to tell him about the experienced advice I got from Dr Alex McMinn in Ormskirk before I left Britain: 'You can't walk away from Africa, can you? You've got to keep trying.' But I think Julian has seen enough to make up his own mind.

As I leave, I wonder where this well-meaning group lies in the Western aid worker's typical career path: initial horror, then understanding, optimism, a can-do attitude, raising money back home and preparing to make the world a better place. But the European dreamer struggles to compete against cold hard African facts: the westerner must face the gritty reality of hierarchies that are difficult to understand, tribalism, cultural conventions stronger than any laws and a labyrinthine bureaucracy. Eventually he or she gives up, disgusted at the Africans' inability to live their lives like us. And that's the crux of the matter; in many cases it would seem they don't want to.

It is slow going to Tambacounda as each pothole shakes the spare tyres behind me into the small of my back. It's exhausting whether sitting or standing, on bends or straight roads, going fast or slow, on the road or on the soft track running parallel to it. One compensation of driving further into Senegal is the emergence of bird life: buzzards, vultures, hornbills and weavers all bring colour and a lighthearted aspect to the drab landscape. There is further interest, no matter how dusty or isolated the villages, in the countless dazzling young women – mostly teenagers – I can see from a kilometre off who sashay down the road swinging bare arms and wearing flat shoes and pristine violets and mauves, shocking pinks and lime greens, or matching lemon outfits with extravagant hair. They look otherworldly amongst the squalor. And perhaps they are meant to.

I plough on towards the Mali frontier. The day gets hotter and I have to stop in Tambacounda for a breather. Parked up in the shade of a large tree, I send a young boy to find me some tea from a nearby stall. I am approached by a rather dishevelled but kindly-looking gentleman dressed in an ancient blue safari suit and broken sandals. He is about sixty years of age, with thinning hair and rheumy, yellowy eyes. He most closely resembles a cinematic version of a colonial-era faithful retainer, the kind that might bring fresh tea to pale families during a heatwave.

'Hello again, it is me!' he says cheerfully in clear English.

The boy returns and hands me the tea. I take a decent swig and shake the man's hand, which feels like unsanded wood.

'Hello. Do I know you?' I ask.

'You come from Dakar today? We meet there, I give you directions.'

He seems certain we have met before. I notice that his teeth are irredeemably rotting and his wizened features sprout hair in three shades of grey, but he has a winning smile and he wants to talk, his voice coated in a film of tea and cigarettes. I still don't know who he is – and I didn't just arrive from Dakar.

'You go to Kayes? I too. I come from Dakar and stop for *essence*... petrol?... and someone take my bag. Thirteen hundred euros and many céfa. Is too bad!'

I notice he uses the local terminology 'céfa' for the Central African Franc (CFA), rather than the archaic term 'franc' that many people employ. He digs into his pocket for his wallet and, standing erect, says, 'Here is my card, sir.'

He presents me with a well-thumbed business card with Militaire Attaché Col Djibril printed on the face. He retrieves it before I can make any further mental notes. My guess is it's his only one.

'I work for ambassador of Mali in Dakar. I travel every week in Toyota Land Cruiser with money from embassy. But this is too bad, the money, the céfa, the euros.'

I eat an apple while he tells me about the life of a military attaché; he is good easy company and it is a relief, even for a few minutes, to converse in English. The colonel recommends the Hotel du Rail in Kayes, which he says he will be going to tonight if he gets his 'situation' sorted. He writes down the name of the hotel manager and tells me to mention the colonel's name to ensure I get a good room.

'We will share a drink later this evening. But I must wait now. You know Western Union? When the money arrive there I can have breakfast, I have not eaten yet today. I will see you at Kayes for a stopover, yes. It will be fine-fine when the ambassador he send me money.'

I prepare to leave but he follows me over to the bike and begins to look uneasy.

He says, 'Some céfa for breakfast will be very good. I cannot eat, I have nothing.'

The colonel keeps his voice low, not pleading, more matter-of-fact. A cautious part of me was waiting for this sting in the tale.

'I can't do that, no,' I say for no reason at all, mainly force of habit I suppose.

'Five hundred will buy tea and bread.'

I realise I've been singed by the slow burn of the pick-up. Now that he has laid himself bare he looks me deep in the eyes, this man of pensionable age. His strategy was certainly more sophisticated than most, but at the end of it all he is still a man in need with his palm outstretched. But, oddly, the mention of the magic word (tea, not bread) and the measly sum requested – about 55p – encourages me to dig into my pocket for the money. The tale was so good and he was so convincing that it was worth the 500 for the entertainment value alone. But I suppose, I try to fool myself, there is always the possibility that he is telling the truth and military attachés in Mali go about in flapping sandals, antique safari suits and two weeks' stubble all the time.

All the way to Kayes I wish both that he really is a colonel working for the Mali ambassador and also that he is an audacious con man with enough nous to see himself through his dotage.

A few hours later I slip over the border into Mali. MALI!

The road from the border is beautifully smooth and I glide through mile after mile of spindly-armed baobab trees in the blistering heat. I reach Kayes, the town with a reputation for being the hottest in Africa, predictably dehydrated in a fug of sweat and exhaustion. Good job I didn't arrive in the summertime.

The town is located on the Senegal River, which flows to the sea at St Louis in Senegal a thousand kilometres away, and is criss-crossed by sandy streets and crumbling buildings populated by slow-moving robed men.

In honour of Colonel Djibril's smooth abilities and memorable smile earlier today, I go to the Hotel du Rail for a beer. The man who appeared and then vanished from my life never shows, of course, but I drink one to the colonel anyway. Cheers!

7
'MANGER, DU THÉ, REPOSER'

Plan your route very carefully.
Raschid Gibrail

Whatever happens, keep going.
Dave Edmundson

Next morning I find an army of food stalls outside Kayes railway station providing identical breakfasts: open fire burning on the ground, a pan of sizzling eggs which are flipped, then stuffed into a baguette and squashed between two dirty hands. This is accompanied by a sickly sweet mixture of a pinch of Nescafé, warm water and a heavy-handed dose of ultra-sweetened evaporated milk.

Big day ahead. I prepare to head towards Kita and then on to Mali's capital, Bamako, about 500 kilometres away... but where's the road? There are absolutely no road signs at all in Kayes and I have to ask four different people for directions to the road. When I see the appalling state of the piste, my heart sinks – loose and stony, hilly and rutted – and previous experience warns me that it can only get worse the further I ride from town. For company, I have donkeys and carts, bicycles, small motos and a few people on foot calling 'white man, white man' as I pass. The Triumph is the biggest thing on the road.

After twenty minutes I seriously consider whether I have done the right thing. The road has completely disintegrated; the rear wheel is sliding out of control over the sandy patches, even at dead slow speeds, and I have to concentrate hard on every metre so that I place the front tyre on something solid.

'*La route à Kita?*' I enquire with everybody I pass, hoping that someone will say 'You're on the wrong road, white man, of course this is not the main road to the capital of our country. Go back to the tarred road where you belong.' I study the map in the hope there might be another route to Bamako but with each stop the realisation becomes ever more certain: this is the road, and I have no option but to take it.

I cross a couple of dry riverbeds and ride over some rocky outcrops where I lose the track completely. I ask for directions in a small village, but I can barely believe the track I've been sent down: an overlapping succession of large boulders emerge out of the ground down a steep decline over which I must wrestle the bike. If I stop or hesitate the bike will certainly go over, and this is not forgiving soft sand; if I drop it here the fall will do some serious damage to it and to me. I fortify myself with advice from an earlier Tea Encounter in Burnley with Dave Edmundson ('Whatever happens, keep going') and get back up on the pegs. The decline in first gear soon segues into an equally steep incline. It's impossible to sit down, even for a second, as the seat bounces around underneath me like a rubber ball.

After a few kilometres, already exhausted, I reach some open country, which offers too many opportunities to get lost. For the first time, an hour after I set out, I am fully aware of the fierce heat of the morning. The enemy – that yellow orb in the sky – is throwing everything it's got at me today. Wringing with sweat I pause for breath, but I decide not to rest and just take a large swig of warm water as there is no shade. The open expanse turns into a narrow track with low bush on either side, which if nothing else cuts my chances of losing my way. The ground is now sandy, talcum powder fine. I can either use the existing bike track or make a new track through the trees so as not to get stuck in someone else's rut. There are more rocks, then more open country; it's up, it's down, and it's through the centre of tiny sleepy settlements from which every person emerges to see who and what is making all the racket. And then of course I find the dreaded deep sand... This is murder.

Eventually I reach Lontou – always a comfort when I am in a place actually mentioned on the map – but although it is an embarrassingly short distance from Kayes, it's already eleven o'clock. It is difficult to reconcile the centimetre showing on the map with the sheer endeavour of today's effort. I have woefully underestimated the distance, the terrain and the effort involved in this stretch of 'road'. At this pace it's going to take me a week to get to Bamako. I unfold the map a little, which is a fearful task with the distance yet to travel, and the enormity of the task before me begins to sink in. Some advice from a Tea Encounter with Raschid Gibrail in Blackpool returns to mock me: 'Plan your route very carefully.' Pity I ignored it.

Breathless, I find some shade and park up for a drink, but the water is now so hot I can't even put it to my lips. If I am to continue I must get fresh water. As soon as I realise I am without it, it is my only thought. I consider whether it is still possible to turn back to fill the jerrycan in Kayes and continue on later. I have to make a decision soon, otherwise it will be too late. But there is also something within me that wants to reach the point of no return so that I am forced to continue. Besides, the idea of going back down this track scares the hell out of me.

After being unsuccessful in three small communities, I'm pointed towards a village up ahead that has *l'eau potable*. I grit my teeth and make my way to a small settlement where people are sitting outside their homes. Once I get my helmet off and kill the engine I realise how quiet it is around me as real life carries on.

Immediately next to me are two elderly men and two teenage boys sitting on low stools.

'*L'eau potable?*' I gasp hoarsely.

'*Oui, l'eau potable... là,*' says the man in robes pointing to a pump some metres away. His son takes my jerrycan and fills it with cool fresh water. I offer a few coins but he waves them away.

Then he says the magic words – '*Du thé?*' – and raises a glass of black liquid.

I look down and see the man is brewing up. He tells me to take off my jacket and sit down in the shade, as if I need telling. Well, actually, I do; I am so dehydrated I feel intoxicated, without any of the pleasurable aspects. He offers to pour water over my baking head, which is the best idea I've heard all day. The water pours through my hair and down my neck. I allow it to trickle anywhere it chooses.

'Mercy... uhhm, *merci.*'

The man is about sixty, with greying stubble, and is wearing stained light-blue robes, a woolly hat and flip-flops. Even though this tea man cannot speak a word of English, he knows what I'm going through. With comprehending, intelligent eyes, which I believe have summed me up in seconds, he knows my whole history: where I'm from, why I'm here, where I'm going. He can see what a state I'm in and that I'm in need of some reassurance. Basically, he can see I need a cup of tea.

He calmly explains, in little more than a whisper, that there is no way I am going to reach my destination today, but so what. I should take it easy and slowly ride to the next town: '*Manger, du thé, reposer... après, Bafoulabé.*'

But Bafoulabé is only another centimetre or so further on the map, and he can see my disappointment.

I am beginning to feel this man's sense of peace, the kind often found in the familiar act of brewing tea, as formal as any religious ceremony. I take the glass offered to me and drink; the tea tastes as sweet as sin, like the first and last pot of tea ever brewed. The moment thickens into something unexpected. Is this the cup I have been searching for? Is this the end of the quest? As a feeling of serenity gradually bubbles up from inside, he looks deeply into my eyes and repeats, '*Manger, du thé, reposer.*'

Even though I am out of my depth, I am meant to be here. It is as if he has been waiting for me, for the last six weeks on the road, for the last forty-odd years, sitting here waiting to give me the advice I need: 'Eat, drink tea, rest.' As Tea Encounters go, it would have to go in the 'poignant' file.

For the first time today I notice the countryside, the view he must look at each day from the little seat outside his home: the mud huts with broad leaves for roofs, the small enclosures for animals, the washing lines, women doing domestic chores, men doing very little, small children running around with ragged T-shirts but nothing covering the bottom half, the sand, the laughter, the closeness, the optimism, the sheer exquisiteness of the human scale of it all, with so little, and so much. But tea is enough to bring us together: tea the healer, tea the great communicator. At this moment, in this place, with this man, it is quite possible that I am drinking the ultimate cuppa. If it isn't, it's a damn fine substitute.

I look down at the glass in my hand and then up into the man's face. I want him to make all my decisions for the remainder of the journey. I am handing over all decision-making responsibilities for the Brew Ha-Ha to this man in a dusty, woolly hat brewing up. I don't want our tea to end – and not only because it would mean I'd have to get back on the buggering road. The absolute folly of today's adventure engulfs me; I don't want to leave this spot. It's time to scale down my ambitions. In an instant I see the trip unravelling – Zanzibar for Christmas? I must have been dreaming. Cape Town by 22 February? Crazy.

I drink as much water from the replenished jerrycan as I can stomach, pour a couple more litres over my head and prepare to get back on the bike. The tea man looks on with quiet encouragement. But I am sure his eyes also say that if I am ever passing this way again he will be ready with another cuppa.

Keep going. I can do nothing else. The honeymoon of the trip may be over but the love affair continues... on to Djamou.

One of the most sparsely populated, poorest and hottest nations in the world, Mali was last in the queue when the natural gifts were handed out. I can attest to those statistics in just two days of travel in this vast country. Even in African terms, this place is struggling. With life here taking place at a noticeably slower pace than in Senegal, the location in the Sahel (lands that border the southern Sahara) defines the character of the country: hardy, determined and tolerant – three characteristics I will have to draw on to reach Bamako.

The road seems to get a little easier for a while and I put it down to the calming influence of the tea. But it doesn't last. It's an ever-changing terrain of sand, rocks, an indistinct stony piste, bush tracks and wild, open country. For the first time the bike seems a burden, a heavy weight I am dragging around instead of a convenient mode of transport. After another hour, during which I neither see nor hear another human presence, the road returns to a twin-tyre track, some of which is well compacted. I save the rear wheel from sliding from under me on numerous occasions while the front wheel has a mind of its own. I get caught in a deep rut and am now heading for wallowy sand. I try and change direction but the bike disappears from under me. The moment I hit the ground I am shocked by an insult of pain in my neck and shoulder; I catch my foot under the bike and land heavily on my bare elbow as my helmet hits a rock. One of the panniers is off, and it's, well, a bike crash.

I try to raise my right arm but my neck and shoulder protest in agony. I look over at the bike, disgusted. My head is pounding and now the sun, always the pitiless sun, is doing its best to put me right off Mali as a holiday destination.

In the silence I take a minute to catch my breath, say a short prayer that the bike is all right because I'm fucked out here if it isn't, and begin the tedious process of taking everything off so I can raise the machine. All the gear on the bike is frying – the petrol jerrycan is untouchable it is so hot, and the fresh water in the other can is already boiling. I look up the track. I look down the track. Nothing. In the distance, bizarrely, I hear what sounds like a train whistle but it's no use to me here – 'A one-way ticket anywhere, please. No, just me, the bike can stay; I'll pick it up next time I'm passing.'

I tackle the bike. One, two, three, UP! It doesn't budge. Keep the back straight, grab the frame, one, two, three, UUUPP! Nothing. Fuck. I look up the track, I look down the track. Still nothing. I notice a trickle of liquid emerging from underneath the bike and realise it is losing fuel from the overflow pipe. If I don't do something pretty quick I won't be going anywhere.

The bike is awkwardly placed facing uphill, so I drag it around on its side so that the wheels are placed over a shallow pothole and try again. This is my last chance. Sod the back! One, two, three, UUUP-AHH... I get the bike halfway up and rest it against my thigh in a crouched position. I take a short breather and... the bike lands on my foot. The exertion has finished me.

'YOU FUCKER!' I shout.

My voice is shocking to myself.

I crouch down on my haunches and consider myself: a brief analysis of the state I'm in. I'm sore in so many places I just want to remain here until someone, anyone, at any time, picks me up and takes me to some fucking TARMAC!

I look down the track, I look up the track... and to my astonishment I see what looks like a group of elderly women walking towards me. A geriatric mirage? One, slightly ahead, looks concerned and motions to the others to run to my aid. By the looks on their faces I assume we all want to express the same thought: 'Where the hell did you come from?' They are very concerned about the way I look, which must be a sight considering the kind of day I've had, and for the moment I know I cannot lie: I am in pain. The sweat is dripping from the end of my nose and eyebrows, my T-shirt is wringing, I must have a face like a grilled rasher, and my clothing is now ablaze with red dust. My shoulder and neck feel as if they are fused together, I've cracked my left elbow, and I've got a headache I'd be proud of after a weekend bender with Amy Winehouse. They make soothing noises but I motion to the bike and make a pathetic attempt to lift it. Shame they're only women, I think to myself. But then with pots, pans, wood and washing still perfectly balanced on their heads, the women lift the bike in one sweet, graceful move. Oh, you beauties.

'À la maison, à la maison!' one of the women says urgently, pointing up the track from whence they came.

I clamber onto the bike and follow them up the track. After a short distance there is a clearing within which is probably the tiniest complete village I've ever seen: seven huts and a small chicken enclosure. One woman carries a pannier under her arm, another holds my helmet as though it were a crown, arms outstretched. She places it gingerly on the ground in the shade of a tree and walks quickly off to one of the huts from which she soon emerges with a bamboo mat and a home-made broom. She sweeps a small area under the tree, spreads

111

the mat onto the cleaned earth and motions for me to lie down. I don't have to be invited twice. She then takes me by the arm and tenderly touches the shoulder as she lays me down. She pulls down my T-shirt from the neck and offers her expert opinion to the others. I close my eyes, exhausted and sore, as she takes a rag and wipes my face, my forehead and chin, around my nose and neck. She then goes to work on the painful right side of my body. She massages with her wrinkled hands all the while making cooing noises as I begin to feel the trauma of the day exit through my pores.

This is not a game anymore, this is not something I can call off anytime and say 'enough's enough'. Contorted thoughts gush through my mind: the poverty of the people, the fact that I couldn't call home on my wedding anniversary yesterday and lying here being administered to by these marvellous old women – it's all beginning to get to me. I have lost my place in my own story. The concern they are showing a damn fool stranger on a bike reminds me of Mr Dunladi saying 'Europeans look for new ways to kill themselves' and of the tea man's advice earlier today: *'Manger, du thé, reposer.'* I open my eyes. All the women, dusty-faced and loose-skinned, kneeling around me on the ground, have now been joined by a girl who looks equally concerned; she is as young as they are old, as pert as they are fatigued. I see the anxiety and tenderness in their eyes and, lying here in their care, I conceive I have never felt so alone yet so connected, so trapped yet so free, and I do the only thing left to me in the circumstances. I weep. I weep for Africa, for these wonderful people, for the toughness of the piste, for my stupidity, for tea, for the mat on the ground and for the heat of the remorseless fucking sun.

The woman ministering first aid believes my tears are a result of the pain in my shoulder and neck, so her rubbing becomes more theatrical; now the arm really is sore, sending shooting pains up to my neck but she's still got hold of it and she's shaking it in all directions. She gets noises of encouragement from the others but the tears keep coming.

I open my wet eyes and try to tell her to rub a little less vigorously, otherwise something drastic might happen, like my arm might come off in her hands. But she keeps on stroking and massaging.

'Easy now. Gentle. Aaargh. You don't have to... it's not necess... AAOW!'

I can't make myself understood and as I look into her face the tears turn to laughter.

Surprised and delighted by my apparent recovery, the women go 'oooOOOOOOOOOoooooooo' as they smile as one, tombstone yellow teeth everywhere.

I blurt out a loud, blubbery guffaw which becomes instantly contagious. We're all laughing now and the wrinkled women believe not only that their treatment has healed me but that they've also found my funny bone. I wipe my eyes. Another woman fancies herself a bit of a chiropractor so she takes my arm and manoeuvres it in all sorts of contortions. She stretches the arm and neck, making circles in the air, and convinces herself that it's nothing too serious. But just to be on the safe side she grabs my wrist and pulls my arm up and down as though she's trying to pump water up from the centre of the earth.

Once she's done, the post-adrenalin low hits me and I begin to relax. I don't understand a single word but I know one thing: I have reached the point of no return on the African

Brew Ha-Ha. Whether I backtrack now or carry on, I'm equally lost. But there is something about our little group under the tree in this village insignificant to the rest of the world that tells me that with human contact, people to be there for people, there is nothing to fear from this trip, from Africa, from life. I am now at the mercy of this astonishing continent. It's what I wanted: to expose myself to Africa, to jump in at the deep end. Well, I tell myself, start swimming.

After ten minutes I sit up and stretch my neck and shoulder to show my crew that I'm feeling better. I manage to extricate myself from their kindly clutches and stand up. I shake everyone's hand with as much heartfelt sincerity as I can muster. And I do mean it.

They help me load up the bike. No one looks convinced that I am well enough to continue; they wave me off hesitantly as if prepared to pick me up should I fall once again. I wave with my good arm and honk the horn, which gives them all a final round of squealing laughter, and I'm gone.

Physically and emotionally I'm shattered and pin all my hopes on Djamou, a town that people say has food of some description and fresh water. But somehow after acknowledging I had reached rock bottom earlier today, nothing about the road ahead intimidates me any more. It's as if a light has been switched on: the one that illuminates my own self-belief.

With renewed resolve drawn from the old women and after two more hours of tortuous riding I reach the town. I stop the bike in the shade of a building and fall over, so exhausted am I.

Djamou exudes an atmosphere of the utterly hopeless: the place is mostly home to disappointed men on low stools drinking tea and playing cards or staring into space dreaming of an alternative to their lives. Some kids play, futilely it seems, with a stick and hoop in the sand.

I go looking for food from hut to breezeblock building crying *'Manger, manger?'* before I stagger to a leafy lean-to with an inviting smell of packet stock cubes.

A woman is sitting on the ground in the shade tending to a young girl.

'Restaurant?' I ask desperately.

'Oui. Riz?'

'Oui, d'accord.'

Rice will do very nicely, considering.

The woman lifts the lid from a blackened cast iron pot on the ground and scoops a generous portion of sticky rice into a plastic bowl. She tops it with two small pieces of vegetable and a tiny whole cooked bird, hands it to me and then returns to her own rice, which she shares with her daughter. Even though I am too thirsty to eat, I resist the temptation to drink from the open well beside us, so the child runs for some bottled water for me. She returns with the drink and a block of ice that has been frozen in a knotted plastic bag about the size of a loaf of bread. I take a shard of ice, wrap it in a piece of cloth to place on the back of my neck and make a start on the water, draining half of it in one go. Then I tackle the rice; I manage a few mouthfuls and leave the little bird intact for the next customer.

Although just existing in this heat is an extraordinary effort, I am beginning to feel a bit more human and I slouch back in the chair to rest. A smartly-dressed man enters wearing pristine brown robes over loose matching trousers and takes a seat and a drink of water from the well. I close my eyes and wonder what Africa has in store for me next. Maybe I should stay here for the night and cool off, rest up, put things in some sort of context. Then again, perhaps I should plug on to a bigger town with more options and, who knows, the road might improve. And this woman tending the near-solid rice might offer me a four seasons pizza to go, but somehow I don't think that's going to happen either.

Then I hear a familiar, extraordinary sound for the second time today. A whistle. I sit up. I know I might be delirious but...

'Il est un train?' I ask no one in particular.

The man sitting opposite, who is now fanning himself furiously, replies, *'Oui.'*

I run outside and see the village is in fact a railway stop – not exactly a station, more a jumping on and off point where people board from some open ground. Women run with food on their heads, children skip over the rails with bags of sweets, fruit and bottles of water, and swarms of passengers make their way towards the rusty railway tracks where a battered train is coming to a halt.

I am galvanised into action. This may be my one and only chance to get off this road. I take the block of ice and thrust some cash into the woman's hand.

I run towards the tracks together with what seems like the entire village.

'Le train à Bamako?' I ask someone.

'Oui.'

I can hardly contain myself. I'm at the very nadir of the trip so far, and a blessed train pulls up outside. Unbelievable.

'*Je voudrais* to put *la moto dans le train* to Bamako,' I say to a likely-looking official. It's the best franglais I can manage in the circumstances.

The man in uniform looks at me while he tries to work out what the hell I'm on about, but he sees the urgency in my eyes and takes me by the hand as we run up the track to the boxcar at the front of the train. I tell a group of guys inside the freight carriage from where I've come and explain that the road has beaten me and the train is my only hope. They love it, and are now determined to become part of my adventure.

The man in uniform says it will cost 15,000 CFA to take the moto to Bamako and a further 2,000 for some local muscle to lift the bike onto the wagon, which seems fine by me. At the mention of 'céfa' I get a sizeable crowd who all want a little of what's on offer. Within thirty seconds the bike and all my gear is lifted bodily into the boxcar. The whole group is tickled with the operation, except for one man. In the commotion, a khaki-suited official arrives and begins arguing with my uniformed helper, the guard in the boxcar and anyone else within spitting distance. He is a severe-looking older man wearing a cap and a monogrammed bag over his shoulder. Who's he? I wait for everyone to stop shouting and realise that it is me and the bike about which he is so aerated.

He goes into a long explanation in French as he walks me towards the office of the *chef de gare*. Crikey, this guy is the station master and I've just been negotiating with another passenger to transport me and the bike to Bamako.

I follow him to the little office and hand over the fare – 5,000 less than the imposter! When I prepare to return to the train I am confronted by a huge wall of a man leading a mob that demands 2,000 CFA for lifting the bike into the train. Nobody else says a word. I pay him happily and he steps out of the way – and allows the sunlight back into my life. Oh, happy days, I think to myself as I skip over the tracks towards the rust bucket train like a child in a playground, energised once again by the exquisiteness of African serendipity.

The air within the metal boxcar is tactile and threatening; the menacing heat assaults the senses. The elderly freight guard, who is wearing something that used to be a suit, sits on a small seat in front of one of the sliding doors staring out at the elephant grass and scrubby scene speeding past. There are other people in the car but I'm not sure why they are all here; whether it's because there is no room in the passenger carriages or they are stowaways or rail employees is not made clear, and never is on the entire journey. There is a man in a red T-shirt who occasionally helps load the packages into the boxcar, another wearing old purple robes and a *kufi* prayer cap who sits placidly on a crate, a serious younger man, silent throughout, wearing a Hawaiian shirt and a yellow flat cap, and half a dozen others who jump on and off in a seemingly random fashion, the fresh smell of male sweat the first indicator that a new body has arrived.

'*A quelle heure le train arrive à Bamako?*' I enquire. (At least I think it's a question.)

Blank faces all round. Someone hazards a guess: '*Peut-être à une heure ou deux heures.*'

I look at my watch. I calculate that if the train arrives at one or two o'clock in the morning that will mean a nine- or ten-hour ride. With time now to reflect on the physical and mental brick wall I hit on the ride into Djamou, I can only be grateful for the chance encounter with this train. I may not be riding into Bamako but the freight car trip still feeds my desire for African adventure. I'm also saving the best part of a week's ride had the road surface continued in the state I found it this morning.

I should make myself comfortable. But apart from the bike and my gear now distributed around the floor, the boxcar is packed with food sacks and crates of fizzy drinks, oversized bags of charcoal and imported rice from Taiwan. It is difficult to find a spot on which to sit or stretch out comfortably; one man lies on a precariously-set mattress, another sits on a moped. A man deep in thought wearing khaki robes has the right idea, sitting in idle contentment with his feet hanging out of the sliding door. I find an empty rice sack, place it on the floor next to him and do the same. This is great. My neighbour and I don't need to talk, in fact neither of us utters a word as we both enjoy the silent pleasure. With the diminishing rock of ice wrapped in a dirty rag on my neck, the wind circulating around my clothing, the scenery changing from plains to scrub to bush and the chunk-a-chunk rhythm of the tracks, it makes for a tremendous mental holiday. I quickly decide that sitting and dangling my feet out of a speeding boxcar door is one of the great things to do and promise myself to do it more often.

The rolling hills are dotted with tiny villages where everybody waves, and we arrive at junctions and sidings where old friends of the freight guard shout welcomes and jokes in through the doors and the passengers have to run for the train because if it stops at all it is only for a minute. At the open door my companion and I notice bush fires ahead.

They become more frequent and burn closer on both sides of the track and before long the train rides through the crackle of burning bush and dense smoke. We are soon both covered in cinders and ash – the white showing up on his skin like snow and the black smearing mine like soot – and we laugh at each other's smudged faces.

At each stop we take on more goods: rice, more bags of powdery charcoal that makes us all sneeze, large metal cases that will rattle and crash unmercifully through the night. Meanwhile, my bike keeps working its way loose from the rope holding it up against the side of the car. Over the uneven tracks the bike walks off the centre stand and we all make a dash to prevent it falling on the fruit and vegetables or on top of one of us.

When I entered the train a man quickly grabbed a piece of floor next to the Triumph and fell asleep, quite oblivious to me. The sleeping man, wearing string-bound trousers and a yellow polo shirt, wakes and impresses everybody by asking me in a loud voice 'WHAT, IS, YOUR, NAME?' which elicits applause and laughter from everyone in the car at his command of the English language.

'Alan,' I answer.

'Alan!' says one.

'Alan!' says another.

'Alan!' yet again.

'Alan!' once more.

'ALAN! MY, NAME, IS, BABOU!' he declares loudly.

More good-natured joshing. He then insists on using my name at every opportunity...

'Alan, *riz*,' as it is thrown on the train.

'Alan, farina,' as semolina comes aboard.

... and announces all the stops and junctions...

'Alan! Boulouli.'

'Alan! Kita.'

'Alan! Sébekoro.'

The last hours of daylight are still extremely hot. At a brief stop the entire train seems to disembark and fight their way to a short string of makeshift food stalls on the station platform. A large lady squats behind two huge pots, each the size of a baby's bath, and serves beans and some sort of meat broth. Passengers are soon lined up at the stalls eating like pigs at a trough. The woman can hardly keep up with demand, her hands a flurry of spooning, serving, rinsing and wiping her hands on the front of her robes. The food is spooned into shared plates and bowls and the hungry passengers shovel the food into their mouths with their fingers. Some use a wedge of bread to scoop it up if they can grab a piece. There is much shouting for rations and with too few bowls to go around the hungry urge their fellow passengers to quickly scoff so they can get their share before the train moves off. One of my companions from the goods wagon encourages me to eat what's on offer but, hungry as I am, the sight turns me off and I shy away.

After ten minutes more people insist I eat; they say there will be no more food before Bamako.

'How long before we get to Bamako?' I ask.

Blank looks.

'Err, à quelle heure arrive Bamako?'

People shrug their shoulders.

I groan and give in to the inevitable. The equivalent of fifteen pence buys me a colossal bowl of beans with sauce and half a loaf of bread to scoop it up as the only spoon is already taken. Even though I have to look away from the others gobbling and slurping on the bench beside me, the saltiness of the food hits the spot. I can't finish it all before the whistle blows and my new friends stretch out their hands to drag me back into the freight car as the train sets off down the platform.

Some stops in the bush are lightning quick while others last for twenty or thirty minutes for a wholly indeterminate purpose. An added complication, especially after dark, is that there is no means of communication between the driver and the freight guard. At one nameless place Babou and the owner of a small moped are halfway to getting the bike off the boxcar when the train moves off without warning.

Babou shouts, *'ABANDONNEZ! ABANDONNEZ!'* (Drop it!)

The man, who is standing outside by the side of the train, pleads, *'NON! NON!'*

The train picks up speed and the man has to run alongside to take some of the weight to prevent it crashing to the ground. Babou is yelling for him to catch the bike as he is about to let it go but the man will not have it: *'NON! NON!'* he begs. But, one kilometre down the track, the situation is saved when the driver notices something hanging out of his train. He stops and reverses to where the rest of the man's belongings are dumped by the side of the rails. He seems nonplussed by the experience; he takes the heavily scratched bike and walks it into the dense bush without a flashlight.

Utter darkness enters the boxcar and I have to look out at the stars often to get my bearings. In the blackness, everybody now seems like strangers and we all allow our bodies to be rocked by the shunting of the train, like so many mannequins. The darkness seems to emphasise the racket of the piled-up freight, the ill-fitting sides of the boxcar and the motion of the wheels over the tracks, which make for a cacophony of noise.

I hear a crash followed by a recognisable voice pleading, *'ALAN! LA MOTO!'*

I jump off the rice sacks and shine the beam of my torch in the direction of a man in balaclava and dark glasses. It is Babou, who has returned to his original sleeping position on the floor of the carriage but is now trapped underneath the Triumph, which has fallen on him. The train is throwing us around so violently that it takes three of us to lift the bike and secure it once again. I am a little worried to see if Babou is at all hurt – I know first-hand how sore a Triumph on your foot can be – but as soon as he gets to his feet he laughs easily, resettles the dark glasses on his nose and accepts my apologies with good grace.

The incident soon passes as though experienced in a dream, for we all quickly return to our corners and resume our fractured dozing. We try to settle but the juddering of the train ensures nobody stays in one place for too long. I lie across a large water container, a crate of Fanta and a sack of rice. It is pure agony. I shine my torch around the boxcar often to see what looks like the final scene from a tragic opera: bodies deposited in dramatic positions across awkward props with arms and legs akimbo. It's an extraordinary sight and every time I flick on the torch we are all in newly comical poses.

By the morning the airborne charcoal dust, the bush fires and the aftermath of the soaring temperature has left us all looking like what we are – grimy boxcar travellers. These guys do this journey regularly, but for me it has been a baptism of fire. The train pulls into Bamako station as it approaches nine o'clock – about seventeen hours after I got on at the siding in Djamou. Had I continued on the dreadful road yesterday I have no doubt I would be waking up now in the bush somewhere – next to the tent I don't yet know how to erect – between two places not marked on the map.

Babou, the last one to leave the boxcar, hands me down the last of my gear from the filthy floor and I strap it all down on the bike. He jumps down on to the platform and holds up a smashed yellow indicator cover. He taps his crown with it, laughing, demonstrating how it broke when it hit him on the head. I give it to him as a souvenir. All I lose is an indicator but I've gained a belief – strengthened over the past twenty-four hours – that if I get myself into a tight corner in Africa, someone will come to my aid.

8
TOMBOUCTOU

Don't forget your water.
Carole Turner

After the long night in the boxcar to Bamako, I take a room in a hotel after checking it has a shower with hot water. It is time to check the bike over, call home, update the blog and scrub every dirty pore on my body. Bamako is the biggest city I have visited since Dakar, but it has none of the perceived threats of the Senegal capital; having said that, the traffic is an assault course. Streets are so narrow that if there is no easy way ahead, bikes jump the nine-inch sidewalk and weave in and out of pedestrians. I quickly learn to do the same.

Refreshed, after doing little more than eating and sleeping for two days, I ride 200 kilometres north-east of the Mali capital to Ségou, where I am surprised to see French sightseers in khaki clothing and walking boots. The small groups of mostly middle-aged 'adventure travellers' are probably here for the scenic river trips to Mopti and Tombouctou further upriver. It reminds me that I am getting closer to my own short-range goal about 600 kilometres north by road.

I find a hotel overlooking the Niger River which is quite reasonable, and if I pay a few thousand CFA extra I get the use of the remote for the out-of-reach air conditioner wedged into the ceiling. I park the bike up against the door of my room and head straight out, keen to see a little of the town while it's still light. I lean on a low wall and soak up the gorgeous location on a wide stretch of the river – it's a relief to see and hear the lapping water after the last couple of weeks on the sandy road from Banjul.

I step into a bar set on the river and order *poulet et frites* that may or may not make an appearance and enjoy the first beer for a couple of days. One of two bar girls in the place is desperately trying to engage me in a tête-à-tête. She knows about six words of English, so the conversation is going nowhere. She keeps saying she has a moto and suggests we go somewhere else to eat. I think. She is now so close to me that anyone looking on would think we were a couple – she a glamorous nineteen-year-old nightfly with feathers in her hair, a shocking orange two-piece and red high heels, doused in half a bottle of counterfeit Channel No 5 smelling out the joint, and I a knackered, bleary-eyed biker with dust in his ears whose height of ambition tonight is scoffing a plate of chicken and chips. Some couple. She pushes off when she realises all I want to do tonight is eat myself to a standstill.

The next morning I decide to exchange some currency at the bank before breakfast and find myself riding the wrong way down a one-way street. I know I'm going in the correct general direction for the bank but can't be bothered to retrace my route despite being shouted at by shopkeepers and approaching moto riders. I reach a roundabout and, managing to avoid the oncoming vehicles, merge into the stream of traffic. But I am immediately spotted by a point duty policeman who whistles loudly and furiously waves me over.

I stop and feign innocence by asking chirpily, 'Where's the bank?'

But he is neither interested in my banking arrangements nor my cheeriness, and berates me for snarling up the traffic as if daring me to challenge him. I look back to the one-way street wearing a surprised look of apology and claim I did not see any signs – mainly because there aren't any.

'*Pardon, monsieur. Je ne voir pas,*' I plead.

He has a book of citations and a pen in his hand and tells me to kill the engine. I take a deep breath and start explaining the trip to him, which takes his attention away from my violation long enough to engage him in conversation. He can hardly believe that I have arrived from England on the Triumph.

'*Oui. Blackburn à ici à la moto,*' I say.

He looks astonished.

'Blackburn Rovairs?' he asks, excitedly.

Bullseye.

'*Oui!*' I answer triumphantly.

The officer puts his book away and shakes my hand warmly, then calls over a fellow officer who is writing a ticket for another motorist. They both step back in admiration at the bike.

'Tree-oomph! Feeleep Yoolezz,' he says, reading out the sticker on the tank.

Philip Youles is now famous in Mali. I could think of worse places to open a branch.

The two officers wave me on after giving me detailed directions to the only bank in town. On my return the police officer whistles me over again. What now?

'*Avez-vous trouvé la banque?* You find... *ze banque?*' he asks.

'Yes, fine. Thanks. Terrific.'

'OK, is good.'

He then steps out into the road, stops all the traffic on the roundabout and waves me on with a salute. Don't you just love Africa?

Next day, 400 kilometres on, I make Douentza, which is as far as I can ride on tarmac before the dirt road to Tombouctou another 200 kilometres further on, which I plan to take the next day. I arrive in a walled encampment just before nightfall and am joined by two small groups of French tourists travelling in four-by-fours. Their appearance is shambolic and weary, and I guess they must have been on the road for a couple of weeks already, but they tell me they arrived just two days ago. Welcome to Mali.

I bed down on the roof of the dorm while the French take the grubby rooms on the ground floor.

Across the road in the village proper I update the blog at the cyber café housed in a tiny radio station with a huge satellite dish in the courtyard, courtesy of USAID. The DJ plays the tunes on a small portable cassette player with the station microphone jammed up against the speaker. At the end of each song he takes the mic in hand and talks excitedly into it while he chooses another cassette from shelves thick with sand. A hole in the wall acts as a window so passers-by can chat and make requests while he is on air. He cannot be ignored because his piercing voice carries far outside the compound of the station. In fact, anybody living within fifty metres need never buy a radio.

An old man in cheerless robes shows me around the two rooms of the station. He picks up a handful of cassettes to prove the extent of their collection, then carefully replaces them on the wall. Curiously, among the local titles there is one by Van Morrison.

'He's from Ireland,' I say.

'*Irlande?* Where is?'

'Near Britain; *après Grande Bretagne.*'

'Aaaahh,' he reflects, brushing the sand off the cassette case with a broad smile, 'Vang Moree-song.'

The level(ish) red gravel/dirt piste to Tombouctou is a joy at eight o'clock with the sun not too hot. After fifty kilometres the road surface turns to deep corrugations, some with fine sand. Despite leaving my heavy panniers on the roof of the encampment, I have two offs (a polite term for ending in a heap with the bike on top of me) and it's generally slow going. People at the camp said the trip would take me four hours, but it takes me nine and a half with some water stops and a fifteen-minute break for rice and a warm Coke at a lonely checkpoint. (The return journey takes me five hours after I take courage and skim over the tops of the corrugations at 80 kph.)

Every time I am gaspingly thirsty, my Tea Encounter with Carole Turner in Blackburn comes to mind: 'Don't forget your water.' It may seem ridiculous, but I never seem to bring enough of the stuff on remote stretches because I don't know how long each day's trip is going to take. It's all pure guesswork. Other times, of course, I carry ten litres through areas where it's readily available, and I could do without the extra weight on the bike.

Finally I reach Fleuve, the ramshackle riverside community at the end of the road, at around half past five. Across the river is Tombouctou. The settlement wears its defiantly end-of-the-line credentials with pride: a thousand-metre spit of land with some nomad tents around the ferry point where women wash clothes and men fish while a few fatigued souls half-heartedly sell some truly dispiriting keepsakes. They are all interrupted by the arrival of the ferry – the last of the day – a battered metal platform with space for about six vehicles.

As evening approaches and the light changes from the eye-squinting brilliance to a soft reddish glow, there is a collective sigh of relief from everyone on the water that the heat of the day is finally dissipating. After getting stuck on a sand bank and returning to the jetty to offload some weight (the people in those vehicles are *mightily* upset), it is night when the forty-minute ferry lands across the Niger River and I claim some space on the roof of a clean hotel.

And if you've ever wondered how far it is 'from here to Timbuktu', it's 9,506 kilometres.

Tombouctou is built on sand and the view from the roof of the hotel confirms that I am on the very edge of the desert. Looking north there is nothing all the way through Mali and Algeria to Morocco. Except sand, that is. I turn my gaze south, but there's not much there either. One good sandstorm could probably bury this whole place and we'd never be found, which is not such a fanciful idea since the desert is growing and one day may reclaim this ancient city.

On a more light-hearted note, the hotel receptionist is a dead ringer for Luther Vandross: the twin brother the soul singer probably never knew he had. He is the same size and profile and has the slight quiff to the front of his hair with the distinctive darting eyes and malty black skin, the effect marred only by his straining khaki safari suit and mismatched flip-flops. He would have a successful look-a-like career ahead of him if he had a voice – and didn't have two rather important front teeth missing. Give me the reason, Luther.

He brings me a pot of tea on an ornate metal tray. The tea is black and not too strong, although still scalding, so it must be sipped, but I'm in no hurry. I settle down in the reception area and enjoy the comings and goings.

Together with answering the telephone and receiving people at the hotel, Luther is tasked with keeping the dust out of reception, which I would imagine was a job for life. When he isn't sweeping the floor he's eating, which helps him maintain Luther's 'fat period' silhouette. Sitting behind the reception desk without taking his eyes off the TV screen he helps himself to unseen food and carefully pours himself water taken from the fridge behind him, savouring it as if tasting vintage wine. Maybe you can be a connoisseur of water in the desert; it makes a kind of sense.

But he is a gentle man and deals with people's requests in a quietly avuncular manner with mock annoyance, the kind where he refuses to admit he enjoys each intrusion. One such interruption comes from a pushy young guide called Abou who arrives in beige-coloured robes and cannot understand why I don't want him to show me around the town.

'I just want to stroll around on my own,' I tell him.

I get the look – the 'you have hurt my feelings and my ancestors' feelings and I shall put a curse on you' kind of look.

'Why you no like me?'

'I don't dislike you,' I say.

'Come, we go now, I show you the mosques and everything.'

'No, you're all right. I'm fine on my own.'

The ride into town has to be taken with caution as vehicles swerve unpredictably over the sand in search of the elusive patch of road with a little grip. I pass the *Flamme de la Paix* (Flame of Peace), a hideous war monument on the edge of town. The memorial marks the spot where more than 3,000 weapons were destroyed to signal the end of the Tuareg rebellion in 1996, but is now a gathering place for untethered goats and resting camels.

The aura of Tombouctou grew in Europe from the late Middle Ages because of tales that it stored unlimited gold and also because it was so difficult to reach. The most direct route for European explorers was to take a camel train across the Sahara, which had obvious drawbacks, or to machete their way through West Africa (largely, my route). When explorers got close to the fabled city they rarely survived to tell the tale – as Mungo Park and Gordon Laing, the first European to successfully visit the city in 1826, found out first-hand.

Tombouctou's location on the Niger River at a meeting point of ancient trade routes between North Africa and sub-Saharan Africa helped it grow as a centre of learning and commerce for desert tribes – Songhai, Wangara, Fulani, Tuareg and Arab – from the tenth century. The desert's most prized commodity – salt – came from the north, and was exchanged for gold from the south.

By the twelfth century, Tombouctou was a sophisticated centre of Islamic learning and commerce with three universities and scores of Quranic schools. During this time hundreds of thousands of manuscripts covering every subject from astronomy to music were written, which helped create the many libraries in the city. But many were ransacked by invading tribes over the centuries, including Europeans. To save the manuscripts from colonial plunder they were buried in the sand or handed down through the generations. Many are being unearthed to this day.

For me the city wears a cloak of impenetrability, and the ancient silent libraries and high-walled mosques of mud and straw add to the mood. The residential neighbourhoods – marked out by communal bread ovens at each corner – are sparsely populated in the middle of the day; those who do venture out into the merciless heat move over the burning sand as if seeking atonement, in deep contemplation.

Sandy streets take me to sandy stores where I buy sandy goods from sandy shopkeepers. In the evening the streets are populated with strikingly diverse tribal groups: the Tuareg with long faces, straight noses and mottled complexions, the Songhai with darker skin and flatter noses and the Fulani people with their smooth, shiny skin, all wearing face scarves against the wind and robes of khaki or blue. A customer next to me pulls down his *tagilmust*, or face scarf, and meets my gaze with a fine layer of golden dust on his own features. I look down to see I am also covered in powdery yellow.

I decide to stock up on some local currency for the long trip down to Burkina Faso in the next few days. The bank is closed (it's Saturday) so I try the Western Union office, where I bump into Abou, the guide from the hotel, who offers to take me to a money-changer in town. I have little option if I want to pay for my rooftop accommodation with céfa. Abou rearranges his robes, jumps on the pillion and takes me to a small grocery store. He says the rate should be around 400 CFA to the US dollar. He goes in to have a word with the shopkeeper while I wait with the bike. He returns to say that the rate has unfortunately gone down to 350. I hand him $100.

A small child, perhaps ten or eleven years old, overhears our conversation and when Abou is out of earshot the boy says in remarkably clear English, 'The rate is four hundred. He is thief!'

I go into the shop where the transaction is taking place and ask for confirmation of the exchange rate. After some significant looks between Abou and the shopkeeper he punches 350 into a calculator and spins it round on the counter for me to read. I can do nothing. I feel stupid for allowing him to change my money; I let my guard down for a second and I get punished for it. I take the 35,000 CFA and vow to return without Abou to sort this out one way or the other. To add insult to the rip-off he insists I give him a lift back to the Western Union office.

I go back to the money-changer an hour later on my own with another $40 in hand. He says 350; I say 400. He shrugs and hands me 16,000 CFA. So the rate *is* 400 to the dollar. On the way back to the hotel I see the small boy who witnessed the con and as a thank you I give him a ride on the bike and hand him a little money for food.

Somehow I've got to get my missing 5,000 back from this dodgy guide, but first I need some leverage over him. Later that evening I see Abou skulking around in the hotel lobby like a hyena looking for scraps – I decide to offer him some.

I make up a story that I have four friends on bikes arriving in Tombouctou in a couple of days who have asked me to recommend a guide.

'Would you be able to look after them, Abou?'

'Yes, most surely.'

He can hardly contain himself.

'It's not too many for you, four people?'

'No, is good, is good,' he answers eagerly.

I ask him to write down his name, address, email, phone number and guide's licence number in my notebook, 'so that my friends will only come to you, Abou.'

Once he has signed away any advantage he had over me and registered an annoyingly smug look of self-satisfaction, I say, 'Right, Abou. You owe me five thousand céfa. This morning you told me the exchange rate was three-fifty but it is four hundred.'

'No, three hundred fifty.'

'I went back to the money-changer this afternoon and I got four hundred to the dollar.'

'M-maybe he forget the rate.'

'And maybe you forgot you're supposed to be a guide, not a con man.'

'I no con!'

'I want my money. I don't have much as it is.'

'I no have money.'

'You spent it already?'

He looks at me with deceitful eyes and goes quiet.

'I will speak to the man and ask for your money,' he says.

'I don't care how you get it, but I want it tonight. I leave tomorrow.' He knows I'm serious and is clearly concerned that I have all his contact details written in his own handwriting.

'You will have your money this night,' he says unpersuasively, then wafts out the door.

He returns half an hour later, empty-handed, and asks Luther to front him the cash by knocking 5,000 CFA off my bill, which he will repay at a later date. I double check; it's all OK. Result.

Abou looks sheepishly down at my notebook in which I am now writing and says he wants the damning page of personal details.

'No way!' I say, gripping the book so tight my fingers turn white.

'Can you...' he indicates that I should scribble out the details with my pen.

I adopt a look of horror. I'm really enjoying this. Abou turns on his heels and slinks out into the night.

9
DJENNÉ, BOBO, WAGGA AND ON TO THE NIGERIA BORDER

Just enjoy it.
Lord and Lady Shuttleworth

Two days later I retrace my route west through the flood plain of the Bani River to Djenné over narrow causeways, temporary lagoons and wide rivers overflowing from the rains. Whole families fish together, wash together, live together; they load wood onto donkeys and carts or punt their way through the water on pirogues. It's an idyllic scene that is ruined by the presence of the bike as everyone interrupts their work to follow me with their eyes; they smile, they wave.

Every building in the beautiful town is built from the same material – one they have a lot of in Djenné – mud. On street corners there are areas that resemble children's sandpits where mud is mixed and prepared for application. The mud bricks are created three or four months ahead of their use to harden in the sun. Other buildings rely on the mud being applied by hand after it is mixed with straw. Following the annual rain, which washes the outer layer away from every building, the whole painstaking process starts over again. The people are very protective of their artisanal skills. A man applying the mud with straw mixture to the side of a building refuses to allow me to take a picture, claiming I am trying to steal his techniques.

The main architectural feature of the town is the magnificent mosque, the largest mud structure in the world. The permanent scaffolding poles, which also lend strength to the building, protrude from the three tall minarets in spiky threat, like a huge weapon of war.

There is an organic atmosphere within the narrow alleyways as if all the buildings were connected in some way, which of course they are, being made from the same material. One could easily believe the buildings grew out of the earth. I toy with the idea that when the inhabitants enter their homes they descend into the ground below to one huge chamber: the earth people of Djenné. The uniformity in appearance of the town extends to the demeanour of its people, who wear mostly simple gowns and sandals, which makes it a very harmonious place in which to stroll. Sand underfoot and the blistering sun complete the – it has to be said – biblical scene.

From Djenné I pick up the main road towards Bobo-Dioulasso in Burkina Faso (which is worth the trip for the tongue-twisting name alone). It's good to be eating up the miles heading south after the detour to Tombouctou. The route follows the Bani River to the west and a ripple of bare hills to the east. On the way, I stop in the town of San for something to eat. That is easier said than done. I cannot find one food outlet; there are no street vendors, nor even a shop that sells anything that could pass for a meal. What do these people eat? Very little by the way many look. I am directed to the *gare routière*, where a few locals are waiting for the next bus or taxi to another life. The area is crammed with people including a loose pack of emaciated kids, shoeless and in rags with the drawn look of the utterly destitute, their oversized hands and feet a sure sign of pitiless malnourishment.

I ask a woman behind a makeshift counter, '*Restaurant ici?*'

'*Oui. Riz avec sauce?*'

My usual, if you please...

The bike has attracted a crowd and I settle down on a low bench that faces out into the open space where frail taxis park. There is a small boy who I take to be the cook's son eating rice and sauce a few feet away, while two more small boys on the other side of the counter try to sell me three bananas.

'No bananas, *merci.*'

They sit back on their haunches and wait, staring at me.

The woman takes a plastic bowl from the ground, rinses it off in a bucket of scummy water then deposits into it a mound of white rice. Then she takes it to another pot from which she dribbles a reddish, lumpy sauce before handing it to me with a large spoon wedged in the side like a spade in hardening cement. Unbidden, she then places a glass of tea next to me on the bench. She must have heard I was coming. The woman shoos the gathering pack of children away from the table to give me some room to eat. It is a struggle to swallow; the rice is stodgy and almost tasteless and the groundnut-flavoured sauce has the consistency of vomit, but I am famished and I have to get some of this fuel down. The one high point of the meal is when I accidentally bite down on a red chilli, tearing up my eyes.

I signal to the two boys that I'll have the bananas after all – they knew I would buy eventually – and wash them down with the tea which has the extraordinary taste of crushed aspirin. I give the food another half-hearted go and notice there is a larger crowd of children now watching every reluctant spoonful that goes into my mouth. They have gone oddly quiet. The atmosphere has changed and the chants of 'white man, white man' have stopped. There seems to be an increase in pressure within the compound and I feel the urge to leave. I push the bowl of leftovers away from me across the low table, at which point about a dozen hungry faces, waiting for this very moment, lunge for the bowl. For some reason my instinct is to quickly grab it back. In turn they all jump backwards to their starting places. The cook shouts something at them, but they stand their ground and stare banefully at her and then back to my bowl of leftovers. A man walks around the side of the building carrying what looks like a whip (but it can't possibly be, can it?), shouting malevolent threats at them all. He strides up to the nearest boy and – yes, it is a whip! – the boy gets a thwwwackk! on his back and yelps away like a mistreated cur. The whip cuts through the air as the children dance and dodge to avoid the swings. Jesus, did I cause that?

The bowl of leftovers is still on the table and the children are daring to edge back to swipe the rice. I see the feral look in their eyes now that my food is almost within their grasp. I look around for the woman who runs the food kitchen.

'What should I do?' I ask, helplessly.

But what should I do? Share it out equally, which would mean a teaspoonful each? Buy a portion of rice and sauce for each of them? But I would surely create a riot and more would appear. Do nothing, even though the man with the whip is still looking threatening? I appeal to the woman again. She seems to know what to do; she picks up the bowl and hands it to the boy sitting next to me who scrapes the contents on top of his own.

'No! He's got plenty of food,' I protest, 'these kids are starving!'

The little sod then starts cruelly playing with the food in his mouth taunting the crowd of kids. I am appalled. I know I've ballsed this up. I consider again giving the woman 10,000 CFA to feed all the children but I am getting dagger looks from her and the whip man. I try to think quickly, but if I had a year to devote to the problem of righting this wrong I don't think I could do it. I take the cowardly way out and leave.

I had my chance to make a tiny difference to one day in these kids' lives and I fluffed it. I had an opportunity to feed a few bellies but instead rode off, confused, anguished and guilty. I take the road back out of town with adrenalin searing through me. I hate myself, knowing I have witnessed something today that will stay with me for years to come.

I can think of nothing but rice and hunger and whips all afternoon until, in a bizarre coincidence, I bump into two South Africans at a remote roadside lean-to kitchen who are driving a four-by-four from Cape Town to Britain. Their presence helps release me from my private trauma. The hirsute John and Mike call themselves the African Surfers. Perhaps it illustrates the difference between the Springbok and Lancashire approaches to trans-African travel that they are doing a surfer tour of the continent while the Brew Ha-Ha just wants to sit down for a nice cup of tea.

They suggest I visit some Zimbabwean farmers in Nigeria and promise to forward details by email. The thought strikes me, 'What are Zimbabwean farmers doing in Nigeria?' – but I don't question them.

John checks out the Triumph and all my gear parked up next to their crammed four-by-four: 'You have so much stuff... and yet, so little.'

I know exactly what he means.

Another curious incident occurs on the road to Bobo later that afternoon. Approaching the Mali-Burkina border – in case you ever find yourself there – there's a T-junction with a *poste de contrôle* at the corner on the left, with three oil drums in the road. An immediate left leads to a roadblock of three more. I drift over to the left-hand side looking for signs of life, a signal, a wave. I see nothing and continue on to the second barrier when I hear a loud blast from a whistle. I look over and see a uniform remonstrating with me from a prone position on a camp bed. I think he wants a word.

Without preamble, he demands, 'Driver registration!'

I hand him my driving licence, which he scans quickly and pockets.

'*Régulation à la droite!* You pay three thousand!'

I fake ignorance. He takes me to the place where I drifted over to the left side of the road. He points to the very spot on the tarmac where the heinous crime was committed and says, '*À la droite* in English, what is?'

'Right.'

'No, is wrong!'

He smiles gummily. He can't speak much English apparently but he can pun.

I claim that I was on the left side of the road because I was riding into the post, it being impossible to get there without actually crossing the centre at some point. He gives little eye contact, returns to his cot and picks up a sheet of paper on which he is tallying up some figures – totalling the weekly fines extracted from unwary Europeans, no doubt. This is what westerners complain about on the African continent: the arbitrariness of officialdom, the disorder and spitefulness, the sheer lawlessness. He is living up to every African-in-a-uniform stereotype for the sake of a few francs.

I walk over to him and once more I explain a little too patronisingly, 'I saw the control post and moved over to look for you. I couldn't see you but when I heard you whistle I stopped, didn't I?'

With an exaggerated look of petulance, he says, 'Me no speak English, only French. You speak me French.'

Are you sure? Have you heard my French?

'Look, I'm sorry...'

'EN FRANÇAIS!'

I take a deep breath.

'Je arrive ici. Je see le poste de contrôle et je ride la moto à la gauche, après oil drums et then... J'écoute le whistle et je voir you... et je arret... Le fin.'

I can see a crinkle of a smile as his eyes roll. I continue...

'Par Blackburn, Angleterre, à ici à la moto, oui. Dix mille kilometres! Après ici je go to Burkina, Benin, Nigeria à Africa Sud.'

In spite of himself he begins to comprehend what I'm saying. He looks over at the moto that has done ten thousand kilometres but still protests weakly, 'You pay, you pay three thousand!'

'*Non, monsieur, s'il vous plaît. Je ne voir pas*, I've said I'm sorry, *pardon.*'

Look pal, I can go on in this ridiculous franglais for as long as you want me to – for longer than you can stand, actually. He walks over to a uniformed colleague and explains my infraction and my trip.

He returns and asks, 'You *militaire?*'

'No, I'm a teacher.' (In Senegal I was a gardener; I feel like a change.)

'What you teach?'

'*Anglais. Je* teach *l'Anglais.*'

He finds this terrifically amusing, an English English teacher teaching English to English students, and I sense his attitude begin to soften. I take out some loose change in my pocket and say pathetically, '*S'il vous plaît* I don't have *trois* thousand, *regardez.*'

A well-timed interruption arrives in the shape of a boy carrying a tray with two perfect glasses of tea. As the song goes, 'Everything stops for tea.' He offers one to the policeman and nods for me to take the second, which I do.

I raise the glass and say, 'To Mali. *Sláinte!*'

'"Slansh." Is English?'

'No, Irish!'

'*Ah, Gaélique!*'

The policeman's attitude has done a complete one-eighty and there are some very pleasant vibes in the air now. My unexpected Tea Encounter acknowledges the salutation and slurps his tea through the froth. My traffic violation has effortlessly morphed into another serendipitous Tea Encounter.

I take a mouthful… eeeowwwurghglglgl. Pure tea syrup. If it was any stronger it'd be solid.

He turns to two junior officers with a shrug. He gives me a little speech in conciliatory tones of which I don't understand a single word and hands me back my licence with a smile that suggests 'no hard feelings'.

'I can go? No *trois* thousand?'

'*Non. Bon voyage, au revoir… et bonne chance.*'

The African stereotype shows its other face. Just when I get exasperated with the chaos and ridiculousness of this place somebody does something so unexpected and humane – and shares a cup of tea. He shakes my hand and for no good reason I turn and salute the other two officers.

'*La frontiere, en kilomètres?*'

He takes his pen and writes: 18. '"Ten eight", is correct?'

'No, "eighteen". *Dix-huit est* "eighteen", OK? How far to Bobo?' I ask.

He writes: 160. He looks at me nervously, 'One hundred… *et*… sixty?'

'*Oui, exactement,*' I answer.

'Is not easy language, the English.'

'Neither is French,' I reply, and everybody fills the empty air with a discharge of unrestrained laughter.

There are few things better than arriving on a motorbike late in the evening in a new city and then ending the night drinking Flag beer and gorging on pizza. Bobo-Dioulasso makes a good first impression on me from my seat in this little restaurant. Afternoon tea with Lord and Lady Shuttleworth in Lancashire some months ago (memorable for the first and only time a housekeeper helped me on with my motorcycle jacket) left me with some brief but important advice for the trip: 'Just enjoy it.' And sitting here in Bobo tonight, I do just that. Until, that is, I go to my hotel room and spend an edgy night haunted by the hungry faces of the little ones I left behind in San this morning.

I spend the next morning in Bobo updating the blog surrounded by Western-dressed business people sending emails over coffee. I am surprised by this oasis of urbanity in a country that has no paved road to its border with Mali.

This 'land of upright people' ('Burkina' and 'Faso' is a forced blend of the dominant Moré and Dioula native languages) is very welcoming to me, and not just because it feels like someone turned down the heat from ten to eight.

The next day I ride 300 kilometres on a largely tarmac road to Ouagadougou (another place name I just have to visit), the capital city. The following morning I stop at a tea wagon called Super Allah 1 in downtown Wagga (as it's known locally). After the first alarming sip I believe I have discovered the very opposite of the ultimate cuppa – on this evidence there's little chance of successfully franchising Super Allah 2 or Super Allah 3.

Later, I go to the only four-star hotel in town, near the airport, for a beer. I meet someone in the bar who speaks some English and he invites me to a Rotary Club meeting that is soon to take place in a private room. He orders me a cup of tea and I sit bemused by the discussions in French. The meeting is very informal – people drift in and out all evening – but they are a friendly bunch. A lawyer member

offers to drive me back to town and as we walk down the
steps of the hotel he points to a little man who brushes past
me, having just exited a limousine surrounded by motorcycle
outriders.

'He is the president,' the lawyer says.

'Couldn't he come to the club meeting?' I ask.

'No, he is president – of the country!'

Next day the stay becomes memorable when someone tries
to sell me a rifle. It isn't a surreptitious rendezvous under a
bridge or in a deserted car park but in broad daylight while
I am waiting for the lights to change.

I make the mistake of using sarcasm. 'If you can find any
room on this bike for a rifle, I'll have it,' I say.

At which invitation the man begins unfastening the bungee
straps to wriggle the rifle onto the back of the bike.

'NON, NON, NON!' I yell, and manage to ride off, leaving
the arms dealer in the road holding aloft two rifles, looking
like Jesse James.

This is only one of many encounters involving people in
the most popular form of casual employment throughout
Africa – the one-item-for-sale street vendor. Phone card
sellers account for a large percentage of them, but I have
also been approached by boys selling tissues in a Senegal
bar, a man trying to sell me a coffee machine at traffic lights,
youths selling warm processed cheese, girls selling underwear
outside an embassy, ties at a police checkpoint, apple corers
in Casablanca, calculators in Banjul. They often approach
me when stationary in traffic but sometimes will run beside
the bike to explain how I cannot possibly live without one of
their kitchen pedal bins or cheese graters. In Nouakchott a
vendor tried to sell me a 'Rolex' ('is very good appearance'),

and when I lifted my right arm to show him I already had a watch he quickly clamped the fake onto my wrist next to my own with a satisfied smile – 'Look! Is much better than yours, monsieur. Is Rolex!'

After a few beers watching a band at an open-air bar on my second night in Wagga I spread all the maps out on the floor of my hotel room and get worked up to a mild panic. I am engulfed by the feeling that I'm at least a week away from where I want to be. It is mid-November already and I have to be in Zanzibar in five weeks. Sitting here staring at the map I know it is a forlorn hope: Benin, Nigeria, Cameroon, Gabon, Congo, DR Congo, Angola, Zambia and Tanzania lie ahead of me. Just writing it down is not so much a disappointment as an embarrassing admission of my own ambition.

The journey to Benin, my seventh African frontier, and onwards through that slender country rushes by like the view from a speeding train. With good immigration control – a brief negotiation for an indistinct stamp in my passport, cash only – and some decent roads, I spend only one night there. For the first time in weeks I ride through hilly country and have time to appreciate the cool breeze and twisty roads, which remind me of the Peak District. Later I spend a chilly and rainy night in an otherwise deserted hotel.

The road from Nikki, the last town in Benin, to the border with Nigeria is a rough narrow track, which slows progress and feeds my doubts about whether I will reach the first town over the border before dark, a constant worry at all the remote frontier posts. There is a checkpoint in the middle of Nikki, and even though I am waved through by a uniformed guard, something tells me I should stop to confirm directions or undergo some formalities, basically the kind of thing that usually happens.

The neglected road continues with huts so close to the track that I can see what people are eating inside. The sun is the overpowering blistering force in this dusty place and the looks on the crinkled faces of the people all the way to the frontier tell me that there is no other subject on their minds; ever, maybe. The golden disc in the sky is a constant presence, like an ache or a troublesome friend: you curse its very existence but you know you just have to live with it.

The border post at Tchikandou is just one man and a stray pregnant bitch with an improvised barrier across the dirt road. As I approach, the man calls into a hut from where an immigration official with terminal exhaustion emerges. He invites me to sit down on a log next to him in the slim shade of a baobab tree. After polite greetings, the sole representative of the Republic of Benin, who doesn't need the aggro of a European who actually wants to cross the frontier, goes back into his hut and returns with two pages torn from a child's maths exercise book. He asks the usual questions, the first of which (and it's always the somewhat redundant first question at the border post) is *'Votre destination?'* As I am standing on the very edge of Benin with only Nigeria ahead, the stop-arsing-about-with-your-daft-questions side of me feels a strong urge to answer 'Ouagadougou', 500 miles in the opposite direction, just to test his sense of irony. But instead I brightly respond, 'Nigeria!'

He slowly and deliberately works his way through his questions, but as African border crossings go it is a thoroughly amiable episode and I almost feel loath to leave after I answer the last question, *'Profession?'*

'*Pêcheur.*' (Professional angler.)

Lassitude is the prescription of the day, but the atmosphere soon develops into one of idle good-naturednees and I wouldn't be surprised if he offers me a cup of tea. I should push on, and I look forward to clearing customs, getting my carnet stamped and making some progress in Nigeria.

'*Douanes est là?*' I ask, pointing beyond the barrier and down the track.

'*Douanes? Non. Douanes est en Nikki, vingt-quatre kilomètres,*' and he points back up the dusty track.

Damn. Damn. I must learn to listen more closely to my instincts – I should have stopped in Nikki after all. That's another round trip of fifty kilometres I could do without. I kick the bike then return to Nikki resenting every bloody minute and every bloody metre.

Half an hour later I reach the small building next to the barrier through which I was waved an hour or so earlier. There is a sleepy inexactitude in the air of this tiny space – too small to be called a building and too temporary to be called an office – so I eagerly hand over my carnet in the hope I can enthuse the officer into some sort of response.

'*Bonjour; carnet, s'il vous plaît?*'

The man in uniform hardly makes a move. He says the officer who has the stamp is not around but should return by three o'clock. It is now twenty past two. He waits for my reaction as his belligerent outward appearance of indifference knows this is not welcome news. In the meantime I am given a chair and we are joined by another two men who spot the bike outside, one in striking saffron robes.

The mood gets a little more jovial as they start drinking Guinness. Then someone switches on a romantic soap opera on a television with an almost unwatchable reception, and within twenty minutes there are six lachrymose eyes fixed to the screen. When the show ends they argue vociferously about the likely outcome of today's episode. I wonder if I'm in the right place.

At three o'clock a large man strolls – actually, it isn't even a stroll, it's more like an aimless wander in the general direction – towards his workplace. He opens the door and looks surprised to see me – to see anyone, I guess – as the uniformed officer vacates the seat behind the desk for him to sit down. My presence there is about as welcome as a turd on the doorstep: a visitor means work. The two men explain to him with the utmost seriousness why I'm here while he considers his options, which to me seem quite clear-cut: either he's going to stamp the carnet or he isn't.

With the look of a man who has just woken up he laboriously reads every used stub of the carnet from all the previous countries while playing with the inked stamp – and my immediate future – between his fingers. Every time he looks as if he is going to make the imprint on the page he has a change of heart and rereads the document just in case it personally commits him to a quarterly book club (we've all done it). The last ten minutes have felt like a week in jail. But I stay silent while boring him with my eyes transmitting 'JUST STAMP THE FECKIN' THING'.

And lo, as the heavens open, the angels sing and the divine light of God shines on his right hand, he sets down the red-inked stamp on the page with no less gravitas than if he were signing a peace treaty. Pressing with all his weight into the desk for a full five seconds, he looks up at me with the satisfied expression of a man with rare and awesome power – and he knows how to wield it. What a berk.

I pull the carnet from under his weakening grasp as he slumps back in his chair: he has done his duty; he has given; he is spent.

I excitedly retrace my steps to the two-men-and-a-bitch frontier. As I approach the barrier I have the carnet ready to wave in the air and the border guard takes more than a little pleasure in raising the tree branch and waving me through.

I wobble down a sandy track towards, well, towards very little indeed, actually. Ahead is an unfinished building with no windows and no sign of life, which could be someone's house or the customs office, the police station or a latrine; there is absolutely nothing to indicate which it might be. Inside, there are two bored-looking officials who go through the litany of questions, which I tell myself I must get printed and laminated to expedite these border crossings. They point me further down an impossibly rocky piece of ground to the customs office, where I see a sight I truly doubt I am actually witnessing. Maybe I am delirious from the heat or it is some kind of hoax, but there in front of me is a car with a cow in the boot. It is not an estate or a hatchback and it isn't a calf but a fully grown cow. In the boot of a car. Mooing. It is in a hugely ungainly position (which I suppose should go without saying), with its head and four hoofs hanging out the back like some ghastly pre-barbecue roadshow.

How the hell did it get in there? Did they promise it a new life in Nigeria? Maybe the car is a shared taxi and it couldn't get a seat inside. One thing is certain: the cow clears customs much quicker than I do.

10
WELCOME-WELCOME

Listen to the hearts of the people.
Rt Rev Nicholas Reade Bishop of Blackburn

My blood races a little faster knowing I have just entered one of the most infamous countries in Africa as far as personal safety is concerned. The email I received from Simon, the security guy from Lagos, returns to me and produces a little extra adrenalin in my body. Probably not a bad thing.

The state of the road towards Okuta is unspeakable, but far from riding into a land of bandits with guns cocked, my entrance into Nigeria is greeted by people cheering and applauding my arrival. This seems a ridiculous thing to write, but I am delighted to say that is exactly what happens. Imagine being cheered and applauded on your inaugural visit to Wigan, or Burnley, or Bolton. Try to picture men downing tools to applaud you, children interrupting hopscotch to cheer frantically, women dropping laundry to wave at the strange figure going past; but this is what happens to a white man on a Triumph in north-western Nigeria. These village people are willing to soak up any little splash of colour in their lives, and today I'm providing it.

The welcome of the people is in direct contrast to riding the hellish road – which is like bouncing a space hopper through a recently ploughed field – and the weather, which is steamy and wet. After I drop the bike in a deep slurry of mud in the fast-approaching twilight, I come to my senses and accept there is no way I can reach Okuta before dark. I take it slowly through a village – still cheered on by most of the people on the roadside – desperately looking for any building that may offer some sort of shelter for the night.

At the village limit, the point at which I need to make a decision whether to stay put or plug on, I can't help noticing school's out, as a wave of kids disperse from a dilapidated building nearby. I am soon surrounded by a crowd of cheering, applauding children. I tell them I am looking for somewhere to stay for the night and hesitantly ask if they know of a hotel. I have to say the word twice, so I know the answer is going to be no. I get a lot of blank looks so I suggest maybe I could stay in the now-empty school or even the nearby church.

Then one bright spark calls, 'To the pastor's house!'

Shouts of glee and 'YES! YES! YES!'

'Where is he?' I ask.

'THERE!'

They all point to a tumbledown building set back a few hundred metres from the road and start running in the direction I should follow, so I fire up the bike and do just that.

'WELCOME-WELCOME!' they shout.

Everyone is running and jumping towards the house, swinging their books and bags, applauding, whistling and screaming with the kind of sheer delight that only comes at Friday going-home time and the arrival of a stranger on a Triumph. I stand up on the pegs and ride off-road fashion. They love it, and so do I. They're all running now, sixty or seventy children, together with a few adults, trying to keep up with the bike as fast as their legs will allow all the way to the pastor's front door.

A young man wearing a plain white T-shirt, ill-fitting trousers and plimsolls comes out of the house and stands impassively on the verandah, which is a pretty incredible feat when you've got scores of screaming kids and a dishevelled biker on your doorstep. The man is followed out by an unkempt woman in a dirty top and blue headdress carrying a baby at her breast. I walk up the steps to shake the man's hand and explain what is going on. The entire crowd goes silent to hear the exchange.

'Are you the pastor?' I ask.

'Yes, I am... the pastor... here,' he answers.

'I'm passing through but I can't find a hotel and it's getting dark and I need somewhere to spend the night and... can I stay here? Or in your church?'

I pause and realise I'm gabbling out of desperation. I can't bear him to say no. He looks at me without expression. It's going to be a no, I can sense it. He surveys the crowd with his eyes, head perfectly still, as he decides what to do. He then looks at the bike, and back to me.

'Yes... you can stay here.'

The crowd, which has now swelled to well over a hundred, erupts into cheers, hugging each other, shaking my hands, applauding and emitting squeals of delight.

A battered sofa is brought out of the house on to the verandah for me to sit down and the pastor hands me a large bottle of water that someone has just brought from the village. I drink half of it in one draught. When I am done he introduces himself as Samuel, which he pronounces 'Samway'. He does not try to control the children who are now crowding around me and the bike, feeling the texture of my protective clothing, or just staring excitedly to see what I will do or say next; instead, Samuel indulges their every joke and enquiry.

I am astounded to see yet more people walking from the village to meet the white visitor and add to the festive atmosphere. The simple thought grows in my mind: Where am I?

Everybody shakes my hand amid formal introductions and bowing, and when I exclaim at the uproarious reception, Samuel says simply, 'This is Boriya. They are happy to see you.'

It is soon dusk in Boriya and a member of Samuel's congregation decides it is time to unload the bike. When all my gear is off and spread randomly about the house they say the bike must come in too. The Triumph is placed in the hallway where it looks huge, and the thirty or so people who can squeeze into the space stroke it with expressions of appreciation and not a little wonderment. I am offered a bench on which to sit next to the bike under their excited gazes and another forty peering in through the two doorways at either end of the hallway, one leading to the verandah, the other to a small backyard. The pastor sits next to me on the low bench, his wife next to him on a chair with the baby feeding, and some of the church congregation in privileged seats immediately opposite. There is an air of expectancy, with constant giggles from the children. Their English is poor for the most part and their interaction consists largely of kindly smiles and encouragement to drink more water whenever I hold a gaze.

The situation moves on when two somewhat smarter dressed men in their twenties arrive and introduce themselves as Gideon and Emanuel, teachers from the local school, whose pupils now surround me and the bike. Their spoken English is good and everyone is relieved that we have someone who can interpret.

'They're so excited,' I say, shaking my head.

'Of course,' says Gideon with surprise. 'You are the first white man many of them have ever seen.'

I am more than just a curiosity, I'm a freak. I get asked a lot of questions from Premiership-supporting kids about English football. I tell them about Preston North End and Burnley FC and Accrington Stanley in the hope that they will be wearing their shirts the next time a biker comes wobbling past. But I think they are more interested just to hear me speak and be part of this event than in what I am actually saying. Still, they enjoy it all with roars of laughter at the interpretations – Gideon has them in the palm of his hand.

After an hour or so of building Anglo-Nigerian relations and mindful of the fact that I am in a stranger's house and have brought a crowd with me, I decide I should try and settle for the evening and return the pastor's home to the quiet calm it must have been before my arrival. On cue, Samuel says his wife has prepared a shower for me and walks me out to the backyard. He swings open an outhouse door and points to a bucket filled with water and a new bar of soap. I hesitate at the door of the pitch-black privy and the mouldy, stone floor and look back at Samuel. He points at the bucket and says brightly, 'Shower.'

Over his shoulder I see we have been followed by a group of inquisitive little faces, waiting to see me take off my clothes. I try to ignore the activity in the yard and start stripping off. Gideon comes out and shoos the kids away as best he can.

'Why are they so curious?' I ask.

'They want to see if you are white... all over... heh, heh, heh,' he says.

After my wash, Samuel's wife, who also steals a few sideways glances at my pale body, interrupts pounding cassava in a wooden tub to give me a brief hygiene check before she lets me back into the house. She doesn't think I would like the cassava so decides to make me some chicken.

I return to the house to be told that all my gear is now in a downstairs bedroom, from which someone has been evicted for the night. I open the door to a grim sight. The only piece of furniture other than a double bed is a tiny table, barely large enough to hold a gas lamp, which is now hissing quietly upon it. The two paneless windows are covered with metal bars, mosquito screens and shutters – all locked. The temperature must be 110 degrees. As I move further into the room I notice an irregular swarm of darting cockroaches on the concrete floor and on the bed. I do my best to wipe the bugs off the sheet but more drop from the ceiling on to my head. I light a slow-burning mosquito coil and hang up the mozzie net in an effort to combat the little blighters but I'm fighting a losing battle.

I open the door to the hallway which remains packed with the curious. People are still arriving, all of whom require greeting in the formal way with a small bow and the right hand placed on the right knee. The food is ready and they want to serve it to me in my new cockroach motel, but I prefer to remain in the hallway and have human eyes rather than insect ones watch me eat.

The chicken leg, boiled eggs, a triple portion of rice and the slurry of hot sauce is very welcome and tasty, the onlookers living every mouthful with me. The cockroaches have infested the house and Samuel takes it upon himself to flick them off my clothing, plate, glass and hair whenever he sees them making progress, to everybody's great amusement.

'The children want to know why you are here,' says Gideon. 'Nobody ever comes here.'

'Tell them I'm travelling through Africa to have tea with people.'

He translates for everybody but I get empty looks.

'My host makes tea and we talk about Africa... and whatever else comes to mind...'

I can see I'm losing them, including Gideon and Emanuel, so I change the subject and ask about life in Boriya, which by all accounts has missed the train called 'progress' and is dreadfully poor. My arrival is greeted as that of an emissary from another world, from what these good people might view as the 'real world'. Although they live in one of the wealthiest countries in Africa, they feel left behind and forgotten. People want me to write down my name, address and other contact details – a common act of desperation – but I know nothing will come of it. The unbridled joy at my arrival is now overtaken by a realisation that they are all frantic for a way out of here and maybe I'm the person who can make that happen. To a large extent, I think these people have been forgotten, an insight which coats the evening with a layer of melancholy.

The tiredness of the day catches up with me, and eventually I have to face the insect-breeding hothouse.

I joke with Gideon, 'I'd better go to bed or no one will ever leave.'

He answers seriously, 'No, they will not.'

Between the crawling bugs in the bed and the unbearable heat I begin to identify more with torture victims than a guest traveller in the home of a man of the cloth. I feel guilty at my own ingratitude, but the night in the crawling pit is not pleasant. Somehow the day's exertions ensure that I get some sleep, but after tickles of crawling feet all over my body remind me where I am, I'm thrilled when I hear noises from elsewhere in the house signifying morning.

I dress quickly and open the door to a hallway full of people. I can't be certain, but I'm sure some of them were there when I went to bed. I ask politely what the family does for toilet arrangements and the wife hands me some loo roll and points towards the great outdoors. I kick the swing door open to see a larger group of people, many new faces, waiting for me to emerge. I can't hide my obvious biological need and there is a ripple of laughter and much indiscreet nudging as the word gets around that the white man is going to take a shit. Purposefully, I set forth into the bush, occasionally glancing over my shoulder for persistent pursuers.

I pack up the bike and prepare to say all the goodbyes when Gideon strides up to the house and, with the look of someone who knows something I don't, says, 'Good morning, Mister Alan. Pastor Samuel has something for you; he has bought tea and biscuits so we can all be in your Africa Brew.'

Samuel comes out on the verandah holding a box of tea, two tins of evaporated milk and a box of plain biscuits. The look on his face is a picture. I am speechless. I think of the welcome the previous evening, the shower, the meal, the bedroom prepared specially, and everybody who came to welcome me and feel a lump coming to my throat. Looking into Samuel's guileless eyes, I want to shout 'YES, this is what the Brew Ha-Ha is all about!' The Bishop of Blackburn's advice for the trip comes instantly to mind: 'Listen to the hearts of the people.' This morning I can hear them loud and clear in Boriya.

We move back into the hallway. The pastor's wife, who must remain 'the pastor's wife' as I am never told her name, comes in from the yard with a plastic bucket full of ready-made tea – hopefully not the one in which I bathed last night. She places a plastic cup down beside it and hands out a variety of mugs to about twelve people now sitting expectantly around a low table.

Gideon asks, 'What must we do?'

With a catch of guilt I say, 'Have tea... that's it. There's nothing else to it, just tea.'

Gideon translates for everyone holding an empty mug and all those, about another twenty, watching from the doorway. They are a little nonplussed by the crude nature of the ritual, expecting perhaps something more exceptional but accept that that's what I want and that's what I shall get. The pastor's wife hands me the plastic cup and I scoop a share from the bucket into my mug and hand it on to Samuel. More tea, vicar? I've never scooped tea before. He does the same. We are soon all having a jolly little tea party, one of the strangest I am ever likely to enjoy, but it's a tea party nonetheless and surely a contender for 'ultimate cuppa'.

Samuel drinks his tea solemnly and ensures I get a few biscuits as everybody is now taking handfuls, no doubt to feed family back home.

He says, 'God has sent you to us for a reason. Now everyone should see you in the flesh. Please stay for tomorrow Sunday service.'

As his English is poor I suspect he has been rehearsing that line all night. I come for tea and Samuel treats me like the second coming.

'No, I can't stay. I'm sorry,' I say. 'I have to keep moving. But thank you for your kind offer.'

A look of disappointment registers on his face but he says nothing.

The crowd in the warm sunshine outside is growing so as soon as we are done I finish loading up the bike. I offer Samuel a spare wrist watch I have been carrying and some money for his wonderful hospitality, which he gratefully accepts as he must be seriously out of pocket from the whole experience, then start up the bike to cheers and applause.

As I ride back to the dirt road I left fifteen hours before, I honk the horn and wave frantically to more cheers and shouts of 'WELCOME-WELCOME' and 'GOODBYE-EE'.

'Goodbye everyone! Goodbye Boriya!'

It is a beautiful new day on the Brew Ha-Ha as I leave the wonderful village of Boriya with a pinched smile, blinking tears from my eyes.

The road improves slightly on yesterday's stretch from the border but then completely disintegrates along the small tracks to Ilorin, 150 kilometres away. The route is lined by lush vegetation encroaching on the road, which sometimes feels like riding through a hedge. When I arrive there I ask for directions to a money-changer from a car driver intent on the same transaction, so I follow him. When we arrive, the driver, who is resplendent in immaculate robes and cap, formally introduces himself as Judge Ola Abdulkadir and gives me an intricate handshake, which I take to be a sign of the Freemason's. I don't know what to do with the signal, so I keep my options open by mustering a knowingly enigmatic smile. He writes down his phone number and says that if I ever need any help during my time in the country I should give him a call. But after the emailed advice from Simon, I hope I shall never need to. The judge also ensures I get a good rate with the money-changer who happens to double as a dry cleaner – handy for money laundering, I think to myself.

I find an Internet café and check my emails. There is one from the African Surfers I bumped into in Mali. They have cc'd me on an email to one of the Zimbabwean farmers they mentioned, asking if the farmer might find some time to have tea with me. There has been no reply yet, but it is encouraging nonetheless. I Google the farms and discover they are around a hundred kilometres north-east of Ilorin in a place called Shonga.

A young man at the next computer who has been reading all my emails gaily says, 'I know where is Shonga. Come. I show you the junction for Shonga road.'

'Great.'

That's made up my mind for me. He stands up, leaving his girlfriend, who is waiting patiently for him, and leads the way.

'What about me?' she asks.

'Wait here. I will be back, can't you see this man needs my help?!'

I throw the girlfriend a guilty look but she scowls, folds her arms and slumps back into her chair.

It all points to good omens, and although the Zimbabwean farmers don't know me, and don't know I'm coming, I sense, with absolutely no good reason or justification, I may be made welcome.

With no direction signs or distance markers, the trip to Shonga is a mystery tour. I have to make regular and frequent stops to ask for directions, to which everybody responds, 'You go to Zimbabwe farmers? Small-small.'

Their reputation precedes them and for as long as I get that response I must be in the right state at least. I am soon on a darkening road, unmarked on my map, going to a village with no direction markers to see people who have never met me and who don't know I'm arriving. I lose my bearings. I could be anywhere. I ride for over an hour and still haven't seen a sign for Shonga, or any other town marked on my map for that matter. I start playing leapfrog with a guy driving a truck full of goats who overtakes me each time I stop for directions.

He shouts out of the window, 'Zimbabwe farmers?'

I give him the thumbs up.

'Small-small, follow me!'

Twenty minutes later we arrive at a crossroads where we immediately attract a crowd. An elderly man on a moped acknowledges me, confirms he will take me to the Zim farmers and sharply sets off with a pillion rider at speed. He turns down a sandy track, but I have to slow as the bulk of the bike struggles in the deep wallowy sand. It is practically dark now. The moped ahead has no rear light yet he refuses to slow down and I do my best to follow an indistinct shape some way ahead with the pillion shouting directions over his shoulder. I am sliding through great swathes of corn and cassava, racing to beat the final shadows of twilight – for tea. This is crazy.

As I become aware of the surreal nature of the experience, reality hits me like a bus over my foot on a cold morning. I hit the deck hard and the bike slides into the ripening corn. It's painful; I've pulled a muscle in my back, I've cracked my elbow and expelled every last breath of air from my lungs. The contents of the left pannier are broadcast in the sand over a wide area and the tank bag is split open. My guides run back to help as I struggle to catch a mouthful of air on my hands and knees. Pathetically, I indicate to them to gather up the strewn belongings and throw them into the box as if my life depended on it.

Soon, through the gloom, I am relieved to finally see the welcoming lights of a homestead up ahead. A guard opens the gate and I limp up to the front door past the kitchen where a woman is preparing an evening meal for two. It's beginning to feel so wrong: I'm in my usual end-of-day sweaty heap – with extra sand in the creases – gatecrashing a Saturday night dinner for two. I knock, but what the hell do I say? A white man opens the door...

'Hello, I'm travelling through Africa on a tea tour...'

... he looks me up and down...

'... and some, ahh, surfers I met in Mali said I might be able to...'

... and says in distinctly southern African tones, 'Don't worry. We'll sort you out, man. Come in and watch the rugby, yah.'

Within thirty seconds I'm watching satellite TV with a beer in my hand and have an offer to do my laundry while I take a shower. I'm not sure Dan and Jenny Swart listen too intently to my incoherent gabbling; they just see a European in need of a few home comforts and any further explanation is unnecessary. Jenny stretches their meal to feed three and I am treated like a returning member of the family. It is as if I have reached southern Africa already: the comfortable open-plan living, the sport on TV, the roast brought to the table, the ready cans of cold beer, the pack of large friendly dogs moving languidly from room to room, the easy conversation.

In bed that night with a full belly, ensconced in beautiful linen on a muscle-soothing mattress and cooled by the air conditioning, I reflect on my previous night's stay in the bug house and consider the bizarre course the Brew Ha-Ha is taking. Despite the obvious difference in lifestyle, Pastor Samuel and the Swarts are cut from the same cloth when it comes to helping a stranger in need.

The next day I find myself enjoying a colonial-style Sunday afternoon tea party (the sort I deluded myself into believing might be served throughout Africa) with four home-made cakes and tea (with milk!). Three white farming couples, Dan and Jenny Swart, Graham and Judy Hatty and Mike and Claire Hellam, are meeting after church to talk about the harvest, their plans for the future and the imminent arrival of fresh livestock. But my hosts are no commonplace farmers; they are practically refugees who until three years ago were helping Zimbabwe live up to its soubriquet of the 'bread basket of Africa'. That was before Robert Mugabe's thugs, risibly known as the 'war veterans', moved in and threw them off their farms with just enough time to pack a few things and leave before things got ugly.

After some time treading water in the Zimbabwean capital, Harare, as the country descended from 'bread basket' to 'basket case', in 2004 the farmers received an unexpected invitation from the governor of Kwara state to introduce commercial farming here. Who better to call on than some recently dispossessed experts with the knowledge that was lacking amongst his rural communities. (It is thought that Mugabe responded angrily to the offer, claiming Nigeria was 'stealing' his farmers. More fool him.)

After negotiating loans and visas, thirteen white Zimbabwean families started afresh thousands of miles from the lives they knew but still on the continent they love. Astonishingly, before their arrival, there was no commercial farming in Nigeria. The successful experiment is attracting attention from other states and further afield throughout Africa – and explains why their project is so renowned along the road from Ilorin.

Graham says, 'I wasn't far off retirement when Mugabe started grabbing the land from the white farmers in his so-called Land Resettlement Scheme. I never thought I'd have to start over at my age, but what's our alternative? Farming is in our blood, so we've got to give it a go.'

We all get stuck into the tea and cake as the wives, more so than the husbands, talk about what they lost under the twisted policy of 'land reform' in Zimbabwe.

Judy says, 'All these people walked onto our farm one day and demanded we leave. The farm was stolen by an army general with no farming experience who hired a Chinese manager to run the operation. I asked him what he was going to do about the school for our workers' children, which we subsidised. He said, "If the school does not pay for itself then we shall close it." The man was a fool. How can any school make money?'

I acknowledge the bitterness and injustice in her voice.

'The school is closed now, and all those families, that whole generation, has lost out. It's a crime. The farm's current production is around fifteen per cent of the output during our time.'

But the human spirit can be resilient. On a short tour of Dan and Jenny's farm, I am astounded at how much they have achieved in only three years.

'From a standing start, we cleared virgin bush and planted one thousand hectares of cassava, maize and soya beans, with a small amount of bananas and mangos,' says Dan. 'We will soon produce fresh milk at the dairy I'm building with two other farmers – the first in the region.'

The last time I had any fresh milk was probably in Morocco. It's great to know they will soon be producing a vital ingredient for the humble cuppa. We walk back towards the house encircled by the early development of a garden, which will complete the colonial atmosphere.

'I lived in a tent while I built this house,' he says matter of factly. 'There was nothing here before, just raw veldt.'

I spend another night and try to commit to memory how comfortable the bed is in the hope it will sustain me in the weeks ahead. After I allow myself to be looked after for a couple of days, Dan and Jenny probably think, 'How the hell is this guy going to make it to Cape Town? He can't do anything for himself.' Two loads of laundry, some excellent cooking, much-needed help repairing the bashed-up panniers, a bike wash, a gear wash, a me wash and some valuable time off helped me recharge the almost-dead batteries. Two nights earlier I turned up in darkness with the lame introduction, 'I'm travelling through Africa meeting people for tea.' The words sounded ridiculous as they came out and I now cringe to think of it. But sometimes it pays to go in the front door and be honest about your failings because the more I continue on this trip the more I have learned to expect the best out of people.

I drag myself away from the Swarts' hospitality and head off towards Enugu and then on to Calabar (thus avoiding Lagos and the TV studios Mr Dunladi recommended). My excitement is boosted knowing that I will be cutting a path through Nigeria in the next few days in contradiction to all the travel warnings. I put in plenty of tarmac miles – which is a novelty – and follow a series of conflicting directions towards Calabar in the south, but I don't pass a single town marked on my map all day so I'm never certain if I am heading in the right direction, nor even sure which road I'm on. I show the map to people who want to help but when nobody knows where they are on the map my own uncertainty is reinforced. I press on through the featureless landscape of scrubby bush hoping to get lucky.

With so few road signs or direction markers, a major feature of travelling around Nigeria is stopping to ask for directions, whether they turn out to be helpful or not.

'How far to Igboho?'

'Small-small.'

'How far to Ilorin?'

'On this machine? Not far.'

'How long will it take me to get to Kabba?'
'I don't know how fast you ride, do I?'

'How long will it take to get to Lokoja?'
'Half an hour, definitely. Or an hour. Or two.'

'Is this the road to Enugu?'
'Yes. Straight, straight, straight... until you turn right.'

'The road to Enugu?'
'It is here. It is close.'

'How far to Abakaliki?'
First man: 'An hour.'
Second man: 'Under three hours.'
Both: 'Yes.'

'The road to Calabar?'
'Like this, like this and like this.'

'Where is the restaurant?'
'If you go directly there you will locate it.'

I stop in the moribund town of Utukpa for the night (I am almost certainly going in the wrong direction) and ask around for a hotel. I get taken to the 'Ocatel' which turns out to be the Oak Hotel, 'the best hotel in Utukpa', a stinking dive up a dirt track with no electricity, no food and an atmosphere of brooding menace. The watchful youth showing me the room asks for 2,000 naira. I look from the pitiful bed in the middle of the room dressed only with a rag to the squalid state of the bathroom and I laugh doubtfully.

I say, 'I don't think so. I'll find one with a shower for that much money.'

He laughs mirthlessly, 'There is no hotel in Utukpa with shower.'

He waits for my reaction. By way of encouragement he points to the tap with a red blob on the faucet as if to suggest I won't need a shower with plentiful hot water from the sink. I bargain him down to 1,500 – about £7 – so I don't feel too bad and take the room. I soon learn the youth's duplicity when I discover no water comes out of the tap with the red blob – it's not even plumbed in. But there is a bucket from which I can have a shower once I fill it from the cold water tap. As I stretch out on the edge of the bed considering my options (beer or bucket shower first?) there is a knock on the door. The youth silently hands me half a bar of Imperial Leather and a damp toilet roll. Have a nice day-eee!

As the hotel descends into darkness, along with the rest of the power-less town, I ask if someone can find me some food, to which I get a lukewarm response. Another guest, the only other, I believe, who is sitting quietly outside in the gathering gloom asks firmly that someone go to the town and 'fetch some food for our foreign guest, who has come a long way. You must treat him well.'

The youth doesn't argue and sullenly retrieves a bicycle from behind the office and rides out of the courtyard in search of my evening meal. The other guest, a guarded individual from Lagos who is in town on some business, strikes up a conversation about the lack of infrastructure in this region of Nigeria, which is especially appropriate as we are now sitting on a battered couch under a tree in complete darkness hoping the lights will come on.

The hotel owner then steps out of an outdoor shower drying his hair with a towel. He flip-flops naked over to the far side of the compound and fires up a spectacularly noisy generator, which pumps power into a few low-wattage light bulbs dangling around us.

The chicken and rice, when they finally arrive slopping about in a plastic bag, are very poor and I eat with little enthusiasm. Afterwards I walk over to 'The Bar', a gloomy concrete-floored space with ancient armchairs accommodating a dozen men glued to a dubbed thriller. I ask if there's any possibility of a beer and one of them stands up without taking his eyes off the screen, unlocks a padlocked door and takes a warm bottle out of an African chest freezer – the un-electric, silent kind. I've had colder tea. I drink it morosely, which is the dominant local style, and steel myself to face the bedroom.

The lights in the small courtyard pulsate to the rhythm of the generator, and together with the laughter of the men in the bar responding to the TV characters, it's enough to signal the end of another day. I lie on the bed and soon I can hear the local boyos drifting in from the village chatting excitedly around the bike. I unkindly wonder if it will still be there in the morning.

It is.

So far, roadblocks – ten to twenty a day on average – have been a necessary interruption; nothing too intimidatory, and as long as I mention the magic words 'Manchester United', 'Blackburn Rovers' or 'Preston North End' (not so much the last one), I can create a diversion which puts them off their usual, 'Do you have something for me?' to which I usually respond 'I'll catch you on my way back!' or 'If I'd known you were on duty I'd have brought something for you! Shame!'

My new tactic approaching roadblocks – sometimes nothing more than a piece of rope stretched across the road – seems to work: I wave, signal as though I have something urgent to attend to on the other side of the barrier, thumbs up, then nod convincingly. This usually results in some bewilderment from the guards, crime control units, bandits or whoever they are; they relax their weapons and uncertainly wave me through, especially when I time it so they are interrogating a car driver ahead of me. For the ones that look more menacing, I slow down to put them a bit more at ease, wave, yell 'THANK YOU!' and then give it some gas. It seems to work well enough until on one occasion a mischievous thug pulls up the rope at the last second nearly garrotting me in the process.

One particularly nasty-looking group of glassy-eyed teenagers swishing machetes who have set up a slalom of roadblocks around some deep potholes look as if they mean business. But there is no way I am stopping for them. I slow down and indicate as if preparing to stop, then manage to slip past all four individuals shouting menaces at me as I weave perilously around the huge holes in the road. Three scream vicious threats and tear after me while another scrapes the tarmac menacingly with his machete, but I'm off.

Despite the machetes, reputation for fraud and intimidatory violence (and the minor anxiety of the open road), Nigeria, on the whole, at least from the seat of a motorcycle, is a terrifically friendly, vibrant and colourful country. Life here seems to take place outdoors. Everywhere I go there are crowds – at stalls, around wells and fountains, walking the roads – which can be overwhelming, yet shouldn't be surprising in Africa's most populous country. The people I have met, with a couple of exceptions, have been delightfully outgoing, laugh easily and above all are LOUD (in 2003 a study rated Nigeria the happiest place in the world). Consequently, Nigerians are very easy to get to know, and after the past few weeks in *L'Afrique francophone* I welcome almost every approach from a stranger who can speak a little English.

Nigeria is modelled on the federal system of government that gives individual states local powers (I have to cross immigration at each state line) and gives some measure of autonomy to the hundreds of ethnic groups here who speak countless languages.

Countless, too, are the number of churches. Nigeria is a stridently God-fearing place in these southern states. If I was looking for salvation or somewhere to profess a Christian faith I could do a lot worse than convert in this country. I used to think it didn't matter to Christians which door they walked through to find God because the ultimate destination is always the same. But here there is fierce rivalry between churches for their congregations, and when it comes to fighting to get bums on pews, every little helps. Where church nomenclature is concerned, however, I would say Nigeria has the market pretty much covered: there is the Zionist Bible Church (salvation and redemption) – which if nothing else makes its intentions crystal clear; the Living Dread Church – which is a little worrying although I'm not sure why; the Elim Ministries (palace of refreshment) – no doubt operating a cafeteria as a sideline; the Jesus Saves Church – fair enough; the Men on Mission – which brings to mind the Blues Brothers for some reason; the Deeper Life Church – suggesting a psychological bent; the Prince of Peace Parish – which seems to conjure up a man in a cape; and God's Chosen Charismatic Revival – which, by the time you've uttered that mouthful, you're saved.

I reach Calabar on Friday afternoon and head straight for the Cameroon consulate for my onward visa, which, through some fluke, I manage to secure in two hours. Feeling as though I have saved three precious days, I celebrate by finding a decent hotel – with not only a red blob on the tap but warm water coming out of it – and sink a couple of Guinnesses.

Calabar is a pleasantly easygoing city with a sea of tiny moto taxis on the street. Men in pinstripes and women in power suits balance on pillion seats as they weave through the clogged port city to their offices. The people I meet look poised and at peace with the world; even when there is what sounds like a shooting outside the hotel and everyone drops to the floor – in fact, the generator blows up – staff and other guests manage to laugh about it. The city's motto could appropriately be 'Don't worry, be happy'.

Next morning the roadblocks to the frontier come fast and frequent. I get everything: federal task force; police; local gangsters with 'Anti-Crime Unit' scrawled in white paint on the side of the vehicles; immigration; neighbourhood boys trying it on; and ad hoc road repairers out to make some naira. But I sail through them all with no more interruption than a few frank discussions on the chances of Man U winning the title again. Nearer the Nigeria-Cameroon border the state immigration checkpoints insist I stop for passport checks. Three or four times I have the same exchange...

'Where do you go?'

'Cameroon.'

'You know the road is bad on the other side?'

This makes a change from people blindly encouraging me down potholed nightmares. Maybe the road is going to get a bit more challenging.

I am the only person at the border control at Mfum apart from a few local traders with desperate cars laden with staples. At the last checkpoint before the bridge to Cameroon I find a policeman who is not in the mood for light conversation.

He slouches back in his chair and sneers, 'Why you here?'

'Just tourism, adventure.'

'Tourist, hah!' He is disgusted at this display of decadence.

'Have you seen all of Europe?'

'I've seen a lot of it.'

'HAVE YOU SEEN ALL OF IT?' he shouts.

This is getting aggressive now.

'No, not all of it.'

'You white people come to Africa, you think you know Africa, don't you? You think you know how we live. Then you go back and write about us!'

I don't like where this is going.

'You can travel anywhere you want,' he spits, 'BUT YOU ALWAYS GO BACK! Get out of here!'

No chance of a cup of tea, then. He throws my passport at me, which bounces off my chest and lands back on his desk.

'Can I go?' I ask.

He responds with a look of such utter contempt that the sooner I leave the better for both of us.

11
I AM THE MUD MAN

Keep going, and don't look back.
Paul Burke

The bridge, barely seventy metres long, separates Mfum in Nigeria on the west bank from Ekok, the Cameroon border settlement over the river. I cross the rickety structure and reach the customs officer.

'You know the road is bad?' There it is again. The puzzled warning.

The police at the checkpoint echo it: 'The road is bad, hey?'

I am directed to a small office in a breezeblock building and enter a darkened room with the curtains drawn. The *chef de frontière du police force* has never before seen a carnet, so I point out the places where I need his precious stamp to enter his country, but he is more concerned that I should want to.

'You go where? There is nothing here.'

His secretary knocks and enters the room carrying a small tray on which are balanced a tiny teapot and two shot glasses.

'I am sure you will have some tea, yes?'

If this is an example of Cameroon hospitality, I can't wait to get in. We both take a large swig of the simultaneously sweet and bitter broth and acknowledge the moment with our eyes over the tops of the glasses. He leads me out onto the verandah of the building.

'We are a race apart up here,' he tells me, 'we are the forgotten people. The people of Mfum across the river and here in Ekok belong to the same tribe, the same families, although they are told they live in two different countries. To them it is not a border, it is just a river. Most Cameroon people speak French but we speak English, but not your English I think. Yes,' he repeats, surveying the ragged border settlement before us, 'we are the forgotten people.'

When he sees my bike and the load I am carrying, he says, 'You should pay a boy to go with you to Mamfé. He can guide you and push you in the bad spots.'

Push? What sort of road is this? We are soon surrounded by a contingent of idle labour ready for hire. Ask a man or boy to perform a task and he will always say yes; ask if he has experience in the task and he will say yes; ask if he will succeed in the task – yes. I have a choice to make.

One man around twenty-five years of age steps forward and asks in clear English, 'Do you need help to go to Mamfé?'

'They say I need a guide for this stretch. Is the road very bad?' I ask.

'It is *bad*,' he says ominously, 'more than the word.'

The man is markedly different from the rest of the unemployment line. Much lighter-skinned and taller than the others, with glassy eyes, he is wearing a baggy T-shirt and trousers tucked into wellington boots, with flip-flops wedged into the tops. He has an engaging sing-song voice and a habit of pulling up his T-shirt to wipe the sweat from his leaking face, exposing his chest. I agree to pay him the price he asks as I am keen to get moving and hope we can reach Mamfé before dark.

'Are you strong? Will you work hard for me?' I ask.

He smiles broadly and says, 'You will be *amazed* what I will do for you on this road, more than the word.'

'You have your own bike?'

'Of course,' he says, and steps aside to reveal a titchy pale blue moto with 'Grande King Made in Taiwan 125' in bold lettering on the tank. It looks like a newborn next to the overweight Triumph.

'What's your name?' I ask, and offer my hand.

'Tabot.'

'Alan. How long will it take to get to Mamfé, Tabot?'

'Tonight, Mister Alan; tonight, I think.'

I buy two large bottles of water, fill both tanks with fuel poured from old whiskey bottles and exchange enough local currency for the ride to town, which looks no more than fifty kilometres on the map. I check my watch – three and a half hours until sundown – and, scattering a herd of goats in the process, we head off.

The Cameroon climate and countryside is a microcosm of Africa: desert in the north, savanna and rainforest in the interior, mountains tracing a spine the length of the country and hot, sweaty beaches on the Gulf of Guinea. I seem to have entered the country through a kind of jungly rainforest, which is dense and claustrophobic after the relatively open road in Nigeria.

Outside the village it is quickly apparent that there has not been a road of any consequence here for some time. The potholed muddy track is almost impassable to everything but small bikes. Tabot says that the rainy season, which lasts for half the year, has extended into November for the first time anyone can remember. As a result, four-wheeled vehicles have dug huge ruts into the soil, sometimes three feet deep, all filled with water. The ruts are spongy at the base and once in deep the Triumph has a mind of its own. Tabot usually leads the way on his moto through the tricky parts and either shouts directions for me to follow or walks back and guides me through the quagmire.

After two hours of this I believe I might be showing signs of doubt and exhaustion. The road bike is not meant for this terrain (mind you, what bike is?) and I'm probably inviting disaster by continuing. My head is spinning with my own hopeless riding and Tabot's urgent directions. I don't voice any of my doubts, but Tabot senses some reluctance and says exactly the right thing: 'Have courage, Mister Alan. With courage you will conquer your journey.'

He's right: 'Keep going, and don't look back,' as Paul Burke advised during a Preston Tea Encounter.

Each time I take a breather, Tabot remains encouraging: 'Lessgo, Mister Alan. Start your bike, lessgo. Gently, gently. It is my belief we will be in Mamfé before dark. It is my dream!'

In dramatic answer to Tabot's dream, I promptly drop the bike again. Each time I do so it takes ten to fifteen minutes to get all the gear off and heave the bike out of the Velcro-like mud; then it's 'take the middle track', 'take the right corner', 'this way, this way', 'have courage', 'more power', 'balance your wheel'.

After each dreadful muddy section, Tabot smiles and says with some accomplishment, 'This spot was my target. It is better from here. Start your bike!'

But it is never long before we reach another unbelievable stretch where I have to paddle the bike through mud up to my calves. I take a firm piece of ground above a five-foot rut but lose the front wheel and the bike falls into the water-filled ditch. I manage to get my leg out before it settles upside down in the mire with my gear trapped underneath. We can't move it an inch.

Up ahead we spot a large overland vehicle tilting at a precarious angle with a white man standing next to it. He wades over to us and watches us busting blood vessels, but he just folds his arms and wants to make conversation.

'Zis bike is too large for ze mud. Yah, it is too heavy,' he says in a thick German accent.

'We got stuck in ze mud, yah,' he says, redundantly. 'We wait for help. Zere are two of us. My friend is in truck.'

'You'll need a crane to get it out of there,' I say. 'How long have you been stuck?'

'Three weeks.'

THREE WEEKS?

'Yah, my friend must stay wi' ze truck. Zere are bandits here. You never know. I stay in ze village every night.'

Well, bully for you for pulling the long straw, pal. The German keeps his arms folded as we give ourselves hernias to get the bike upright with another four men who arrive on motos.

Before we leave I am accosted by someone Tabot knows (actually he knows practically everybody on this route) who gives me a history lesson about the legacy of colonial rule and diplomatic relations with Nigeria; then it's the connection between governmental corruption and the role of international aid.

'And did you know,' he continues, 'the government ignores us because we speak English here in north-western Cameroon. The people who rule us are French-speaking, so they do nothing for us. We are the forgotten people. That is why we need your help.'

We leave him trudging on foot to the next village and press on. The cycle of dropping the bike and heaving it out of the mud continues. I lose an indicator here, a mirror there. The bike is getting scratched to hell. I'm slipping the clutch horribly to get some traction on the unpredictable surface, the engine is racing, I'm sweating bullets, Tabot is shouting encouragements, but there appears no end to this track. I am running out of steam. There is no room in my mind for thoughts of home, nor of any reality outside this short section of mud ahead of me. My life, every sinew and every brain cell, is now devoted to reaching the bend in the road fifty metres ahead – and then continuing on to the next. My mud-caked feet must weigh four kilograms each, my face is cracking with drying muck, and everything I possess is unrecognisable, covered in slippery caramel-coloured slime, as am I (Tabot remains relatively mud-free). I wonder how I must look to the people along the route. Fearsome. I am the mud man. Goo goo g'joob.

It continues to be very hard going in the brutal heat and we – I – have to take frequent breathers. Also frequent are the number of impromptu roadblocks, which are basically a couple of logs placed across our path at waist height manned by apprentice bandits on extortion duties. They have usually cleared a short pathway circumventing a section of chewed-up road, so they see the 'toll' as fair reward for their toil. Each encounter brings loud and sometimes scarily vicious arguments between Tabot and the gangs in a tortured form of English Tabot calls Cam-Tok. They typically ask for 1,000 CFA (about £1) and settle for 500, sometimes 300, and I wonder if all the arguing over a few pennies is worth it. But at the same time if we don't reach Mamfé tonight I will be very short of local currency, and every 500 saved is 500 I can spend on food and tea and beer further up the track.

Sometimes I am sure it will come to blows, and as everybody carries a machete, or at least has one close by, where these encounters could possibly lead does not bear thinking about. These youths in their late teens are unpredictable, and if things turned violent we would not be able to defend ourselves, nor have any authority to call on – the jungle is a world apart. I now understand what Daniel in Casablanca meant when he said, 'Don't stop for anything, just throw money.' I cannot rely on reason to dig myself out of a situation that gets out of hand; if it does, it's going to take cold, hard local currency to fix, which I don't have. When we give in to their demands and negotiate a payment, Tabot makes sure the fee includes them pushing us through their patch of swamp. They are usually all smiles on the other end and happily wave us off – 'Come again, white man!'

After four torturous hours we emerge from the dense forest to reach a small village as dusk descends and the rain begins to fall. Wet through, we park up outside a bar, the atmosphere moist and stagnant. We order food – mostly offal and some cow's ears – and I ask Tabot if there is somewhere we can stay tonight, wash up and dry off.

'We eat and then continue on our journey!' he announces.

'Tabot, have you noticed? It's pouring with rain... it's pitch black... *we've had a big day*!' I say, trying to stifle my incredulity.

'Water cannot hurt us. Do you not wish to continue? Does your Tree-oomph not have lights?'

I met this man only a few hours ago but already I can see that sometimes Tabot can be both ingeniously practical and simultaneously away with the fairies.

'Tabot, you've got to be joking. It's hell out there,' I say, pointing to the great unknown. 'If we go now we'll never be seen again!'

He laughs out loud with his trademark light-up-the-jungle grin, pushes up his shirt and says, 'You are right. I am tired, more than the word. Tomorrow I will see my son who is two weeks one day. Tonight we stay at Club Two Thousand.'

Club Two Thousand? This I have to see.

Club 2000, located on the far side of the village is, technically speaking, a hotel. In my room there is a bare single mattress sitting on a double-bed frame in the middle of a concrete floor, the clichéd bare swinging light bulb and a sheet acting as a curtain draped over the window, which is merely some torn insect netting forced into a hole in the wall. It looks like a room in which a hostage might be held.

But on the bright side, the hotel proprietors are terrifically welcoming. The husband immediately takes my muddy gear and boots and washes them outside; then he moves my bike under some cover – in case it rains! His wife, who wears the metaphorical trousers in the household, is sitting on a couch in the reception area adopting the demeanour of Dame Barbara Cartland dictating a novel. She is flamboyantly dressed in a shocking purple, lime green and pillar-box red two-piece outfit and headdress and talks with elegant waves of her hand. Her English is quite good and she is keen to hear all about my Tea Encounters, even though I'm traipsing mud around her hotel like it's going out of fashion. She does not even flinch at our appearance.

'Tea? If I had tea I would give you tea,' says Dame Barbara. 'Perhaps tomorrow. Always tomorrow!'

Tabot has other plans: 'Let's share a Top' – which is his way of indicating that he wants a few beers, so we head off back to the village on his bike to eat more and drink a suitable quantity of alcohol equivalent to the kind of day we've had. After watching football on TV in a bar and answering lots of questions from other drinkers about the 'outside world' (including the guy we met on the road who has been watching too much *Panorama*), I have had enough, so Tabot drops me back at the hotel. He asks for an advance on his fee and heads back out for more beer and who knows what else.

Soon the cacophonous tin roof of Club 2000 threatens to implode with the falling rain, like a snare drum pelted by marbles. My heart sinks at the thought of all that fresh mud on the road ahead.

The next morning Tabot is waiting for me when I wake at half past six. I stagger outside in my smalls and wince at the sight of my still-soaking trousers and boots.

Tabot knows what I am thinking: 'You have no choice, Mister Alan.'

I ease myself into my wet gear with all the enthusiasm of a man going for root canal dentistry, then continue on the jungle road – without tea or breakfast – where we left off yesterday: mind-boggling mud, near impassable tracks, monster-sized ruts.

Tabot shows his big-hearted side when he stops to pick up a boy of about eleven who must get to school in the next town to take an exam today. It is a picture: Tabot shouting instructions to me through the mire and the boy on the tiny pillion hugging his school books and notes for today's test. I look across at Tabot laughing and joking with the youngster and I know I chose the right guide at the border post. Loyal to lost causes perhaps, but it is terrific to be in his gang.

'I HAVE NEW SON,' he shouts to his pillion, 'TODAY HE IS TWO WEEKS AND TWO DAYS!'

Life goes on outside of this mud after all, I think to myself.

At one point we reach a wide, deep section of road completely rutted with a soft bottom and no obvious route through for the bike.

A man on a tiny moped skids past at walking pace. 'Welcome to Africa,' he says with a cheery wave. 'If you get out of here you must tell them to build a road,' he says. 'We are suffering here.'

The man is perfectly serious. He did say 'if', didn't he?

I call after him, 'Nobody's going to listen to me. You must tell your politicians yourself, you must insist that they lay some bloody tarmac.'

He stops his bike and looks back over his shoulder.

'But you are the white man. You can build a road.'

I am lost for words; it is not the first time I've heard this infuriating fatalism.

Meanwhile, the bike still needs shifting. Tabot insists on taking my bike through the monster ruts then returning for his own. Somehow, and to my teary-eyed astonishment, Tabot makes it. The boy pats me on the back; even at his tender age he knows what the trip means to me. And at this moment it means everything.

Tabot rides on through the deepest ruts yet, slipping the Triumph's clutch and revving hard. The exam boy and I push as best we can while schlooping our feet in and out of the mud on either side of the beast. I am now, like yesterday's performance, head to foot in the stuff while the boy's school uniform is a sight and his books pebble-dashed. Tabot has to slip the clutch hideously to find some grip under the tyres. The engine can't take much more of this.

'Don't slip the clutch, use the rear brake to keep the speed down,' I yell. 'DON'T SLIP THE CLUTCH.'

'It is difficult, Mister Alan, IT IS NOT EASY!' shouts Tabot over his shoulder.

Don't I know it. Eventually, inevitably, predictably, the clutch gives out. Tabot is now in first gear revving like a banshee yet perfectly motionless. If I had to choose one place not to break down on the whole trip so far, it would be here on the road to the increasingly mythical town of Mamfé. At this precise moment I don't believe there is anything in this world more immovable than a Triumph Tiger stuck in a three-foot, water-filled ditch in Cameroon.

When Tabot accepts the bike has had it, he says with some urgency, 'We cannot stay here. It is too dangerous on the road; we must push to a village.'

Tabot rounds up some help to heave the Triumph out of the ditch and on to relative safety, which is like pushing a stubborn hippo uphill. After two kilometres that leave me gasping for oxygen we stop at a mud hut to rest. I am totally banjaxed: my muscles are going into involuntary spasms, I can feel the pulse racing in my neck and can hardly focus on anything. My head is about to burst from the effort and the heat of the afternoon sun, and I collapse on a low verge.

Tabot soon comes over with two oranges, the first food of the day for either of us.

'Eat!'

I eat. It's not enough so he brings me four more.

When I can get the words out, I ask him, 'How much further to the village?'

'This is village.'

OK. That tells me everything I need to know.

'More oranges!' I demand.

Tabot explains what's going on to the gentle people who live in the hut, who seem remarkably unperturbed by our presence; maybe they've played host to other stranded bikers in the past. Tabot leaves to find some help and takes the young boy with him, who is fretting a little over missing his exam. I promptly fall asleep on a straw mat in front of the hut.

I am woken an hour later in a pool of sweat by a young man wearing a Juventus football strip who doesn't want a kick-about; he says he wants to fix the bike.

'Where is clutch?' asks the centre-forward.

He wants to repair my bike but he doesn't even know where the clutch is.

'How many of these bikes have you worked on before?' I ask by way of assessing his suitability for the work.

'One.'

My heart sinks.

'Triumph?'

'Bee-em-dubber.'

Imagine a weary sigh here.

'Do you have any tools?' I ask.

I get a look of considered bemusement.

Tabot arrives and says, 'It will be OK. You have some tools? We manage. We take out the clutch then I take to Mamfé to repair, then we put back the clutch and we go. What is problem?'

Life is all so simple to Tabot sometimes.

The centre-forward empties the oil into a filthy basin and gets the clutch out. All the springs, bolts and washers are in the dirt around the bike now and I just hope he can recall where everything goes.

'I will find someone to repair the discs,' says Tabot.

'OK.'

'It will cost money,' he says plainly.

'All I have are a few francs, some euros and pounds,' I say.

'I will find a money-changer for euros. We could be in Mamfé tonight but you must go further.'

He's right. I have to make sure I have enough for the repair, petrol and food and even accommodation for both of us. I cautiously take out two fifty-euro notes, the last euros to my name.

I look at Tabot coolly as I hand over the money. 'Tabot, this is it. There is no more. We have to pay for the repair and make sure the balance of the hundred gets me to Douala. I'm relying on you.'

What I actually mean is, 'I know this is a lot of money to you but please don't scarper and leave me even further up this shitty creek than I already am.' Although I'm not sure I'd blame him if he did.

'It will be two hours through the mud but you will see me once again. You will be amazed.'

Tabot wraps the discs in a rag, jumps on his little bike and he's gone, followed by the Juventus mechanic. I am left standing outside the hut with the bike in bits and six little kids staring up at me like a troop of nosy meerkats. I am hungry (more than the word!) and there's only one thing for it.

'More oranges!'

I am still eating oranges and drinking the house water from a gruesome-looking bucket as dusk comes and I accept that Tabot will not return tonight. In the gathering gloom I prepare a space on which to sleep outside the hut and consider this capsule of existence I have earned for myself. The parents sit on upturned logs at the side of the hut, the father silently eating the *fou-fou* his wife has been pounding all afternoon in the large wooden tub; his wife's two hours of cooking has produced a meagre repast. The father squeezes the *fou-fou* together into a ball then adds some coarse green leaves and dips it into a fiery red sauce before throwing it into his mouth. The scene has the distinct whiff of disappointment, of lives unlived, never really begun.

When he has had his fill, the mother calls the children in and tips their father's leftovers into a metal basin. She puts the food on the ground inside the hut and next to it places a storm lantern. In the growing darkness the little scene looks like something from the Stone Age: the hut with a sagging leafy roof, the dirt floor within, the shaven heads of the children backlit by the glow of the lantern, the tiny hands going into the bowl, sharing, not fighting. It is a sight that will stay with me forever.

I know people go hungry in the world, but to sit here and see the guileless expressions of gratitude, to smell the cooking pot, to hear the sounds and giggles of these children is overwhelming. But these people are not starving. They have some food today. They go out into the jungle and gather it from trees or farm the cassava hand-to-mouth. These are the lucky ones. Someone once said that man at his most extreme is man at his most dignified. That was always an interesting concept, but now I see it is true: their very survival is their greatest triumph, and I have no suitable words to honour that.

The sound of squelching footfalls interrupts my thoughts. It is Tabot. He has arrived by his traditional form of transport – on a wave of optimism – and is wearing a smile that could light up Broadway. I am delighted to see him, more than the word.

'I wonder how you would feel here with no food and I tell myself, "I must return tonight." Can you imagine!' he says. 'I have eaten, now you must eat.'

He hands me a black plastic bag in which he has carried a soggy spaghetti omelette and a tiny loaf of bread from the next village. I take one bite of the omelette and look across at the children scraping up the leftover *fou-fou*. I put it down and call the mother.

'Please give this to the children,' I say. Tabot translates.

She takes the food then touches me tenderly on the upper arm. Either she is going to tear up or I will, so I turn back to Tabot.

'What's the news? Where's your bike?'

'There is a very tough spot up ahead so I leave it beyond. There is no electricity in Mamfé. All the power is off.

It happens. They cannot repair the discs so we wait for tomorrow. I will go to my village tonight and keep the money. I will return, you will see.'

Once the children have finished their windfall supper, I nail up my mozzie net above the mat in front of the hut and prepare for a night under the stars. People walking along the track stop and enquire whether I will be sleeping there all night.

'Don't worry,' they say, 'you should be OK,' in a way that heavily suggests I may not be. But no one spells out the dangers. Bugs? Bandits? The rain?

A neighbour joins the family on the bench outside the hut.

'Will you sleep out here tonight?' the neighbour asks.

'Why? Is there a problem?'

The man offers me some lumpy palm wine in a plastic mug and says, 'There are some bad people about. But… I am not far along the track if there is trouble.'

O, crikey. I give in to the pressure and move the mat inside with the kids. The children are thrilled that the white man will spend the night in their home and their parents are relieved I'm inside, where they can keep an eye on me. The mother and father sleep in one bed with the baby; the three other kids share another behind a drawn curtain. I lie down in the empty space behind the front door with my gear around me, all now obscenely irrelevant.

Artist and writer William Morris once declared, 'Have nothing in your house that you do not know to be useful or believe to be beautiful.' I wonder if he'd ever been to Africa because there's certainly nothing superfluous here in this darkened space. Useful shelter, beautiful people.

Everyone in the hut is awoken in the night by a loud noise outside. The whole family gets up, mum and dad, babe in arms, kids looking tentatively behind their father – me looking tentatively behind their father. He stops to listen, then carefully approaches the door. We hold our collective breath. I can hear my own heart beating. Cautiously, the father slips back the two bolts that separate us from whatever is out there and pauses momentarily before pulling on the handle to open the door. I'm thinking, 'If we're all so frightened of what might be out there, surely it would be better to keep the damned door locked and go back to bed, wouldn't it?' I shine my torch on the door as he swings it open. Father boldly steps outside into the moonlight; the rest of us remain rooted to the spot. He turns around with the first smile I have seen on his face all day. It's the bloody bike. The side stand has sunk down into the soft ground and it has toppled over.

We pick the bike up in our underwear under the rays of a moon so luminous we can almost feel its heat. The whole family is soon hugging, bathed in the ethereal glow. We are alone, how alone we all are. But these people in this mud hut at least have each other and they know it, and the more they are aware of it the more they hug each other. I have to concede that their show of love accentuates my own aloneness and I want to hug them all. The moment dissolves into laughter at our unfounded suspicions of what might have lurked outside the hut and I can feel the kids warming a little towards me as they giggle at my baggy pants – the underwear that Lycra forgot.

The next morning the mother leaves early for a funeral, which is two days' travel away. The children eat another paltry meal that has been left for them, but there is none for their visitor. I go outside to my place on the mat and watch a constant stream of men walking down the road, each one shirtless, each carrying a machete, raising it in greeting, 'Good morning'... 'How are you'... 'Welcome-welcome.'

The husband tells me he is going with the others for some kind of communal farm work and strides off resolutely with the still, purposeful blade at his side. It is a remarkable scene: taut, muscular bodies going forth to eke out a living in the jungle, some with machetes in make-do holsters draped over their shoulders like gladiators going to battle.

It's now just me and the kids. At about eleven o'clock, the eldest girl, who is about nine and therefore by default in charge of the household, puts down her chalk and writing tablet – it is rare to see paper or pens in these remote areas – and brings me five beautiful oranges. I greedily suck on them. In return, and in the clichéd 'white man patronisingly hands around candy' tradition, I give out my last three boiled sweets. They are a big hit.

We are later joined by more little ones who emerge cautiously out of the bush.

'Sweetie *bonbon*?' one asks hopefully pointing at my tank bag.

My adopted three take great pleasure in telling the gathering crowd of children that there were only three boiled sweets in my bag and they, still licking their lips exaggeratedly, had had them. So there. One unhappy child wearing shorts down to his ankles can hardly believe his poor luck and asks for evidence. All three stick out their fruit-coloured tongues with satisfaction and the disappointment registers on everyone else's face. One small girl in a denim dress impulsively kisses one of my brood on the lips to get confirmation that she's missed out on the rare treat and enjoys the second-hand sugary taste.

'Sweetie paper!' one says, suddenly alive to the possibility of seconds. This starts a frantic search around the yard for the discarded sweet wrappers: they are found, licked, sucked and enjoyed every bit as much as the sweets were ten minutes ago. One child chews and swallows one of the wrappers to everyone else's scorn, but the delight is apparent on his face. A little child in a Celtic FC shirt is waddling about interrogating stones, asking, 'Sweetie?'

One of the neighbours is an older boy of about ten with clear eyes and a little spoken English who confidently informs the others, 'This is the bike that will fly.'

'Well, no, it won't fly but...' I am loath to correct him.

'Will you go down this road?' He asks with a mature, troubled expression.

'That's the idea.'

'But there are some very bad spots.'

He exaggerates the last word with a shake of the head as if the spots were fiendish traps.

'When you reach those spots you will have to fly. Nothing can go on this road. You will be stuck for many days in those bad spots; there will be no way out!'

He is holding the handlebar of the bike now with his left foot on the peg. I can see what he's edging towards.

'Okaaay, jump on,' I say guardedly.

That was the cue they were all waiting for. Fourteen children push and fight their way on to the seat of the bike brrrmm-

brrrmmmm-ing their way down an imaginary highway with vibrating lips and screeching sound effects, twisting the throttle and slapping the hindquarters of the immobile bike as if it were a stallion.

Of course now I've made a job for myself and have to make sure everyone gets a spell on the bike or there'll be tears, so I spend the next ten minutes lifting smiling kids on and pulling scowling kids off until the toddler in the Celtic shirt and a permanent leak of snot on his upper lip becomes overexcited by the whole experience and takes a piss on the pillion seat.

'OK, that's enough! EVERYBODY OFF!'

Later the kids are running riot when the father returns and order is quickly restored. I feel like a student teacher who has been reprimanded by a headmaster, so I go back to my place on the mat where I can do less harm while the kids are found chores to perform.

I sit for hours waiting for a gear to engage – I still just about have the energy to pun – and for something, anything, to happen. Later in the afternoon I hear a small bike approaching. It's himself with my precious rebuilt discs stuffed crazily into his jacket. The mechanic is close behind.

'I have done it,' gasps Tabot. 'The road is very difficult, can you imagine!'

I'm delighted to see him offer me the change from the 100 euros before he collapses in the shade, pulls up his shirt, Tabot fashion, and waits for someone to bring him water and oranges.

The mechanic fits the remade discs, but after replacing the clutch cover and pouring back the old oil I notice there is one disc left over. Even I know that's not good.

'No fit!' he says with a shrug.

There is nothing more we can do. If it takes me down the road, even a little way, it's progress (I'm thinking more like an African with each passing day). The clutch lever has hardly any play and the gear shift requires extreme violence to engage first, but I decide to make a go of it and, although I've lost all sense of how far it is, try once again to get to Shangri-La, I mean Mamfé.

'Lessgo!'

The little kid who warned me about the 'bad spots up ahead' was not wrong. In fact he was precisely correct. Tabot and I turn the first bend and are greeted by an extraordinary churned-up sea of mud that resembles a huge, frozen brown wave. It's the mother of all ruts, two metres high, fifty metres long and full of menace. I attack it with the dodgy clutch without fear, skidding and slipping towards its core and manage to get through with only a couple of falls. Once we scale that there are two long narrow channels that were originally worn by trucks and four-by-fours until the ruts were too deep for them. Then only small bikes could get through, which in turn have worn them down to around eight feet in depth. That's not a typo: eight-foot deep ruts. The channels are so narrow the bike only goes a few metres before it gets wedged; when I get off it remains upright. We dislodge the bike with help from another uncompromising gang who immediately impose a windfall toll.

Despite the appalling conditions people are still picking their way through this madness between the villages, walking or riding pillion somehow, or finding a path through the trees. They often drop the well-rehearsed ironic comments – 'Welcome to Africa' or 'Now do you see how we are suffering?' – and occasionally more barbed ones – 'You English take our trees but you do not build the roads'.

But Tabot tries to keep my spirits up with key patented phrases: on tricky bits it's all 'gently-gently' or 'gradually-gradually' – I never learn the difference but there is an important distinction for him – and as we approach a slippery bit it's 'slicing here' and after I've dumped the bike in the mud it's 'lessgo, lessgo, mount your bike, start your engine, mind your side stand… jussgo.' And when he sees the terror and hopelessness in my eyes he tries to toughen my resolve: 'With courage you will conquer your journey. It is difficult, Mister Alan, it is not easy. We will soon be beyond this nonsense.'

As we approach a settlement, Tabot calls out, 'We must stop. I must see Samuel. TODAY HE IS TWO WEEKS AND THREE DAYS!'

We ride into a sizeable village of perhaps two hundred people and park up outside a breezeblock compound where Tabot lives with his extended family. Three women are sitting on low stools carving up some cooked pork on a cracked piece of linoleum laid out on the ground. I am introduced to his mother, his 'junior' (younger) sister, his silent, shy wife and his absolutely minute two-week-and-three-day-old son. At the far end of the courtyard is a pigsty housing some huge porkers, next to which is Tabot's home. He stuffs a change of clothing into a plastic bag while I buy a sticky bottle of Coke from a neighbour, then we head off.

We finally reach Mamfé in the early evening. As we hit tarmac I announce our arrival by blipping the throttle hard to get rid of all the mud from the rear tyre. Tabot is loving it and is laughing and teasing people he knows along the way.

He shouts across to me, 'Your bike is fast, so fast! It is unbelievable!'

That's the word for the day. Unbelievable.

We park up at a bar next to a tiny workshop where Tabot's side stand is repaired (he has lately had to lay his bike down on the ground or lean it against a tree every time we stopped) and we sink a couple of large Guinnesses. We soon attract a group of friends and relatives and my bar bill is ticking up like a taxi meter on the space shuttle. More people join us, including one of Tabot's 'senior' brothers – not such a coincidence as he is one of twenty-three children by the same father – and the talk turns to the condition of the road. Everybody is well impressed that we brought the Tiger through what Tabot is now referring to as 'this nonsense'. I have no idea how far we have travelled from the border, but in this terrain actual distance means very little.

Then one of our drinking buddies drops a bombshell: the road onward to Kumba – my next destination – is every bit as bad as the one on which we've just spent three days. Tabot looks at me.

'I was on that road last week and it had some tough spots. Lots of gallops. More nonsense,' he says. 'It is even further than this road. Kumba is a long distance.'

Then a short pause, long enough for the fear to sink in.

'Do you want me to go with you?'

'Of course I do but the money is draining away, Tabot.'

I probably have about £15-worth of local currency left, the change from the clutch repair and a stack of sterling that I can't give away.

'I know a man who will change your English money in Kumba,' says Tabot.

We agree an additional fee for Tabot to continue with me, but I don't hold out much hope of changing the few pounds I have left. It would be a first if I managed it.

'Tonight we eat and drink some beer and we will be ready for the road in the morning,' Tabot says. 'The mud cannot hurt us, we are muddy today and look – we have survived,' he laughs with a worryingly maniacal edge.

I pay the waitress for all the drinks and suggest we find a hotel of some sort. There is more than a little euphoria in the air: we are both a little drunk, Tabot's side stand and bearings are repaired, we're riding on thin tarmac to cheers from indistinct figures along the road in a blacked out town, the cool air rushing through our loosened clothing. I grab his hand and pull him and his little bike through the streets of Mamfé – City of No Light. After so many muddy miles at walking pace we laugh incredulously at the smoothness of the road, the effortless speed and the sound of the rushing air.

After we dump our gear at a hotel that looks more like a derelict industrial unit (not in a good way), Tabot says he's ready to hit the bars. I feel the same. I've still got a thirst on me I wouldn't sell for ten thousand francs. We take his bike into town and recklessly spend the last of the local currency on beer and implausibly perfect grilled fish prepared by a *maman* tending a little brazier.

'I have eaten, I am satisfied,' Tabot declares and pulls up his shirt to rub his belly and show the rest of the bar his chest.

A friend of Tabot's arrives, a girl who wants to go somewhere to dance with him. I just want to keep on eating and drinking having spent the previous thirty-six hours living on sodding oranges.

'Mister Alan, you come and drink,' Tabot encourages, 'if we stay together you will be safe.'

'OK,' I say, 'I'll drink as long as it has no vitamin C in it.'

Tabot slaps me on the back, 'No vitamins tonight, heh, heh. Only beer!'

We go to an empty bar with a tiny dance floor and Congolese music videos playing on a TV screen. Tabot and his girlfriend are soon grooving while I get in the Guinnesses. I watch their effortless moves jealously – Tabot has found something else I can't do. But sometimes you just have to abandon Western cynicism and join the end of the conga line, so I get up and do my best inebriated-white-man-on-a-dance-floor turn – simultaneously rooted to the spot with arms flapping wildly around the room. It is not a pretty sight, but the music is infectious and I manage to lose myself in the moment.

Tabot watches me with some interest, and after a little thought says, 'It is difficult Mister Alan, it is not easy!' which is the phrase he has been using all day to describe my off-road riding and which says everything you might need to know about my sense of rhythm. Some stereotypes are true. There is incredulous laughter as they both imitate me and end the evening in the belief that this is how we all 'dance' back in Lancashire.

Tabot takes me back to the hotel on the back of his bike while the girl follows on a pillion taxi to spend the night with him. Nothing is said or explained before or after about the girl.

As they go to his room Tabot asks, 'What would you have for breakfast?'

'Tea would be nice. But somehow I don't think we're going to get any here. Good night, good night.'

Tabot's one-night stand must have gone home last night because she arrives early as we are loading up my bike. She is carrying a flask, and it's full... of TEA! The girl is delighted to become part of the Brew Ha-Ha – although I don't think the pun translates very well. Tabot's eyes are agog waiting for my reaction and I shake him on the shoulder in appreciation. It's good to be reminded that the tea tour is not yet abandoned.

The tea girl, who looks worryingly young in the morning light, waves us both off on what is to become the toughest day yet.

'After Kumba it is tarred express all the way. We will be in Kumba by two o'clock. It is my dream,' says Tabot.

One kilometre from Mamfé we find the gooey mess otherwise known as the road to Kumba and a horde of cars and trucks transferring goods and passengers to tiny mopeds for the route ahead.

'More nonsense,' is Tabot's only comment.

The route onward is truly appalling, more like a slow motion amusement park ride than a road. Occasionally the dense tropical bush opens into a clearing and I am able to appreciate the countryside about me: the lush greenery, huge standing trees, silent witnesses to the pristine jungle, an Eden of useless beauty. Nobody comes here. Nobody stands back and admires the stupendous views. And even when I give it more than a fleeting glance, the landscape does not know it is being admired, nor when it is ignored, unaware that it's loved or unloved.

Everyone believes life is better for those living in francophone Cameroon while these north-western pidgin-English areas near the border with Nigeria are treated like stepchildren. Whatever the truth of the situation, there is no doubt that living conditions are shocking in this region and if it wasn't for the wild, freely available oranges and mangoes, planted cassava and plantain and the occasional ear of corn, things would be desperate. Villages are ramshackle at best, vehicles – mostly small motos – are held together with a hope and a prayer and plenty of string. The people scuff about in either flip-flops or wellingtons or remain barefoot. Most homes – barely standing – are eccentrically built mud huts with dirt floors and leaking, leafy roofs. It's depressing to ride through, and with children chanting 'white man, white man', men hissing at me on the roadside, and whole families stopping to gawp open-mouthed, I begin to get a little troubled by it all. I'm not sure anymore if 'Welcome to Africa!' is a greeting or a threat. I'm frazzled, and losing my composure and any sense of perspective of the trip. There is no beginning or end to it now, just an infinite series of present moments played out in front of a tortured audience. I'm shouting at the jungle, my brain aching with the effort of thought and knee deep in this nonsense with only a slim thread of camaraderie stretching between Tabot and myself keeping me from going completely and utterly IN-SANE!

As usual, Tabot finds the right words to say, 'We will reach Kumba today. I will see my son tomorrow. Today he is two weeks and four days!'

There's no answer to that. I blow a huge sigh, and before Tabot can utter the famous phrase, I call out wearily, 'Lessgooo!' When we make it through a tough patch or blag our way past some particularly nasty gangs he says, 'That was my target and we have beaten it,' and so it goes on, sweetening the unpalatable as if things will start to improve from this point. But there is always another 'worst bit'. This is Tabot's outlook on life: have hope for the future but don't fear it and take pride in your past accomplishments.

Which is just as well because nothing, sweet Jesus, nothing prepares me for what we encounter halfway to Kumba. We stop our bikes on the edge of a swamp. The road looks as if it has been churned in a giant food mixer and left to set for a month. In between mountainous ruts lies a menacing, viscous goo. People are staring awestruck. There are no discernible dry spots to aim for, and the surrounding jungle is too dense for even the most determined machete-wielding gang to cut a path through. Tabot suggests we swap bikes for this stretch. I think about his suggestion for less time than it takes me to stall the engine and I get on the little Grande King, which feels like a toy after the Triumph. I put it in first gear and prepare to head off for a test ride towards the undergrowth at the side of the road. The slack in the chain jolts it forward with a jump, the steering is random, and it seems as though every rattling component will drop off at any moment. That's enough. I pull the brake... and then I pull it again... I squeeze the lever with all the strength in my fingers but nothing happens. Now I can't find the rear brake. The bike keeps on course for the thicket of trees as I dig my boots into the ground to slow myself down and avoid a(nother) catastrophe.

'TABOT!'

I shut my eyes as I OOOMMPH give the trunk of a large tree an excruciating shoulder charge and topple off into the brushwood with the bike on top of me.

'JE-SUS CHRIST!' I bellow.

Tabot and a moto taxi rider run up to me laughing hysterically.

'I no have brakes!' Tabot informs me.

'I noticed! How the hell do you ride without...?'

'Since yesterday. I manage!'

Unbelievable.

Tabot and I agree that he should ride my bike through the nonsense and then return to collect his own. He, of course, is relishing the challenge. I walk alongside to help balance the bike for as long as I can keep up but I soon get stuck up to my knees and then lose my footing, topple over and get a face-full of Cameroon's finest. I look up and see Tabot disappear around the bend of the road at walking pace.

That's one problem solved. It takes me twenty minutes to walk the length of the slurry in the sinful heat looking like the Swamp Thing. The undergrowth and trees enveloping me are as exhausted as I am; limp and lifeless, they droop in sympathy with my spirits and with every wickedly heavy step. I reach Tabot as he is trudging back to get his own bike.

'You do not look good, Mister Alan. Stay cool and rest. This day is very hot, yes. I get my bike and we will continue,' says Tabot with characteristic certainty.

Whatever. I'm not sure how much more of this I can take. I thought the road to the tarmac would take around three hours but it's been three nights already; the sprint has turned into a marathon and I'm still nowhere near something you might reasonably call a road.

I find some shade and take a swig of hot Coke as an elderly couple on a small moto slither past following Tabot into the mudbath. They are wearing smart, clean clothes and are loaded up with an unfeasibly large stack of goods and parcels on the back. With mud up to their ankles they move slow as molasses, as if it were a Sunday afternoon drive out to the country, admiring the scenery, chatting occasionally.

A little further on they wobble a bit and without a struggle fall as one into the mud – SSGHLHLHLOOOOOP; the bike, husband, wife, goods, they're all in. I jump up and wade out towards them. They are completely engulfed in mud down their right sides. It is a comical sight with their left sides perfectly clean. I'm trying hard not to laugh as the woman extricates herself from under the bike. She refuses to help us lift it, preferring to shout at her husband for getting them into this mess. The weary look on the husband's face tells me 'say nothing'.

Our feet are making dreadful sucking noises in the mud and there is no sure footing to get any purchase on the big lift.

'One, two, three... UP,' but instead of lifting the bike the man sinks even lower into the goo. He's almost up to his waist and we're making no impression on the bike at all – all I can think is 'don't laugh'.

'My shoe, my shoe!' he exclaims.

He pulls up a bare foot from the mud. His wife, with gloop dripping from her right side, gets down to search for the shoe. By chance the husband and I get on to a better footing in the mud, just enough to right the bike. He starts the engine as the wife gets on board (without his shoe), and I push until the bike is safely away, getting covered in the muddy backwash.

Tabot arrives as I am walking back to the shade.

He scolds me, 'Alan, I am confused. You must sit in the shade and stay cool but no, you push other people through the mud and all the nonsense.'

He opens his hands in disappointment.

I tell him about the falling couple, the tiny bike, the goods, the shoe, the mud and the harridan for a wife and I break out into pure hysterical laughter. I'm just laughing at someone else covered in mud. Why is that so funny? It's hilarious. I can't get the words out, I'm in fits and Tabot and a passer-by start laughing too, but I know they're laughing at me.

'They were covered in mud. Can't you see? That's... what I look like... all... the time. I AM THE MUD MAN!'

I'm breathless with the laughter, struggling for air and shouting riotously at the jungle. Nothing can hurt me now. Nothing. This is it. This stretch of Kumba road has officially pushed me over the edge. I am in so deep on this bloody journey that the only way out of this mess is... O, for a cup of tea. I wipe my muddy hands over my face, blacking up, and holding them aloft call again: 'I AM THE MUD MAN... ON A TEA TOUR!'

I've crossed some sort of thin line into craziness and it is a great release of emotion – and a huge relief that we have surely conquered the 'worst ever' stretch of road. Yeh, right, I'll believe that if I ever get to Kumba.

'Mister Alan, mount your bike, start your engine, lessgo, lessgo. Continue.'

With dirty hands I wipe the tears of laughter and incredulity from my eyes, mount my bike, start my engine, and all that stuff.

I start to wonder what else the road has planned for us. It cannot get any worse, surely. As that thought enters my mind I try to delete it from my brain but it settles in instantly, the challenge to throw something more at me. And then it happens. When things are bad, there is one thing that is sure to multiply your problems: rain.

Some welcome cloud provides a little relief from the heat of the sun, but before I have time to appreciate the relative coolness the sky turns angrily dark and people run past us along the road.

'Quick, Mister Alan, the rain is up. Continue!' calls Tabot.

With no more warning the rain pelts down as if someone is emptying a bath of warm water over us. The ground quickly turns to a greasy sludge – even the solid bits – and the bike slides out of control off the edge of the road. We pick it up but I have to keep it down to a cheek-rippling 10 kph in first gear to prevent coming to grief again.

I paddle with both feet as I protest through the roar of the downpour, 'Tabot, we can't go on like this! If I went any slower I'd be in reverse. This is *ridiculous*!'

He has an answer for everything. 'But we are moving, are we not? Keep going!' he says, echoing the Lancastrian Tea Encounter advice of Dave Edmundson and Paul Burke. At this moment, I hate them all.

Drenched through, we make it to a small village and I run for an outside bar with drinkers sheltering under a leafy awning. Tabot stays outside to fool around with a group of children sent out to shower in the rain – about a dozen naked brown bodies gambol in huge puddles, some with bars of soap washing each other's backs. It is an amazing sight. Tabot walks around in the rain as if taking a shower too, upending his legs so the collected water down his wellingtons drains away. They soon fill up again in the colossal downpour and he dances around like a man with a bumblebee down his Y-fronts. Everybody in the bar and all the kids are in fits at my hilarious, remarkable guide.

The drinkers are a merry crowd. It's Saturday and a few are already drunk on Guinness; some order tiny one-shot sachets of spirits to follow, while others suck the bones out of a fish stew the *maman* is spooning out. Oh, how I would like to join them; I could seriously make a hole in a pint of the black stuff right now, and last night's grilled fish seems aeons away.

Tabot wants beer. Meanly, I say if he wants a drink he can pay for it himself, although I don't think he has a penny to his name. Considering the state of my – effectively our – finances, alcohol is now a luxury. Our situation will be desperate if we don't reach Kumba and find a money-changer before dark.

After doing my sober best to enjoy the merry atmosphere in the bar, Tabot asks me for a hundred francs, about 10p. I automatically dig out a coin and hand it to him, thinking he might need to buy some time for his dead cellphone to call home, but instead he orders a sachet of whiskey and quickly sucks it down. At least now one of us feels better.

'We will reach Kumba tonight, it is my dream!'

Which is turning into one of those self-delusory phrases like 'I think that lap dancer really likes me' which nobody is expected ever to believe.

One of the men overhears our conversation and says, 'Do you go to Kumba? But Kumba is very dangerous! Do you know it?'

Tabot is still sucking the dregs out of the sachet.

'Yes, it is *dangerous*, more than the word,' he says. 'Kumba is most unsafe, everybody knows that. Even I am scared.'

Oh, great.

'So we have to get there in daylight!' I respond urgently.

'Yes, we must get to Kumba tonight,' he says with a bead of whiskey on his upper lip, 'because Barcelona play a match on TV, they are my team. I cannot miss.'

He throws the spent sachet on the ground.

'And now I feel so good I will sleep with two women tonight!'

Tabot lifts his shirt on cue like a man who knows his priorities. He wants to leave the bar but despite the urgency to reach Kumba (for local currency, not Spanish football and whores), I say we'll wait until the downpour stops.

'Maybe it does not rain everywhere,' Tabot says frankly. 'We have been wet before, Mister Alan. We know the rain cannot hurt us.'

I say nothing.

After sitting glumly in the shack for far too long, and just as Tabot seems to be itching for a second shot of whiskey, the rainstorm eases off and we move out gingerly through the waterlogged road.

The rain steadily dries up and after an hour Tabot excitedly shouts over to me, 'NO RAIN HERE. LESSGO!'

We reach Kumba by six o'clock. We're all smiles when we hit the tarmac; in fact I'm ready to break into song.

After finding the money-changer who takes the sterling off me we go for my favourite – fish and beer.

'Any chance of a fork, Tabot?'

After the past four days I really feel as though I deserve some cutlery.

'Fingers is for the fish! You must touch your food!'

Amused, he calls the waiter but the bar does not possess a single fork so he borrows one from someone on the street.

I believe we are both becoming aware that we will soon be parting. With nothing to plan for, I am already missing the challenge ahead. I think, but don't express the thought, that it might be fun to continue our adventure. Now that it is coming to an end, I am again becoming fuelled with ambition. Speaking of which, although I have always thought of myself as quite an optimistic, self-sufficient person, in the last few days I have discovered there are gaps in my character that Tabot could easily fill, attributes of his personality that I never knew were missing in mine, such as his extraordinary ability to let go of the bad times in the past, to relish every challenge. Tabot's refusal to acknowledge the material evidence of his circumstances is heroic, especially in someone who sees the hidden possibilities of the future as a potent motive for carrying on. In other words, 'Keep going, and don't look back.'

Tabot cannot fully relax in the bar and gives off an unnerving crackle of high-voltage tension throughout the evening. I think he is a little out of his depth in Kumba. He was more at ease in Mamfé; actually, he was the star of the show in Mamfé. Although he seems jumpy about the dangers here, it doesn't stop him adopting his usual alpha male display, sitting spread-legged in the bar displaying his midriff. He has now perfected a new move, which consists of holding his arms out as an impassioned gorilla might while his T-shirt is pulled up and held under his chin. People in the bar are fascinated by him; even by local standards he is compulsive viewing.

After a few beers Tabot walks me back to the hotel and then... goes back out on the prowl with most of what was my cash in his pocket. If I've learned anything about him in the last few days, it is that he can't look at a line without wanting to step over it.

Next morning after the predictable one-egg omelettes and dry bread for breakfast we both sup the last of the lukewarm tea from two flasks brought from the hotel kitchen – our second Tea Encounter together and quite a poignant one on the Brew Ha-Ha. None, surely, will be drunk with such a backdrop of racing thoughts. I can feel a delayed slingshot effect as the wave of experiences from the past few days catches up with me and I recap with a mental replay of incidents and people, of mud and water, and of my own emotional limits.

We wheel the bikes out of the restaurant where they spent the night and take them down to the corner where a posse of boys are washing cars and bikes on this sticky morning. They quickly go to work, each fighting over who will wash the Tree-oomph even though it is twice the size of the Grande King 125 Made in Taiwan.

'You must wash away the bad luck of the last few days,' Tabot says. 'You can't take it with you. I want your bike clean-clean for when you enter Douala.'

We sit back on the bench and watch them hose off the worst of the caked-on mud before starting with the huge soapy rags as the congregation in the church with no windows next door gets into song, filling the run-down neighbourhood with a joyous sound. Tabot fields questions about the bike from the crowd that has gathered. His Cam-Tok is impossible to follow but I can tell what the subject is because he has no local substitute for 'Blackburn' and the answer to the most popular question, 'One hundred and forty meelez an hour,' which brings gasps of astonishment.

'You will be amazed what I will do for you on this road,' Tabot had said. Looking into his glassy eyes, I knew then he was making a statement of fact. I was amazed. Despite every natural and unnatural obstacle thrown in our way (and with such little tea!), we had proved the truth of his catchphrase for me: 'With courage, Mister Alan, you will conquer your journey.' With courage, yes, but also with Tabot's blind optimism and his astonishing ability to find a solution to every obstacle while I was being overwhelmed by the problem. Armed with little more than a pair of wellingtons and a charm that could win wars, he used his wits to make sure this part of my journey succeeded. He is the same man I met at the border a few days ago and he will be the same man after I leave. But my time with Tabot has changed me. He has taught me not to dwell on difficulties – especially when there are so many – but rather always to look for solutions, to do positive things, not just utter positive words.

Now sitting in the shade with the soapy water draining around our feet and the church choir providing a spiritual soundtrack, the feeling is one of exhilaration, as if I have come up for air after four days' swirling downriver on a fast current with just enough strength to keep my head above water. For the first time on the Brew Ha-Ha, I allow a glimmer of pardonable pride into my twirling thoughts, in myself, in the bike and most of all in Tabot.

I look across the bench at him. The perverse thought returns: I want the challenge to continue. Something is drawing me back out there.

'Are you sad?' I ask, without taking my gaze from the bikes.

'Yes, I am sad also,' answers Tabot. 'It is over. If I could, I would continue with you to the border of Gabon to make sure you are fine-fine. You must go on with your journey. You had courage and you have succeeded.'

He looks me in the eye and adds deliberately, 'More than the word.'

It is a tribute I hardly deserve but one for which I am deeply grateful. With the bikes clean-clean we ride to a petrol station to fill up.

'The nonsense is now over for you.'

Neither of us can summon any sensible words to say here at journey's end; we've left them all behind in the experiences in the mud.

'I feel very strongly that we will meet again,' he says as our tanks fill up with four-star, 'It is my dream. It is funny, is it not, I want to visit Europe and you want to see Africa.'

He then turns a little pensive, 'How would you feel if we were swap, if you would stay here and I would continue on the Tree-oomph?'

I note the sadness in his eyes, this adventurer stuck in one place.

'I would be sad, too,' I answer. 'I couldn't live in this... nonsense. But you've got a family here now.'

We shake hands and both somehow resist the urge to embrace; then we start up our bikes.

'Safe journey.'

'Look after yourself, and baby Samuel.'

'TWO WEEKS FIVE DAYS!' he hollers, and lifts up his T-shirt. We both chuckle.

Our bikes face in opposite directions for our onward journeys: me to the city of Douala and hopefully a new clutch, him back through the nonsense to his village, his wife, baby Samuel and the pigs in the pen.

I ride off first and he yells after me, 'TARMAC EXPRESS... ALL THE WAY!'

12
THE X FACTOR

What's important is the truth of the journey.
Dr George Ogola

Thankfully, while the road from Kumba was not exactly 'tarmac express all the way' as Tabot claimed, it was mud-free, which meant I could go easy on the dodgy clutch during the eighty-kilometre ride to Douala, Cameroon's largest city.

I call Philip in Blackburn to send a replacement clutch. I tell him Cameroon has at least four thousand holes of its own, and I seem to have fallen into most of them. He is reassuringly calm about the problem with the bike – 'It'll be 'reet' – and I settle down to recharge after the gruelling Mamfé road. Then I borrow a waiter's cellphone, buy some credit and call home. I give Olive the number and she calls straight back. It is difficult to empathise with what's going on at home and I find it impossible to describe the last few days with Tabot, but she can hear in my voice that I will have a story to tell when I get back.

'I love you; take care. I know you can do it,' Olive says.

It's just what I needed to hear.

In utter contrast to the tiny villages strung along the Kumba road, Douala, set on the Gulf of Guinea, is a hectic port city. While its importance can be seen in the number of Europeans here on business, the city's crumbling streets are filled with a combination of leprosy-afflicted yellow Toyotas and small moped 'bendskin' taxis, pronounced 'benzakeens'. I use them every day while the bike is laid up, more often than not looking for an embassy to apply for an onward visa. You might think that people would either know where an embassy is or not. But in common with almost all taxi drivers I have hired on the Brew Ha-Ha, the ones in Douala believe that just knowing the name of a destination will miraculously spirit them there.

I ask, 'You know where this is? You're sure? You've been there before?'

'OK! OK! OK!'

And we immediately get lost. At each traffic light they ask other baffled bendskin riders where the Republic of Congo embassy is. The first one drops me at the Central African Republic embassy; the second takes me to the DR Congo embassy; the third rides away when I jump off the back to ask a policeman. I never find the embassy. Mind you, I'm getting a great tour of the city.

I leap off a bendskin for something to eat in the centre of town after the third circuit of the city looking for somewhere that probably doesn't exist. Food of some description is always available on the street from children who carry plastic containers on their heads filled with sweating doughnuts and other foodstuffs going off in the blazing sun. Cooked food is sold at tiny makeshift kitchens on the pavement, which basically consist of a middle-aged woman with three or four buckets of food and a ladle; diners sit on narrow benches in the shade and eat from plastic dishes.

I buy a soft drink and something grilled from a street trader where a pack of vendors usually congregate when an open truck full of uniformed police and soldiers storm the area wielding scaffolding poles and wooden batons. Perhaps the vendors are illegally pitched, but even so the violence is extreme. The traffic stops as they run amok through the neighbourhood, smashing to pieces all the stalls and terrorising the vendors who try to protect their goods. Many of the women flee, grabbing what they can or leaving their livelihoods behind screaming in terror. Others try pathetically to save their packets of chewing gum, nuts and phone cards. One of the thugs in uniform uses a tatty parasol to charge at an elderly *maman* who won't give up her merchandise. She screams boldly at her attacker as a passing Good Samaritan grabs the sunshade from the soldier in a rare act of defiance. Like most onlookers I step into the street to avoid getting thwacked. I feel helpless. I warn the street vendors all the way back to my hotel about the soldiers on the loose, after which they pack up and step back into darkened shop doorways for cover.

That evening in the hotel bar I get chatting to a smartly-dressed man called Anthony who has international business interests. He takes me in his Mercedes Coupe to the downtown area of Akwa for a perfunctory cup of tea. There is a large outdoor seating area at the Greek restaurant where at least half of the tables are taken by scantily-dressed young prostitutes who sit alone, bored as can be with a half-empty glass of something fizzy in front of each of them. The girls are largely disregarded by the Europeans eating Central African moussaka except when they slowly strut into the place and their spectacular arrival temporarily kills all conversation. Their black bodies are an exaggeration of womanly curves: the blue-black skin, glossy as melted chocolate, playful breasts, buttocks like canonballs under Lycra, juvenile make-up and garishly bright clothes leave little doubt about their profession as they make their way to an empty table – the long way. They sit playing with their cellphones trying to look as if they're enjoying themselves sipping a drink alone, waiting for a customer to come along and make their evening worth their while.

Work is hard to come by in Cameroon – I've seen what the hinterland is like up around Mamfé – and women have to find a way to put food on the table. These girls are no doubt doing their best to claw their way out of the desperate situation in which they find themselves. Anthony is also preoccupied with employment in Africa.

'I spend some of my time in America, where my family lives. Americans work hard. But the black man doesn't want to work. Look at that pothole,' he says pointing out to the street, 'it's been here for years yet the people who live here complain but do nothing about it. It is laziness. We are blessed in Cameroon with a climate that means no one is cold all year round and there is always fruit on the trees, so no one goes hungry. The black man doesn't have to work to stay alive. In England, where I lived for a while, you work hard, otherwise you freeze. A Cameroonian man would die of the cold in England. I guarantee it.'

This international businessman is looking back over his shoulder and he doesn't like what he sees. Throughout the evening his cellphone rings constantly. Each time, he checks the number then kills the call.

'I do not want to go to her,' he indicates towards the annoying ringtone, 'she eats in local places and I cannot trust them to be clean. I prefer these international restaurants. Cameroon restaurants you cannot trust.'

Towards the end of the night, as the bar girls drift away, an attractive young woman, whom I suspect to be the one calling all evening, arrives and sits down at our table. She has a Guinness and waits silently until he is ready to leave. He drops me at my hotel and takes her home with him.

On my third day in Douala I get news that the bike parts have arrived from Britain. I retrieve the new clutch from customs after giving them the shirt off my back and find a mechanic. I brace myself for another financial shock but am relieved that he accepts my first offer – African prices – and he leaves excitedly counting the cash.

After three days stationary in Douala without the bike, I relish the 200-kilometre ride to Yaoundé, Cameroon's capital and second-largest city, where I will apply for three onward visas. Feeling as though I've overcome a major hurdle on the trip – the absurd Mamfé road – I rediscover the joy of leaning the bike into bends and overtaking cars with a satisfying twist of the throttle. On the way, I buy a watermelon taken off a waist-high pyramid of fruit on the roadside from a group of children who all take turns sitting on the bike. I arrive in the city after dark and find Les Boukarous, which in many ways is typical of mid-range West African hotels: let's say its redeeming features are so well hidden it would take Hercule Poirot to locate them. OK, it's rubbish. After poking my head in through an open door on the first floor, I tell the receptionist that the room she has offered me is in a near state of collapse – 'but the room be cheap,' she says without a flicker. I check in, as she knew I would.

Before unloading my gear I have to put a hole in a large beer. The bar doubles as a behind-the-scenes lounging area for waitresses. The largely outdoor restaurant, which has recently undergone refurbishment, has seating for around a hundred, with all the tables set up with tablecloths, wine glasses and cutlery; there is also a dance floor and a stage under cover. Unfortunately, the advertising hasn't worked because there is only one family of four waiting for food. The staff – three barmen, five waitresses dressed in brand new black-and-white outfits and two other suited men looking for something to do – comfortably outnumber the customers.

It is almost certainly the first night of waiting-on for the hapless girl who is tasked with serving the forlorn family out in the restaurant. She places two bottles of fizzy pop and glasses on a tray and brings them to the table. Common with convention in Cameroon she tries to open the bottles and pour the drinks while they are still on the tray in her left hand. Just as she is about to catch the edge of the bottle top with the opener the tray slips away from her and she has to rebalance the bottles and glasses. The deadpan intensity of her expression and her attempts to flip the bottle tops then pour the liquid into the glasses is a performance worthy of Buster Keaton. The anxious girl returns to the bar to pick up a bottle of wine for the two adults with perspiration dripping into her eyelashes. The barman is transfixed with worry as he brings out two corkscrews; nobody can work out how to get the screw through the seal and into the cork to liberate the wine. In whispers, lest the family should hear their ineptitude, the waitresses feverishly offer suggestions to the poor girl. Finally, they all convince her that she does not need the vital half of the two-piece corkscrew to uncork the bottle and send her out to her doom with just the curly piece of steel. The look of terror in her eyes is alarming. She balances the bottle of red wine and two glasses on the tray in one hand and confidently swings the half-a-corkscrew in the other – a useless gesture of bravado. Everybody else, including me, is peeping out from the bar with breaths held, like watching a fawn edging towards a trap.

She reaches the table and, still balancing the trembling bottle and glasses in her left hand, begins stabbing the top of the sealed bottle with the screw. It is pure slapstick. The other waitresses are now descending into uncontrollable, stifled hysterics and despite my sympathy for the girl's predicament I am going to the same magnificent place. I try to control the giggles so hard that the beer starts coming out of my nose as I hold my entire face in my hands. Every time the girls look at me with sheer hysteria etched on their black faces I have to hug my shoulders to prevent myself from falling off the chair. I have never laughed so little and so much simultaneously in my life.

The family pretends not to notice the girl's quandary and choose to wait patiently for their drinks. She is still stabbing the top of the bottle with the end of the corkscrew as she looks fitfully over at the others behind the grill for aid – anybody, for Jesus' sake, somebody help me, scream her blinking eyes. While the entire family, who have all finished their dinners by now, look away, she thinks to creep with the bottle back to the bar for assistance. Nobody wants to take responsibility for the wine but instead all stare at it as they might an unexploded bomb. The barman finds another corkscrew and manages to get it halfway into the cork, then sends the waitress back out with the device sticking out at an eccentric angle. She puts it down on the diners' table and, while she is mopping her brow and preparing herself for another go, the mother puts the bottle between her legs, pulls the cork, pours two glasses and takes a large swig without saying a word.

Now that I have been in Africa for a couple of months, I have developed certain personal criteria when choosing a hotel. If it can satisfy the basics, I bargain like hell and it's usually a goer. Is there space for the bike in reception or in the room next to the bed? Is there water? Electricity? Food in the hotel or nearby? Air conditioning or fan? And if it's late and I'm desperate for a drink, I ignore all of the above and take the first grotty place I chance upon, which is how I came to choose Les Boukarous.

The hotel is quite acceptable, especially when compared to many others on the trip, as I spend most of my time on the street and it satisfies my criteria of a 'goer' – electricity, water, (asthmatic) air conditioning. The bike is secure in the courtyard, it's in an interesting location, the staff are all rehearsing for parts in the next Michael Frayn farce, and as I was told, 'the room be cheap'.

On my first morning I apply for a visa for the DR Congo. The receptionist takes my passport and a significant amount of cash and says it may be ready in two days. I prepare for a prolonged stopover in Yaoundé as I must also apply for Republic of Congo (or Congo-Brazzaville as locals call it) and Gabon visas in turn.

One of the attractive features of Yaoundé is its setting on a number of hills that divide the city into distinct neighbourhoods. From the top of one you can see the peaks of four or five others, giving an open aspect to the city, while the overcrowded and crumbling neighbourhoods nuzzle in between. But this also makes it easy to get lost – to a stranger's eyes, one neighbourhood of shacks and one-item stalls looks very much like another.

The hills also make it difficult for the taxis to get about, especially going uphill, as no taxi driver will ever shift out of top gear, no matter how torturously slow the going gets. He will be hunched over the steering wheel trying to kick the accelerator pedal through the floor with a look of mild despair on his face while the bronchitic car strains and creaks and rattles and shudders and the engine threatens to cut out before it reaches the summit. I want to shout, 'FOR GOD'S SAKE, MAN, CHANGE GEAR!' but I remain silent, shudder and rattle along with the loose interior and pretend it's perfectly normal to be going nine kilometres per hour in the outside lane. The drivers' body language changes dramatically on the downhill sections when they slip their cars into neutral and freewheel as far as the traffic allows. Then they're all smiles and slip off their baseball caps to wipe the sweat from their faces in preparation for the next minor Kilimanjaro.

Taxi drivers constantly attempt to overtake other taxis (which are going equally slowly, of course) without a hope of either getting past before the next junction or before the oncoming vehicle reaches us. If the oncoming car bottles it and pulls over – often onto the pedestrian section – we have instantly created a new forward lane and other taxis follow behind us, squeezing the oncoming traffic, which now has to use the margin of the street up against the shop fronts.

Taxi interiors: there aren't any. Door trims, handles, window winders, arm rests, and ceiling trims are often missing. What happens to them? Do passengers steal them? Perhaps there are special-edition Cameroonian Toyotas that are sold without these (one would have thought) quite important features. The seats are often split and torn, exposing their innards, and sometimes covered with a blanket to hide a multitude of sins and past misdemeanours. Sitting in the front seat, while occasionally more comfortable, is fraught because I get a kaleidoscopic view of the dangers ahead through a starfish-shaped crack in the windscreen. Many side windows are missing and have been replaced with hardboard. The interior light is always disconnected so at night the passenger steps into a darkened car save for two one-watt blue fairy lights located above the forward doors. Very romantic. Speedos don't work, dash lights refuse to illuminate, and the dials are dead.

Outside, almost every panel on every taxi shows signs of Yaoundé's Wacky Races–inspired driving. Exterior trims have dropped off, other cars' paint is etched down the bodywork, and bonnets and roofs are dented. How on earth do you dent a roof?

But to compensate for what some passengers may view as drawbacks, the driver often adds outlandish embellishments to attract custom: an oversized Mercedes logo stuck on the bonnet of a Toyota Corolla, an unfeasibly long radio aerial, flashing lights on the roof, or aftermarket side skirts – designed for a different car, of course.

In the meantime, the driver battles on to his next fare unsure when the uncertain source of his livelihood will give up the ghost. Perhaps this is why, when they stop at a petrol station en route to my destination, the drivers put in only 1,000 or 2,000 CFA worth of diesel (£1–£2) to keep them going for the next hour or so; any more might double the value of the car. On one occasion the driver asks me for the fare up front so he can buy some diesel before he can move an inch. But, full tank or empty, the look on the face of my driver remains – a grim resolve to reach the next set of traffic lights before the whole damn thing falls apart.

Late one afternoon a taxi drops me at a cyber café so I can update the blog and send some emails. As I step out of the still-moving car I notice a change in air pressure compared to this morning, when the city was bathed in brilliant sunshine. The ions start spinning, the birds stop chirping, and the sky darkens; there is a new physical presence in the city. An eerie light is reflected now in everyone's face, every car and building, and there is a collective expectation that we are being prepared for something wholly out of anyone's control. The rain is up.

One or two fat raindrops fall from the sky, huge globules of water, signalling our one-minute warning to either get undercover or prepare to take a shower. I step inside as the terrifying thunder crashes overhead. It shakes the building to its flimsy foundations as the spectacular lightning illuminates everything in gigantic flashes of monochrome that threaten to fuse the city's lights. Then comes the rain sounding like an approaching locomotive, angry and animalistic; huge waves fall from the sky, lashing the streets and buildings.

The water is simply dropping out of the sky now. Large puddles appear in indentations in the poorly-laid tarmac where there is any, and in muddy pools where there is none, and wide streams attach themselves to every doorway, trapping those inside. The once-busy street is soon a shallow river; pity those at the bottom of the hill. Within minutes the city's drainage cannot cope with such a deluge, and garbage, wedged in corners, culverts and gutters, now edges its way down the hilly streets. Objects lose their colour in the darkness; the brightness of the clothes of the women, the gaudy street stalls, even the lush trees fade to grey. The sensation, at first refreshingly cool, soon turns mouldy and rank.

Up and down the street people with sopping feet huddle under small porticos in shop and office doorways or dive under street vendor umbrellas. They catch their breath in awe at the interruption then stare wide-eyed at the rain bouncing like dice over the tarmac. A few cars bravely crawl through the downpour, but mostly the city has come to a sudden, sodden stop. The only thing happening now is the rain and it's hard to believe it is dry anywhere. Maybe it's raining all over the world.

The next morning I get myself a street breakfast at a grimy stall. While I wait for the omelette and dusty bread I read a discarded copy of the bilingual *Cameroon Tribune*. Beside a sycophantic story about the president's wife with the headline 'Le Beau Geste de Chantal Biya, First Lady Extends Largesse to Limbé', I see a photograph of a student riot in the north of the country. I look closer. The riotous town is Kumba, the place where even Tabot was scared. We must have arrived in a lull during the riots because, although we were aware of a highly charged atmosphere in the town, we saw no street clashes. Neither did we see the smoke from the police station that was burned down, according to the newspaper report, nor the bodies of the two students who were shot dead. Tabot was surely aware of the precarious situation on our arrival but chose to focus on my quick exit from the town the following morning.

Anyway, back to my street breakfast... As I'm eating, I notice a crowd gathering outside a swish hotel. They are joined by camera crews and there is an excited buzz in the air. I strike up a conversation with a couple of teenagers who are here to take part in *Stars 2 Demain* (Stars of Tomorrow), a TV talent show similar to *The X Factor* which is holding auditions today. I poke my nose into the hotel and the show's directors let me have a backstage view of the auditions. It is terrific fun. All the familiar elements are here: the excited friends egging each other on; the lads there for a day out; the girls phoning home with the fantastic/devastating news; the 'born to be a diva' without a hope in hell's chance of getting through. I am sure some are going to faint as they approach the head of the queue, and when they get under the lights they habitually go to pieces.

At the very sight of many of the acts the cameraman cannot help chuckling, especially when a young man in blue robes does a little involuntary jig to a song he has written himself, sending the camera up and down in time with his shoulders. There are warm smiles from the judges when he finishes and wins through to the next round.

The contestants are given no instruction whatever, just handed a dummy microphone, told to stand on their mark in front of the camera and do their best. They have one minute to impress the judges in which they are asked to sing one song they have prepared, usually in French, and also two further songs: one in the language of their village and one in English. Popular English choices are 'I Will Always Love You' and 'We Are the World', which for some reason is always sung 'You are the world, you are my future...'

One feature that doesn't come across on TV shows like this is the uncontrollable nerves of many of the contestants – they may be singing calmly on the top half but their legs are often shaking like some nervous stringed puppet. Some clearly have talent but mostly it is all uncontrollably funny, as the truly tuneless are always the ones who are so convinced of their own talent. When it goes wrong it goes horribly wrong and as with a Triumph heading for a pothole, there is nothing you can do but avert your eyes, brace yourself and shout 'next'.

On my way out of the hotel, I am approached by two men – one in a raggedy suit and tie carrying a portable cassette player, the other clutching a small video camera.

'*Bonjour monsieur*,' says the suited man.

'Hello.'

'English?'

'Yes.'

He turns to the other and says excitedly, '*L'homme est anglais. Parfait!*'

'We make video for my song,' the suited man says. 'This my brother.'

The camera is waved at me as proof as he switches on Congolese-style dance music at African volume through the little speakers.

'I do not wish to insult... but we would have a white man. It will look sharp!'

'OK,' I say.

First I'm a co-opted *X Factor* judge, now I'm starring in a music video.

'What do you want me to do?' I ask.

'Sit only. Do nothing. Look sharp!'

I sit down on the hotel steps in my baggy trousers, tatty T-shirt and scuffed shoes and do my best to look sharp but everything inside me says the guy is getting a raw deal. He rewinds the tape to the beginning, straightens his tie and wipes the sweat from his face. When the music starts he erupts into a menacingly extravagant dance around me with flailing arms and thrusting groin as if he is trying to attract the attention of passing aircraft.

In between miming the lyrics (I have no clue what he is singing about) he shouts directions to his brother – *'l'hotel et l'homme blanc, l'hotel ET L'HOMME BLANC!'* – who is doing his best to keep up with his gyrations while keeping both me and the hotel sign in shot. Feeling simultaneously left out and self-conscious, I start to tap my foot and generally sway to the rhythm with the occasional knowing glance to the camera.

But the singer notices me getting into the music and shouts, 'NO! Sit only. Look sharp!'

So I remain sitting stiffly motionless – and looking sharp – while the budding star continues to jump around me as though he is trying to cast some kind of voodoo spell on a reluctant missionary.

By the third day in Yaoundé Les Boukarous restaurant, so far as I can tell, has still not attracted another paying customer. That poor restaurant review in the *Yaoundé Times* must have done for them. I take a lonely seat. They still have half a dozen staff kicking their heels with just two guys playing CDs through the sound system on the stage stretching out a single beer between them. Apart from that and the occasional passer-by attracted by the music, absolutely nothing is happening.

Then something strange occurs. The two men turn off Papa Wemba and put on a George Michael CD. Now I am not what you would call a big fan, in fact I have always found his music inane, but as soon as those recognisable chords begin streaming out of the huge speakers I find myself swooning in a bath of nostalgia. I realise I have not heard any Western music since I left Britain nine weeks ago. The familiar melodies and predictable rhymes stab me with a shard of homesickness. God, I've been away from home too long.

A few days later, with visas for Gabon, Republic of Congo and the DR Congo stamped in my passport, I look forward to getting back on the road – the road that I've been on for exactly two months (it's 1 December). I am way behind any vague plan I ever made for this trip because of the wasted time with the clutch in the Sahara and being stuck in the mud with Tabot. All I know is that I have to get to Zanzibar in three weeks for Christmas with Olive. Now that I have run out of time to ride to the east coast, I plan to ride to a major city – perhaps Kinshasa in the DR Congo – and leave the bike somewhere safe before flying to Zanzibar.

I check the bike over but can't get the panniers to fit snugly on the frames, which is hardly surprising considering the treatment they've endured. The hotel cleaner, Entudi, suggests he take me to a welder who may be able to help. We weave through the city to a group of guys working on the roadside making some superb metal gates and doors. The young man in charge quickly sets about the repairs with a hammer and a welding kit but not much else. For 3,000 francs the panniers are sorted in twenty minutes while we sup tea together. Entudi is surprisingly voluble, talking animatedly about his life and his two girlfriends, both of whom are pregnant.

'Which one to marry?' he asks. 'I have problem, yes?'

'You've got two problems!'

'No, four!' He laughs.

We have a couple of large beers before Entudi shows me the way back to the hotel via a painfully dilapidated neighbourhood – his own. He leans off the bike shouting greetings and shaking hands with every other person on the street, in the shops, selling at the stalls and with other riders on little mopeds all the time weaving past stray goats. He's loving it and so am I.

On the way, I see a vast building project in the centre of town – a shockingly rare occurrence on my travels. Entudi tells me it's going to be an indoor sports stadium, which accounts for the large contingent of Chinese on the streets. But as we approach the construction site it becomes apparent that the Chinese are not here merely to offer their expertise and financial backing; they are also labouring while impoverished blacks look on. I have seen this in the most unlikely places – Mali, Senegal and all over Cameroon but, I wonder, why are there so many Chinese on the continent when these menial tasks could be performed by unskilled local labour? Many people have told me that foreign-financed projects are the result of under-the-table deals and ministerial corruption, and I have to reconsider the advice I got from Dr George Ogola during a Tea Encounter in Manchester: 'Do not gloss over what's bad – what's bad is bad anywhere in the world. What's important is the truth of the journey.'

It is a fascinating time in the history of Africa, especially with commodity prices at their highest for many years and the countries of the world beating a path to its door for the oil, cobalt, gold, diamond and coal reserves. Money should be flowing into the continent, but there is not much evidence of it in Yaoundé.

The next morning I pick my way through rush-hour traffic and ride on tarmac past huge sentry-like trees all the way to the frontier with Gabon around 200 kilometres away. The weather at the border is overcast and still, and the pewtery light reminds me of England. It's a strange sensation to ride cool and not arrive somewhere in a sweaty heap.

I stop in the small town of Bitam over the border for the stamp in my passport. I walk into the police station at the very moment two officers are interrogating a line of bedraggled men shackled around their wrists and ankles – and to each other, chain-gang-style. They all have pitiful expressions, which is not surprising, as they regularly have a pistol shoved into their faces. My guess is they're illegal immigrants. The building is divided by a ceiling-to-floor cage, which separates the front of house from the business end of the operation. I have to hand my passport through the cage to a man in uniform who then pushes his way through the chained men to a room behind. It's an extraordinary scene, one that brings to mind the degradation of slavery. In front of me the bound men are led outside to have their photograph taken. Bizarrely, they line up as a football team, six kneeling in front and eight standing behind. They even smile for the camera when asked, which gives the police officers a giggle.

What is immediately noticeable at my first stop in Gabon is the relative seriousness of the Gabonese compared to the

Cameroonians and Nigerians. Although there are no other whites in Oyem that I can see, the locals pay me little heed. Where in Cameroon I was often received with interest, here it is indifference; there it was familiarity, here it is politeness. Oyem's main street is full of women selling either beer in tiny bars or fish from small braziers and tradesmen in small cubby holes busy with woodwork, tailoring or barbering. It is a lively place with an air of permanence about it that large parts of Cameroon did not possess. Still, if I leaned on one of the shacks, the whole street would probably go down like a stack of deck chairs.

I stop at a bar with two tables under a flimsy awning and a cement-floored bar inside. I desperately want a cup of tea, but there's no way this decrepit little place could entertain that desire. I sit outside and wait for service but am instead approached by a small child of perhaps eight or nine who asks me something I don't understand.

I reply, 'Bonsoir mademoiselle,' and smile.

She walks away a little confused. Oh well. I wait ten more minutes before I look into the bar to indicate that I'm still waiting to order, whereupon the owner yells at the little girl for not taking my order the first time. The little girl *is* the waitress. She comes back to me and meekly asks a second time what I would like.

'Un Guinness, s'il vous plaît.'

It feels absurd to order a beer from a girl who should be playing with her toys but the little one runs to the back of the bar, retrieves a bottle, flips the top and pours me a stout like an old-hand barman.

Although I find the people in Gabon get less excited about things, the eight riotous guys in the bar behind me are trying their best to make up for it by being hopelessly drunk and yelling simultaneously at the middle of the table, which is crowded with empty beer bottles. It is ten past five in the evening. I order fish from the shack next door as the uproarious laughter that can only come from copious amounts of alcohol reaches bursting point, with now absolutely everything everyone says being the funniest thing ever uttered on God's earth. They want to include me in their hilarity, and I eat in the middle of a jolly crowd. It is an extraordinary atmosphere in which to enjoy a fish supper.

Compared to some I have bounced down, the road south from the tea-less town of Oyem is as smooth as a polished desk. Built for the huge logging trucks – 85 per cent of the country is rainforest, a major foreign currency earner for the country – the route is marked with directional signs and distance markers that actually provide usable information, the first in black Africa. The villages are appreciably tidier and cleaner than in any country since Morocco, and most have names – the rectangular metal signs at the town limits are identical to those used in France. I have also noticed modest homes with well-tended graves out front elaborately decorated with tiles, not unlike small water features. The largely Christian population must want to keep their dear departed close to home.

After six hours I reach a large sign on the side of the road: *Vous Franchissez L'Équateur*. Wow; this is what you call a milestone. I park up, hoping I will find someone to take a photograph of me with the bike at this momentous juncture, but I wait for twenty minutes during which I don't see another person. I can't even have a cuppa to celebrate. I toy with the fanciful idea that after 14,000 kilometres I have reached the pinnacle of the trip and from here it's all downhill.

I reach Lambaréné late in the afternoon, a town set in a sumptuous location on the Ogooué River offering great views in an atmosphere of pleasant sleepiness just short of actual lethargy. I am instantly drawn by the sign advertising the Bananas Hotel. Sometimes my weakness for engaging names leads me astray, however – the Dicky Hotel in Oyem was a damp, dark pit and the less said about it the better.

Lambaréné is most famous for the Albert Schweitzer Hospital. Named after the Nobel laureate who founded the institution in 1913, the hospital is a melancholy place set amongst trees that go down to the water's edge with what looks like long-stay wards for children and five-foot signs warning against the dangers of SIDA, the French acronym for AIDS. I get a few curious looks from patients and staff as I bounce down the track towards the original part of the hospital which is now a museum. A man steps out from one of the wards to see what the noise is all about and gives me a salutatory nod. I don't know it now, but this man will become important to the trip further down the line.

13
BAD SPIRITS IN NDENDÉ

Be careful about your health
and drink a lot of water.
Dr Ahmed Sahab

Take a smile with you.
A smile gets you out of anything.
Debbie Robinson

I leave sleepy Lambaréné and, after being warned several
times about the state of the road ahead, reach Mouila after a
hard stretch on dirt roads in what I expect to be my last day
in Gabon before the Congo border.

There are few things more dispiriting than being woken by
a crack of thunder and the taunting applause of rainfall on
the tin roof when you know you've got a 300-kilometre ride
on a dirt road the next day. With a ten-month rainy season,
I suppose it was unlikely I would avoid some precipitation
in the Gabon rainforest. Lying in bed, I consider spending
another day in Mouila, but I change my mind in order to
make some headway towards Ndendé. I pack up and prepare

to leave in utter silence; there is not another soul in the hotel. I count my thin wedge of cash and consider briefly the idea of doing a runner. But I think, no, the bad karma will probably catch up with me and I would rather leave with a clear conscience. I leave 10,000 CFA under the disconnected telephone in the small office and get going.

The huge loggers are behind me now as the scenery turns to open scrub, with playful birds hopping from the ends of branches. The road is quite tricky in places, but it seems to be drying out, and the surface is no worse than twenty others I've struggled with on the journey – slushy puddles, gravelly dirt and churned up ruts.

About thirty kilometres from Ndendé I see a small herd of goats in front of me. My usual approach would be to head straight for the animals knowing they will scatter, but this time I swerve a wide arc around them until, unexpectedly, the soft ground forces me into a shallow culvert. Then things go black. The next thing I'm conscious of is that I am on the ground with searing pain in my right lung and having great difficulty catching a breath. My head thumps and I can't focus on anything. I check my two legs... OK; left arm... OK; right arm... bloody hell, that's sore. A shocking pain transmits itself down my arm from my neck, which I now feel for. There is a hideous lump where my collarbone should be – I'm sure that protrusion wasn't there this morning. I compare it to the other side, and collapse as much in annoyance and disappointment as in pain.

'FUCK NO!' I call out. 'NO! Collarbone... OK... that's not serious,' I try to convince myself. I roll over on to my back but the pain pulling in my right shoulder and ribs is excruciating. I try to find a position where I can lie without too much agony and inhale a breath. I roll onto my left side, knees up, from where I can see the bike in a perfect mirror image of its prone rider: stranded in the road, headlights staring back at me wild-eyed, its dirty body torn, broken and bruised.

I can't stand up. I can barely move. I am suddenly gaspingly thirsty, but there is nothing I can do except wait for a passer-by to help me. My mind drags up a suitably inappropriate piece of advice from a Tea Encounter in Liverpool with Dr Ahmed Sahab: 'Be careful about your health and drink a lot of water!'

The blood roaring in my ears, the tearing sensation down my right side and the physical torture of breathing all fuel my racing mind. All I can hear are my own sounds: the struggle for breath, a wet gurgle in my throat, my boots scraping the dirt to prove to myself I am not totally disabled. Nightmare visions of my immediate future simultaneously play themselves out: the distance from a town (let alone a hospital), the tough terrain, the absence of any other traffic, the state of the bike lying next to me. Shit.

Fifteen distressing minutes later – that feels like a couple of hours – I hear the arrival of a vehicle. Soon a man is standing over me. He rolls me onto my back.

'Aaaarglglhh.'

I take my hand away from my neck and the man recoils in shock.

'Ooo, la laaa!'

Is that good?

'L'hôpital à Ndendé?' I croak.

'Non. Mouila.'

Damn, I've got to go back to Mouila. If I ever get out of this mess I'll have to come down this bloody road again. The man helps me up and manhandles me into his TLC. Then I hear him loading my gear into the open back of the vehicle and talking non-stop with some urgency, but it isn't easy to hear anything over the disappointed silence in my head. I ask if someone could ride my bike back to town.

'*Non.*'

That's that, then.

This Good Samaritan was certainly not an ambulance driver in a previous life, nor in this one. He stands on the gas all the way back to Mouila through the potholes as though his life depends on it. It is sheer bloody agony. The trip would be quite fun, I suppose, if I didn't have mild concussion, broken ribs, a stinging gash in my hip and a bone sticking out of my neck.

We reach Mouila within an hour – another occasion when I could have kissed the tarmac – and the driver despatches me to the hospital *urgences*. He explains everything to the duty nurse, a large, mild-mannered man with huge hands and a pencil moustache, by whom it is my great good fortune to be admitted – whose name I later learn is Ngoma Serge Dimitri.

There is only one problem: they clearly don't expect sick people to be admitted on a Sunday – the hospital pharmacy is closed. After taking X-rays, the nurse looks at me with some embarrassment.

'*Vous avez besoin d'antibiotiques. J'ai besoin de quinze mille francs.*'

Serge is asking me for 15,000 CFA (about £17) for drugs. I have nothing left in me to argue and I hand over the cash. He returns from town an hour later with some bandages, a large box of Elastoplast, a few antibiotics and a strip of painkillers, and then takes me to an empty room on the surgery ward. He keeps more bad news for this moment: there is no linen for the bare mattress and no food or drink available. Then Serge calls in the one and only surgeon on his day off to take a brief look at me. Although the doctor's body language shows that he isn't too keen to get involved, he agrees with Serge's analysis – double fracture of the right clavicle, various ribs broken or bruised, ribcage out of alignment, serious blow to the head, open wound to the hip. Serge stretches the bandages every which way over my shoulder, dresses the wounds then administers the drugs.

I send someone to buy some cellphone credit, charge up Serge's phone, then call Olive.

'I was just beginning to worry. I haven't heard anything from you in days. How's it going?'

'I've had a bit of an accident…'

Once I feel a bit more comfortable, Serge says goodnight as his twelve-hour shift has just ended. I lie back on the mattress and consider the events of the day. I am soon interrupted by another nurse who comes into the room and stares at me, not knowing what to say or do. I have just taken my first deep breath of the day and I know only one thing will fill the gap in my life at this moment – a cup of tea. This is definitely one of those moments when I need someone to say, 'I'll put the kettle on.'

'*Thé?*' I ask.

'*Thé?… Non,*' replies the nurse without expression.

Oh brother, what a day.

An hour later, at nine o'clock, Serge walks back in holding a piece of cake and a Fanta he has bought for me in town.

'You eat now,' he says.

My appetite is the last thing I'm concerned about, but I appreciate the gesture. I explain that I must retrieve the bike from the roadside tonight. Right now. Despite having finished his shift, Serge and I take a soon-to-expire taxi to find a policeman in the pouring rain. We're in luck, the little office is open. With the second-hand stench of alcohol hanging in the air between us, two police officers scribble on a used scrap of paper the information about the accident and location of the bike, such as they require it. It is quickly apparent these guys would not go out in the jungle for their mothers let alone an accident-prone European. When they have heard enough and want to get back to their girlfriends waiting in a van outside, Serge asks them for a lift to the hospital on their way back to town, as it is still teeming down. They reluctantly agree and we squeeze in next to the two good-time gals who both jiggle about and giggle incessantly at private jokes. This is doing wonders for my spirits, as you might imagine. The bastard driver stops at the top of the road about 500 metres from the hospital and swings open the van door. We both step out into a deep water-filled gutter.

I hold the weight of my arm in my left hand and gingerly walk down the middle of the road to avoid the huge puddles, which hardly matters as we are getting drenched. Serge walks half a step behind me in case I need a helpful arm to lean on all the way back to my hospital bed.

'I go now,' says Serge, 'my wife with *bébé* soon. She is...' he balloons out his tummy.

'Pregnant... expecting a child,' I say.

'Child, yes. Very soon.'

I am glad to get back into bed, or rather, clamber back onto the mattress. The condition and whereabouts of the bike and the future of the journey have me gripped; it is the only thing I can think about. And if the bike is still there tomorrow, major parts will almost certainly be stolen from it. I am haunted by the possibility that the African Brew Ha-Ha might end right here, right now, in this grim environment two degrees south of the equator. Ha Ha. A less suitable place for its conclusion I could not have found.

In between bites of the cake and Fanta – which bring on a wave of nausea – it is a terrible night of disappointment and anger at myself, and I feel for all the people waiting for my arrival at Original Tea Bag Designs in Cape Town. There are shouts and moans all night from the main ward across the corridor from people with serious illnesses, while strangers continue to walk silently into my room until midnight. They take a quizzical look at the white man and wander out again.

The next morning the door to my room opens at ten minutes past five – a female nurse wants to take my temperature. It is the first of countless interruptions that continue throughout the day; I am never alone for more than ten minutes at a stretch. It is a revolving door of nurses, cleaners, orderlies, garbage men, maintenance men, lost visitors who cannot find their families, all of whom have heard there is a white man in the hospital. Some sit down to gawp at me while others talk incessantly in French. *'Je ne comprends pas,'* I say, but it does nothing to stop the flow.

On one occasion a nurse leaves my door open while she treats the ugly wound on my side and three other people follow her in, including a Lebanese shopkeeper from town who believes it's an opportune time to make conversation and, ignoring my moans of pain, says, 'Ahh! I know you. You come to my shop yesterday. Yes, yes.'

He looks to the others for affirmation. 'I know this man!' he announces. 'He is my good customer, yes.'

I turn over onto my left side, shut my eyes and try to imagine myself away from here. In another universe, possibly.

Later in the morning, I return to the police station with Severin, another male nurse, to get the paperwork done – hopefully with people who are sober this time. There is a strange mellow atmosphere at the office; some people listen to my nurse's explanations, some ignore him, but there is plenty of cautious discussion about *le touriste*. The upshot is that the police will do nothing to retrieve the bike from the Ndendé road, nor protect it from theft. I don't even have any curiosity value; they simply want to see the back of me.

Back at the hospital I decide to take matters into my own hands and insist the doctor, who can speak some English, hears me out. He cuts short his morning consultancy to come to my bedside.

'Doctor, I'm sorry for interrupting you but no one speaks English on the ward and I'm more concerned about retrieving *la moto* from the Ndendé road than my injuries right now.'

The doctor doesn't catch every word and has no instant solutions, but someone who walked in with the doctor takes up the challenge. Alexis, a short young man with oversized facial features, a square head, flattened nose and a beaming smile, says he has the answer. He needs 8,000 CFA to take a taxi to Ndendé, then pick up a truck and return to the spot where the bike fell and bring it back to the hospital. I have no choice. I hand him the responsibility – and the money – and lie back and wait.

Now I can start worrying about my shoulder, which is in bits. The painkillers are hardly working, the Elastoplast couldn't hold a stray hair in place let alone reset the twice-broken bone, and no matter how I hold the arm I'm in agony. Where is Serge my moustachioed nurse when I need him most?

I ask everyone who comes within shouting distance of me if they would redress the wound but they either chuckle or answer, '*Je ne comprends pas.*' Some irony.

Then, later in the afternoon, even though he is not officially on duty, Serge opens the door. Hallelujah.

He indicates that he is going to sort out the useless bandage. Severin joins us and makes himself useful by holding the bone in place with his thumb while the new sticking plaster is stretched across my shoulder. Once that is sorted they take me down for more X-rays to see how the clavicle is setting, although even I think that might be a little premature.

At four o'clock Alexis swings open the door to my room with a big lippy smile, '*La moto. Allez!*'

By the time I walk around the far corner of the hospital, the bike is off the four-by-four and standing in the car park. The four men who recovered the Triumph are standing proudly around it. If ever there was a time to get misty-eyed about an inanimate object, this is it.

The bike is a mess. The front end is smashed in like a squeezebox, but it is all there, nothing is missing, and it's the best news I could have had right now. I gladly pay 50,000 CFA (about £55) to the driver of the truck as Alexis wheels the bike into the hospital. He takes it into a spotless room used by nurses to wash up before and after their shifts and a short cut to a few emergency beds. With a flourish, Alexis pulls out a key and locks the exterior door.

'I have key only,' he says and slips it into his pocket. Well, at least that should be safe for the time being.

Later in the evening, Serge arrives in a white gown, cap and mask on his way to assist the doctor in surgery. He knows I'm upset at the possibility that my trip may be over. In response he sits down on the squeaky mattress with that uniquely Central African ability to be close and say nothing without embarrassment.

After a short while he says, '*La moto*... is good... OK, I go to my job.'

He doesn't have much to say, but it's good to know he's around, this man who met me on arrival in the *urgences*, diagnosed the injuries, bought medication and bandages in town, got the doctor to come in on his day off and dressed the collarbone, then after his shift took me to the police station and walked me back in the rain, found me some food, rearranged the dressing, took more X-rays and liaised with the hospital administrators, who are now communicating with my insurance company. Now that's what you call nursing.

Sounding like something from another existence, a representative from my insurance company calls the following afternoon on Alexis's cellphone.

The stiff female voice says, 'We are arranging to bring you back to the UK, Mister Whelan.'

'No way; send me to a better-equipped hospital in Gabon. I'm staying in Africa.'

'The cautious course of action is to bring you home. Our advice is…'

'I want to continue on the Brew Ha-Ha.'

'What?'

'I have to finish my trip.'

'The underwriters are not going to like this.'

'I don't care!'

Within thirty minutes I have packed some essentials into a pannier and get Severin's help to strap the rest of my gear to the bike, watched by nurses about to go into surgery. Severin and Alexis accompany me to the airstrip which has to be opened specially for my 'mercy flight'. Both take pictures with their camera phones, amazed that a plane should be sent for one person.

By three o'clock I am on a hollowed-out jet done out like a flying ambulance on my way to Libreville, the capital of Gabon, for admittance to an insurance-approved clinic. I'm quickly hooked up to oxygen, pulse monitor, drip, blood pressure monitor and painkiller drip which is more paraphernalia than in the whole of Mouila Hospital. In the air I try not to allow myself to even consider the possibility that the Brew Ha-Ha may be over. But I am worrying about how I am going to get to Zanzibar in exactly two weeks for Christmas with Olive. 'One thing at a time,' I tell myself.

After a 300-kilometre flight north, as we prepare to land at Libreville, I notice smart cars moving about the city, the palm-fringed beach, the concrete buildings. Let's hope one of them is a decent hospital – with a few spare painkillers.

The glass doors of the Polyclinique El-Rapha whoosh open and I am pushed in a wheelchair into the air-conditioned calm of a Western-style hospital. Two doctors, one an orthopaedic surgeon, and a senior nurse are waiting for me in an examination room. They take an X-ray of my shoulder and swiftly decide to strip all the heavy bandaging from my chest, neck and shoulder – along with copious amounts of hair.

'Bandage not good,' says the surgeon.

'What is zis?' He asks, jabbing at my shoulder.

'A hairless shoulder,' I say.

'OK. Shouldair must be… like zis,' at which he stands up with his shoulders stretched back exaggeratedly.

Dr Zakaria and the other two each take their places and without warning one pushes my shoulders back, one pushes my spine forward, and the third straps me into a large figure of eight foam bandage that loops over the shoulders and ties under both arms with industrial-strength Velcro. Now that was painful. My eyes are scrunched up in agony and watering with the shock of the manoeuvre. But strangely it is also a great relief to have my back straightened and my arms stretched away from my body, although I can't help thinking it feels very unnatural.

When they seem happy that I am well and truly trussed up, Dr Zakaria asks, 'How do you feel?'

'Like a plucked chicken.'

The night for me is pure distilled misery. The braced bandage around my shoulders is excruciatingly tight and has the effect of coarse sandpaper under my arms. It's as close to imprisonment as I ever want to get. The pain down my right side is agony: my ribs feel like they want to burst out of my chest and I still can't take a deep breath, the bloody gash on my side is sticking to the bed sheet, my hip is black and purple, my head is pounding like a pneumatic drill, and every time I move the room seems to float away from me.

I take a moment to realise that I am desperately hungry. I have hardly eaten at all since the morning of the accident three days ago, but rather lived off adrenalin. A cuppa would go down well right now, but I could die of thirst waiting for a nurse in this place. Eventually the torture of being prone is too great and I force myself through the pain barrier to get out of bed and inch towards the bathroom across the empty corridor.

It is a great relief to be out of bed, but I get a shock when I see myself in the mirror. My face is torn with agony and heavily lined, I have a week's stubble, and my hair is a fright. I've aged a decade or more since the accident through worry, pain and the unavoidable Mouila Hospital Diet, and even before that I couldn't say with any truth that I was well-nourished.

I catch my own eyes in the mirror: 'How did you get yourself into this bloody mess…?'

I use my left hand to splash my face with cold water.

'… and how are you going to get yourself out of it?'

I stagger back to bed. It is five o'clock.

The doctor arrives at seven and asks, 'You still feel like chicken?'

A week after admission my time is up at Polyclinique El-Rapha. My stay has been a bizarre mix of rest, frustration and farce. I used to think nursing was a vocation, a profession that attracted people with deep reserves of empathy, caring and a desire to ease other people's pain and discomfort. But at El-Rapha I have not received one moment of real care.

Serge, my nurse saviour from Mouila Hospital improvising with little medication and non-existent supplies is worth a dozen of these idlers. I miss him.

While the nursing is conspicuous by its absence at El-Rapha, the food is actually not bad – but the meals are brought by two silent women in their twenties dressed in doctors' cast-off white coats with faces as long as a late breakfast. The woman on reception takes rudeness to a new level. She ignores me no matter how close to the desk I stand and regardless of what I say in English, French, sign language or Morse code. Her idleness makes me want to shout, 'I'm sorry for interrupting but I'M NOT WELL!'

I can't wait to leave the hospital, and yet I dread the thought of having to cope in Libreville on my own (getting about is still a struggle and I can't even shower myself). It is a shock to go back out into the real world – and Libreville, after the hospital stay, is shockingly real. The first thing I do is arrange a three-connection flight to Zanzibar in a few days to meet Olive (I'd almost forgotten it's Christmas). I would love to have ridden there on the Triumph (which hopefully remains secure in Mouila Hospital), but that is not uppermost in my mind at the moment – a week's rest on a tropical island sounds like what the doctor ordered. I find a grimy hotel and grit my teeth until then.

I arrive in Zanzibar airport and wait for Olive's later flight from Manchester. Even though I am the only white man in arrivals, she doesn't recognise me when she steps off the plane. When she notices me she finds it difficult to hide her horror at my dishevelled appearance. To make the arrival extra special, Olive's suitcase – packed with her new holiday clothes and a valuable list of essentials for my trip: chain oil, batteries, underwear – fails to appear at the luggage retrieval desk.

I spend the few days over Christmas mostly eating and being showered. I feel guilty at being barely able to move and Olive bites her tongue about my extreme weight loss and general incapacity. I'm sure too that she harbours doubts about me returning to finish the trip, so I don't ask. After five days' recuperation that pass like a summer's afternoon, Olive says she will be in Cape Town to meet me at the top of the mountain before the final descent into Hout Bay. I can barely wait for that day.

Taking the flight back to Libreville is the hardest single decision of the trip so far: Olive leaving for Manchester and me going west across the continent to continue this nonsense. But judgmental decision-making sometimes makes no sense on a continent that relies on instinct. Most people would have taken the insurance company's offer two weeks ago to fly back to the UK for treatment. Nobody expects me to continue but, and it is a big but, how would I feel if I didn't finish the trip, if I gave up now at the first major crisis, if I lost sight of the blinding light? I try to answer my own nagging questions, 'What am I doing this for?' and 'What am I trying to prove?' But perhaps I won't know that until I reach Original Tea Bag Designs on 22 February at 2.30 p.m. for the tea party. There's no way of describing how far away that feels right now.

I arrive back in Libreville on the evening of New Year's Eve. I go back to the same grim hotel and count the minutes to midnight and the three-month anniversary of the Brew Ha-Ha. I raise a glass to friends back home who are probably now dancing around the kitchen to ABBA songs and direct my thoughts to the quest ahead.

I have another three weeks before returning for more X-rays, at which time I will get the prognosis, which I have to admit does not feel too good from where I sit.

The trip has come to a grinding halt. The busyness of my life while I was on the road has vanished, and there are times when I feel totally lost. I get no purchase on the events of the day, and I torture myself by imagining the places in which I might now be had I not had the accident. For the first time, I am seeing people on a daily basis rather than excitingly brief *bonjours* and *au revoirs*, and irrationally I begin to resent their familiarity. In fact, I am probably grieving the death of my closest friend for the past few months, the journey itself. The longer it went on, the bigger its personality became, the more fascinating its history, the more people's lives it touched. I tried to shape the journey, and then the journey shaped me. I am eaten away with absurd resentment at the bad luck of it all.

Libreville, a large seaport with a well-established commercial sector, is bolstered by a large community of expat French contract workers – mostly driving well-maintained four-by-fours. I should imagine the city is quite draining when you're well but it's bloody exhausting when you're crocked. Simply hailing taxis, haggling for food and fending off the vendors and hawkers on the street is enough to stress me out. And because I've lost so much weight I have to traipse the streets holding up my trousers with my good hand like some out-of-work circus clown. On top of all that, it is agony to do anything and I still cannot take a shower. The doctor insisted the figure of eight bandage across my shoulders must not be removed, which means, quite frankly, if I were me I wouldn't want to get anywhere near me. Jesus, do I stink!

One curious incident shakes me out of my stupor. One night at midnight, while I am listening to the BBC World Service on my tiny radio, I get a frantic rap on my hotel room door. The waiter outside urgently demands my presence at the bar. This had better be good. It turns out that the hotel has double-booked my room and the incoming guests have just got off a flight from Douala, Cameroon. Nobody is very happy about the situation but another room is found for the couple to occupy.

The next morning I join the displaced couple for breakfast and do my best to apologise.

The man says, 'It is not your fault. You have a long journey ahead of you.'

'How do you know that?' I ask.

'We have met before.'

Curiouser and curiouser.

'Where?'

'In Lambaréné, at the hospital where I work. I saw you ride in on a big black moto some weeks ago.'

It suddenly dawns on me that the person I am having breakfast with is the man who acknowledged me at the Schweitzer Hospital. And last night I slept in the very room he had reserved. I may be clutching at straws here, but for some reason I take this incredible coincidence as a sign that this trip has to continue, no matter what.

In an attempt to relight the fire of the trip, I reflect on some of the Tea Encounters before I left for Africa. One piece of advice comes to mind from a Tea Encounter in Manchester with Debbie Robinson – 'Take a smile with you. A smile gets you out of anything' – which is just what I need to do. Smile. There's nobody here to get me out of this mess and, short of hitching a pillion ride from the next passing biker to Cape Town, I have to get myself into gear.

First off, I order a pot of tea, which amuses the barman no end – he normally serves me three beers and a large glass of ice for my G&T I take to my room every evening. As I drink the tea alone at the bar my mood changes instantly. 'I'm on a tea tour, for crying out loud,' I tell myself, 'go and find someone to share a pot.'

I leave the hotel and call a shared taxi, all of which use a system that involves yelling in through the driver's window your destination and suggested fare. If he agrees to your offer he honks and pulls over.

A Toyota going in my direction approaches with one spare seat.

'*Centre ville, cinq cent francs,*' I shout, starting with five hundred.

He doesn't stop.

Another cruises by...

'*Centre ville, sept cent francs.*' (Seven hundred.)

... but also drives on.

And another one...

'*Centre ville, mille francs.*' (A thousand, I'm getting desperate now).

... honks, and pulls over. I don't know why I always start with five hundred francs because no taxi driver has ever accepted so little from me, although I notice locals paying even less.

On my first night out in town at the poshest hotel around – and in spite of the foul pong coming from under my arms – I meet up with a jolly group of people and pick up an invitation to tea and some lunch. Africa hasn't beaten the Brew Ha-Ha just yet.

'No, of course it's not too late to come for lunch,' says the female voice down the line of the borrowed cellphone, 'I'll send my driver.' Click.

Within ten minutes a brand new air-conditioned four-by-four arrives to take me to the home of Madame Marie-Hélène Mathey Boo, one of my new friends I met last night.

The traditional *rouge* with vegetables has obviously been kept warm, but the food doesn't look as if it has suffered at all, and I can barely wait to tuck in. The cook serves rice and the *rouge* fish dish to each of us in turn: myself, then madame sat at the opposite end of the table and lastly her assistant, Christy, on my right.

The dining table is formally laid out with tablecloth and linen serviettes, heavy cutlery and shining porcelain, water and wine glasses. It is surprising to me, who is not always the most formal individual, how pleased I am at such a simple thing as a set table, a courtesy not shown since visiting the Zim farmers of Shonga.

A tubby, middle-aged woman who looks as if she is about to burst, Marie-Hélène is director general of the Centre International des Civilisations Bantu (or CICIBA, if you happen to notice the personalised registration plates on the three pristine four-by-fours in the driveway), which is a multinational cultural organisation created to protect and nurture Bantu heritage. Until very recently Marie-Hélène was the DR Congo ambassador to Gabon (she has not yet been replaced so is still addressed as *Madame Ambassadeur*), which she happily admits, apart from the perennial refugee problem on the border, was a very taxing round of cocktail parties, golf dates and networking opportunities. Life's tough.

Christy, also from the Congo, has a good command of English – you can't underestimate the importance of that on a lunch date – and wants to talk about everything from movies to black magic.

Christy says, 'It is a dream for us to go to Europe. I think I would like England the most but I am embarrassed for my English.'

'No, it's good, the best I've heard in Libreville.'

'I wonder why you would come to Central Africa at all,' she asks.

'Just adventure. It's been a great trip so far, in spite of the accident.'

'Gabon is rich and comfortable, but you go now to the DRC, my country. The war will not end; many bad things have happened that we cannot forget. I worked for a time with the child soldiers who learn to shoot before they learn to read. They know no different. Killing and dying is a playground game when you are taking drugs so young. It is difficult for them to learn to play childhood games. But when they do they become children again, not soldiers. You will see them on your journey if you continue. There is also black magic that way, the slave route; it has many bad memories for Africans, bad demons.'

A visitor arrives after lunch in the form of Henri Tchikaya, another Congolese, a well-dressed individual and a great conversationalist (even though I don't understand a word of whichever one of the many Congolese languages he may be speaking). Henri has the demeanour of someone who has come for a job interview. He is in the home of the outgoing ambassador and wants to make a good impression, but his downfall is when he is asked if he would like a drink and opts for a whiskey. Then another. He thinks it will steady his nerves but merely adds to his unease. After his third drink, he begins dramatising his conversation, whether serious, comical or flirtatious, with extravagant hand gestures, which is a bit like taking part in a one-way game of charades. The housemaid makes some tea in an elegant pot and brings china cups and saucers as I ask Henri (who is getting a lot merrier than the rest of us) for some advice on the road ahead.

Using Christy as his interpreter, he says, 'Remember, Gabon is the centre of traditional beliefs in Africa and Ndendé is the centre of those beliefs in Gabon. You must ask yourself why did the accident happen in Gabon... you were not meant to continue with your journey by that route. Ndendé was the centre of the slave trade many years ago, so people believe there are many bad spirits there. Did you take a charm with you? Did people back home raise the spirits to protect you?'

I shake my head.

'No? Then it is too late.'

He opens his hands with some finality, 'It is the way your trip is meant to be. Think of the places you have been and the people you have met, is that not enough?'

Marie-Hélène adds seriously, 'The accident has told you to find another way; you cannot carry on by the route you had planned. This happened for a reason; do not fight against it.'

So, I was not meant to go down that road. But in the car on the bumpy road back to the hotel I tell Marie-Hélène's chauffeur about my desire to ride to Cape Town. He leans back, shakes me by the hand and utters one word.

'*Courage!*'

'Thank you,' I say, 'I appreciate that.'

And I do. I try to balance the concern shown to me by Marie-Hélène and Henri with earlier advice such as, 'Whatever happens, keep going' and 'Make up your own mind', both of which are almost taunting me now. And whatever happened to 'Never lose sight of the blinding light'? Perhaps the light is fading a little in the face of shadowy African spirits, after all.

I go back to the infamous Polyclinique El-Rapha. To my eyes, the new X-ray shows the bone is setting in a very awkward position. One fracture has reset the bone straight, but the second is fusing at a gruesome angle, and rather worryingly I can still wobble it about. With the outlook for the Brew Ha-Ha not what you might call rosy, I enter the doctor's office with the damning X-ray under my arm.

Dr Zakaria slips the negative into the light box and I am stunned to hear him say, 'Eez very good. Zis iz fine.'

'You're kidding. Look at it! The fracture is nowhere near healed, and I'm still in so much pain.'

'Take off shirt and bandage, *s'il vous plaît*. Do you still feel like chicken?'

He loves that joke.

I ease the bandage off. The sensation in my arm and shoulder is extraordinary, at once feathery light and concrete heavy as though it might drop off from the neck at any moment.

'Lift ze arm,' says the doc, '... and again. Ze bone is fine, but you must go to... *physiothérapie*. Your muscles and ze area around ze bone eez veee-ry bad.'

He steps back and looks at my bare torso with a squint.

'Have you always *asymétrique thorax*?'

He shows me how one side of my ribcage is sharply out of alignment.

'No, that must be from the accident,' I look down aghast. 'And now that you mention it, the sternum makes a rather worrying clicking sound when I move.'

'Eez no problem,' he says, and laughs my concerns away.

He looks closely at the gash in my side: 'Eez OK,' he pronounces.

'Eez sore!' I reply.

He's laughing at everything now; he thinks I'm making a drama out of this. He dismisses my apprehension and writes down the name and address of a physiotherapist in the city centre.

'*La moto*, is OK to ride and continue to Cape Town?' I ask.

'Of course, in two weeks; *après physiothérapie*.'

YES! I practically skip down the stairs of the hospital. So, two weeks of physio and the African Brew Ha-Ha should be back on the road.

I immediately spot a taxi: '*Centre ville, cinq cent francs*,' I call.

The driver honks and pulls over. Yes!

14
RETURN TO MOUILA

At some stage you have to say,
'Tomorrow I'm doing it.'
Martin Higginson

Mindful of Martin Higginson's advice over tea in Lancaster exactly a year ago – 'At some stage you have to say, "Tomorrow I'm doing it"' – well, tomorrow I'm doing it.

On the fifteenth day after the appointment with Dr Zakaria and following almost daily physiotherapy, I investigate ways to get back to Mouila, 400 kilometres south. I have only four weeks to reach Cape Town. Although I am warned about the dangers of travelling by bus or shared taxi, I discover that bush taxis leave for Mouila most days from PK8, a *gare routière* on the way out of the city.

I stop at the cyber café on the way back to my hotel. The young guy who runs the place recognises my improved mood and mobility and treats me like an old friend, although we've hardly had a conversation before. I suggest we meet for a beer and we agree to hit the town later in the evening.

Everigne takes me to a couple of hectic bars with impromptu dancing between tables and in every other available space. *La musique congolaise* is played at ear-piercing volume to customers who feel quite at ease spending an evening in a shack listening to shattered speakers turned up to eleven. I have never seen the Gabonese so loud and gregarious. I get a hundred invitations to dance – a little exercise for the shoulder – and people buy me beer all night. Maybe it's the booze talking; perhaps they drink so much because they are naturally so reserved, like the English. I am so excited about getting the Brew Ha-Ha back on the road I get completely bladdered.

It's an early start after a very late night – so late, in fact, that I'm still drunk. Incredibly, Everigne is already at the cyber café on the main road, and he offers to take me to PK8. He soon finds a shared taxi heading for Mouila for only 14,000 CFA – £15 for a Mitsubishi to take me 400 kilometres through the jungle.

Compared to many of the overcrowded and overweight cars and small buses doing their best to asphyxiate us, my shared taxi is a reasonably comfortable four-by-four. Although it is wearily shabby, it appears the most roadworthy vehicle on the street. With me on the back seat are a young mother and a child of about three years; in the front passenger seat is a teenage girl. The driver, a smartly dressed twentysomething, accelerates away from the kerb and is clearly intent on getting to Mouila as fast as is humanly possible in a motor vehicle. He overtakes in wince-worthy style over potholes and on blind bends; the terrain – gravel, mud, deep puddles – makes no difference to his speed.

The landscape is mostly dense bush as opposed to the huge forests of timber in the north. Consequently, the road has been left to disintegrate in these parts because there are no loggers to lay smooth tarmac for their trucks. The roadside settlements also become poorer the further south we travel; the relative riches of Gabon – and it is rich compared to most African nations – are denied these communities.

The woman beside me gets tired holding the child and wedges the boy between us to prevent him being thrown about the car like everybody else. The bouncy journey helps me regain some of the momentum of the Brew Ha-Ha. The wind hitting my face through the open windows and the juddering over potholes serve to reinvigorate my sense of adventure. My thoughts shrink to the stark certainty of my quest, and a shared pot of tea in Preston with Mike Finnigan nine months ago surfaces...

'Many people have a common problem, which is "my attitude needs to be sorted" and if you can sort that you can pretty much sort anything,' Mike said. 'Like the people who only talk about setting out on a quest but never actually do it. All they see are the obstacles. Once you can create the quest in your mind, the success will emerge from that desire. What is your dream for this trip?'

'To ride into Original Tea Bag Designs in Cape Town. That one moment will mean a lot to me; and of course to find the ultimate cuppa,' I answered. 'Do you have any advice for the trip, Mike?'

'Never lose sight of the blinding light. For me, that's the only piece of advice people need in life. As long as your blinding light remains your goal you will succeed.'

I wake to find the child asleep in my lap and his mother snoring with her face pressed up against the closed window. The collective sweat in the car could drown a goat and even with the other three windows open it is difficult to get a good lungful of air. After five hours over the gallops we stop in Lambaréné for something to eat at an outdoor lunch counter serving the ubiquitous thrice-cooked *poulet et riz* in Maggi stock cube with optional rancid mayonnaise and hot sauce.

On the way out of town our driver manages to get into a fight with a ragged crowd of men manning a checkpoint. The uniformed officer in charge, who looks as though he last heard a joke in 1992, sneers menacingly and is up for a fight. He waits for the driver to end his rant before launching a fearsome attack of his own while all the time banging on the bonnet of the car with his clenched fist for emphasis, leaving a huge dent. The officer now decides he wants to test the roadworthiness of the Mitsubishi. Roadworthiness? In Gabon? Then he levies a 1,000 CFA fine for an unspecified violation which leads to a full-on nose-to-nose shouting match. Indignantly, the driver takes out his cellphone and takes a photograph of the officer and his men, which causes a huge scuffle. All the while there is a mood of resentment and incredulity in the car at the driver's stubbornness. Personally, I can't help feeling the two of them are lacking in the blinding light department.

Still protesting the injustice of the fine, the driver finally pays and storms back to the car – twenty-five minutes after he stopped at the checkpoint. Needless to say, he now has time to make up and we are all in for a bumpy ride, which is a bit like saying a Blackpool rollercoaster goes up and down a bit, and we spend the next hour with our hearts in our mouths as he takes the road like a rally driver who's overdosed on Red Bull.

We arrive in Mouila at six o'clock – nine hours after we left Libreville – exhausted and dripping wet, with stratospheric blood pressure. My shoulder and ribs are tearing at my side after the trial-by-pothole. I give the driver 1,000 CFA as a tip to cover his fine and ask him to drop me at the hospital because, frankly, I don't know where else to go. As we reach the familiar bridge over the Ngounié River near the hospital, I say a short prayer that the Triumph and all my gear are still where I left them seven weeks ago.

I step up to the hospital's open-air reception. I can't help feeling a shard of affection for the place in spite of my painful admission, and speculate whether the pharmacy, laundry and kitchen now open on Sundays. As I consider what I'm going to do next I notice a man in an ancient doctor's white coat, arms folded, leaning against the desk.

'Mister Alan, welcome.'

I am astonished to see it is Severin, one of the nurses. I haven't seen him for weeks and nobody knows I am arriving today, but he stands there as if expecting me.

'Can I see the bike? Is everything all right? Is it still here? And all my stuff?' I babble.

'Do not worry,' he says, evenly.

'Is Alexis here?'

'Why Alexis?'

'Because he's got the outside key to the room where the bike is locked up.'

I get a blank look.

'Alexis has *la clef pour la chambre*,' I say.

'But the room is open. It is always open. We use the room... every day.'

My heart is now in my boots; all my gear and the future of the trip is (or was) stored in that room. Severin registers my shock – and my gaping mouth – then leads me by the hand to the far end of the hospital.

'Alexis *promised* that the outside door to the room would be kept locked and that only he had the key,' I say, desperately.

I brace myself for what I am about to find. Severin opens the door on the steamy room and I step inside. The white-tiled floor is spotless and ahead is a sink with nail brushes and anti-bacterial scrubs. To the left of the door is the Triumph with all my gear strapped on top, exactly as I left it. I stand there blinking at it all for thirty seconds. Severin's face is a portrait of pride.

'My God, it's all here,' I say, trying to hide my astonishment.

'Yes,' says Severin, simply.

It is apparent the room is both a popular access route to this side of the hospital and a rest and clean-up area for the nurses. They walk past on their way to the emergency beds and some welcome me back when they recognise me. I feel the need to thank every one of them for looking after my bike and, it sounds ridiculous, for not stealing any of my gear, although the curiosity for some must have been overwhelming. The worst thing that's happened in the humid, stifling room is the thick layer of mould now growing on all my stinking gear, clothing and inside the helmet.

Within an hour we find a mechanic in town whose eyes pop out of his head when he sees what he has to work on, and we perform a quick check of the damage: the battery, predictably, doesn't want to play; we can see the radiator overflow is broken in a couple of places; and the whole front of the fairing is so crushed we can't turn the handlebars. There's plenty for us to get on with tomorrow, and I hope the man in the overalls has the equipment and tools we need.

Severin takes me to Hotel La Métisse nearby so I can check in to a room. He says he will call Serge to tell him of my return, and I offer to buy them both dinner tonight.

Later, Serge arrives looking precisely like himself, with a brilliant smile on his face that provides the only light in the dark courtyard. Like a planet, he attracts people to him like gravity. He gives me an elaborate greeting gently touching foreheads left-right then left-right again while shaking my hand.

'You are well, Mister Alan?'

'I'm great. Look,' I lift my arm gingerly to shoulder height. 'Everything's OK now,' I lie.

'Where did you go?' He asks.

'Libreville. They put a brace on for a month and then physiotherapy. I'll get the bike running tomorrow, hopefully... *la moto... demain... peut-être!*'

Serge is serious and concerned.

'And then what you do? Do you go home?'

'No. Congo!'

He looks at Severin and they both laugh. Then all three of us laugh at the preposterousness of it.

As our drinks arrive – I'm on Guinness, teetotal Serge and Severin both have fizzy pineapple – a large woman who is looking for mischief comes over to ask after my recovery. She says she was a patient in the hospital when I was there but I don't remember her. She is especially interested in the progress of the gash in my side, so she must have been one of the many who gawped at my gory injuries when I was doing my best to pretend I was in another solar system. She doesn't wait for an invitation to join us and is included in the next round of drinks. The woman is Congolese and has huge laughing eyes and a permanent smile that instantly bring more warmth to the gathering. But most curious of all is her shape. She seems to have bulges in places that I've never seen before, in fact where they shouldn't be at all. Her crowning glory is a bright red wig precariously placed on her head and on top of that a yellow baseball cap. If a cartoon character mated with a Congolese *maman*, this would be the result.

With little warning the heavens open and the rain pelts down on the flimsy lean-to under which we are drinking. Even though we are still dry, the woman takes off the yellow baseball cap, careful not to dislodge her wig, and puts a plastic shopping bag on top, then replaces the hat. She now has three layers of cover – four, counting her own hair. I suggest discreetly to Serge and Severin that we order some food but they think the meals are too expensive in the hotel, at three to four pounds a pop, and recommend we go somewhere cheaper, perhaps find a *maman* grilling fish on the street.

A taxi is called, I say goodbye to the redhead and we make a run for the car through the rain. I get in the front seat and look behind to see the woman has jumped into the car next to Severin, squeezing his slight frame up against Serge who slides in the other side. I say nothing.

Table for four, *s'il vous plaît*.

At the roadside grill the redheaded, plastic-bagged, baseball-capped cartoon character is determined to keep up with me Guinness for Guinness and is soon doing a star turn of gags in French for Severin and Serge; I don't understand a word, of course, but it's a great night. We all eat heaps of fish and rice and before we go Serge asks for another grilled fish, which he wants to take home for his wife at home with their newborn baby.

On the way out of the bar, as the rain stops, I am thrilled to bump into the doctor from the hospital, who takes a look at the collarbone. I give him a brief update on the last few weeks.

After listening intently, he asks, *'Maintenant?'* ('Now what?')

'CONGO!' I say.

The doctor laughs and shakes his head with disbelief. Serge says something ironic about *le blanc* and they're all in fits.

Our unintentional date for the evening turns left on the way out of the restaurant and the three of us turn right towards my hotel.

After walking a short distance, Serge says, 'You must be very careful. The women. They like only the money.'

'Right. No different to Lancashire, then,' I joke.

'This woman, she want to sleep with you.'

'Bloody hell. No way. Serge...?'

'You know her?' Serge asks.

'I've never seen her before. I thought she was a friend of yours.'

Severin says, 'No, we do not know who she is!'

Serge slaps me on the back in relief and we hoot all the way to the hotel as they translate all the rude and daft things she said to them during the evening while I imitate the balancing act with the wig and the hat and the placcy bag.

The next morning I'm up early to meet the mechanic at the hospital for seven o'clock. He shows up wearing a bright orange jumpsuit and a pair of dark glasses, and is holding his entire toolkit in his right hand: a pair of pliers. This is going to be fun. But fuelled by the encouragement of almost everybody who comes through the room we manage to make some progress. Nurses pick their way past us with barely a complaint that we have all my tools and bike parts on the floor, we've lost about a litre of fuel and a cupful of oil on the spotless tiles, and each time we nudge the bike we dislodge crumbling mud picked up on the Ndendé road. Even the doctor comes over to urge us on – 'You will succeed. Be brave.' I can only imagine the kerfuffle if this was happening at El-Rapha – or the NHS!

We manage to straighten the frame at the front of the bike that holds all the electrics and switch gear, clear out the radiator and overflow dirty with mud, and – as there is no running water in the hospital – catch the rain dripping from the rusty tin roof to replenish it. Replacing the broken radiator connectors proves trickier so the mechanic goes to town in search of something that will make do. Work comes to a standstill until he returns.

After I scrub all the mould off my bike gear and helmet, I go up to the outdoor reception area and chat to a line of girls, about nine or ten years of age, who are waiting for their parents visiting relatives. It is a good spot to watch the comings and goings of the hospital. It is Sunday and many visitors are carrying food parcels either bought in town or carried in pots, perhaps leftovers from their meal at home; some bring the food in the very containers in which the food was cooked. Many are young mothers; it is rare to see a teenage girl without a baby on her back. Serge told me last night that he treats girls as young as eleven through their pregnancies. I look across at my young companions who probably have a year or two left of childhood. It's a solemn thought. Soon they're going to be producing kids, taking dirty washing to the river and pounding cassava in wooden tubs until they're sick to death of the stuff.

I am greeted by both patients and staff who recognise me from my stay last month. Everybody wants to gawp at the scarring and other injuries, but they are delighted at my recovery and all wish me well. It is also great to see Alexis, and I make a point of thanking him properly for rescuing the bike and ensuring the future of the trip. He is as spirited as ever, demonstrating the undervalued quality of saying nothing charmingly. He soon moves off to make somebody else smile.

As dusk approaches I walk into town and order tea. The unusual request prompts some quizzical looks then fires the young waiter into such excitement that he leaves the bar and never returns. The very drunk, very boisterous customers are at the stage where each request for beer is accompanied by lewd remarks to the young waitress. She must be about fourteen, and each time she gets up to fetch a drink from the back she hands her child to a customer. She flips the top and places the bottle on their table while trying to ignore the crudely suggestive comments.

Most of the people within view are intoxicated. Across the road a man in a loud Hawaiian shirt is selling palm wine from a filthy yellow jerrycan to people lining up with empty whiskey bottles and mucky jars of various kinds. One old woman staggers around with one foot nailed to the ground while the other searches vainly for something a bit more solid. She holds out a plastic beaker and when it's full slurps it down, the milky liquid dribbling down her dirty cheek as she struggles to remain upright.

As the palm wine queue gets shorter I see behind them a rudimentary stall on which is laid out a selection of bush meat: porcupine and a large python sliced into meal-sized pieces. A four-by-four pulls up in front of me and the back opens to reveal a freshly shot adult monkey. The driver pulls it out by its limp arm and throws it on the table next to the porcupine, the ugly gunshot wound still visible.

A little way up the road there is an uncannily inebriated man with an empty bottle in his hand lying face up in the middle of the traffic. Occasionally one of his limbs or his head shoots up into the air for no apparent reason. The shirtless man is regarded by oncoming vehicles as no more than a temporary traffic island; they do not even honk, but rather swerve off the thin tarmac onto the dirt and swing back again.

A man in a dark suit clutching a bible approaches my table and asks if I have found God. I look around at the warm full-blooded scene of Mouila on a Sunday: the drunk lying in the road, the chaos in the little bar around me, the adolescent waitress with the baby on her hip, the bush meat laid out in undignified poses, the copious amounts of palm wine slipping down the throats of the good people of Mouila, and the sheer frantic scramble for life. Or escape from it. Did God want this for them?

'I don't need your God,' I say gently, and the preacher steps to another table.

Without tea I go back to La Métisse and ask if they have anything in the way of food. I am directed inside to the bar, which is used mainly by the owner's family, for the bar area doubles as their front room. And they do what people usually do in front rooms: argue and fight, eat food on their laps in front of the telly, change the baby's nappy, smooch up on the couch, drink beer. It's a recognisable domestic scene but one that doesn't exactly encourage spritely service when a paying customer (me) wants to eat in the middle of a crucial African Cup of Nations quarter-final or when you have to interrupt an argument to get a drink.

I am handed a menu which is two pages long, one headed *Gastronomie Europene* – sausages, pork and spaghetti bolognese – and the other *Gastronomie Africaine* – *gazelle*, *porc pic* (pig), *crocodile*, *tatou* (armadillo), *python*, *chevrotin* (goat), *antilope*, *sanglier* (wild boar) and *singe* (monkey). I can feel my taste buds reeling in anticipation, but as is often the case in Central Africa the menu reflects what the kitchen would like to cook rather than what's actually available today. Maybe those items are available on special occasions, or certainly rare ones, such as the sighting of a comet or a gay wedding or a change of president (the last being the least frequent, of course). Yesterday I ordered an omelette and got chicken and peas; tonight I am given the only thing on offer: chicken and chips.

The next day the mechanic and I take around six hours to correct the tricky problem with the overflow tank using makeshift items from the town dump. Then I somehow succeed in using two thin strips of electrical wire to jump-start the bike from the battery on the hospital ambulance.

By the time the bike fires into life there is a mixed crowd of the sick, the lame and the plainly curious all cheering me on.

I take the bike around the hospital car park a couple of times in the rain, which is a strange sensation for which I am unprepared. The sheer speed of the bike relights my sense of freedom and purpose, and it is exhilarating. I knew I was missing the bike, but I had not allowed for how much I physically craved the act of riding, how my muscles had missed certain repeated functions. Now that they are required to be of use again all the comforting, familiar routines start to re-engage. When the crowd sees me smile, I get a round of applause.

Ngoma Serge Dimitri has two jobs, neither of which fully exploits his sacerdotal gifts. He is both a nurse at Mouila Hospital and a joiner; I am sure there must be crossover benefits for both sets of customers. On my third day in Mouila, once the bike is back on the road, Serge says he wants to introduce me to the family. Time for tea! We both jump on the bike and he directs me to a simple shop where he buys frozen saucissons for some reason. I buy some biscuits so his children can learn the joys of dunking.

Serge's house is off the tarred road up an overgrown muddy track with just enough space to walk between the vegetation. He jumps off the back of the bike and guides me up to his home in front of which is a score of people, even though it is still a bit of a mud bath after the rain today. Children are running around in bare feet and men are lighting fires while women are making the most of the dry spell to hang out their washing.

The three-room house, quite large by local standards, is of wooden construction and built on stilts about a metre above ground. Access to the house is gained by a crude ramp dotted with coloured plastic shoes and flip-flops. I offer to take off my muddy boots but Serge insists that as a visitor I should remain shod. The house has bare wooden floors and unpainted slatted walls, which display some curling photocopied pictures of Serge's wedding and a few quotations from the bible. In the main room there is a table and four chairs, a chest with a small television atop and the bones of a sideboard which he is evidently constructing; an ancient Singer sewing machine is placed on its shiny surface. Up against the far wall is a blackboard on which is scrawled some after-school instruction for the children. Behind me is a doorless opening with a curtain pulled across, and beyond that a narrow verandah looking onto a clutch of banana trees which Serge is proud to say he tends.

His wife, Lyda, who has given birth since my last visit to Mouila, is nursing the infant in another room but, Serge explains, 'My wife, she make the water before she sleep.'

On the table are placed three cups with saucers, a few tea bags and a container of dried milk. I sense Serge is a little nervous. As a guest in his home I wait for him to take the lead, but he has an Englishman in his house for tea and he's not sure of the etiquette. It's an awkward moment.

'So you found some tea, Serge.'

'Yes,' he says, pleased that I have noticed. 'I bought for you.'

Yesterday Serge told me, somewhat bewildered about the Brew Ha-Ha, that he never drinks tea and he has never had it in the house. The packet before us has two bags left, so this has probably been borrowed from somewhere.

Serge reminds me of an earlier character on my travels. Tabot and Serge might inhabit opposite poles with regard to relationships with women, family and booze, but where it counts they are matched: both are perceptive, generous-spirited individuals in the face of overwhelming odds, with a talent for improvising and doing the right thing.

I show Serge's children some photos from my trip and spread out the large maps of Africa on the bare floor to explain where I have been.

'Africa!' I say, and run my hand over the beautiful shape.

I point at Mouila, 'This is where you live.'

They all watch their father to gauge how excited they should be by the fuss I am creating. The family, none of whom speak any English, then gape at the map as I might stare at advanced calculus.

As we prepare to have tea one of Serge's young sons is despatched to fetch water, which he brings to me in a plastic bucket. He places it at my feet and holds out a new bar of soap two-handed, like an altar boy aiding a priest at mass. I wash my hands with some embarrassment.

The water for the tea is in a complicated-looking flask that we have to upend to get a slow trickle into each cup. It's sufficient. The tepid water is just warm enough to stimulate the tea out of the bags, and with some lumpy powdered milk on top, it at least looks the part. Then Lyda emerges from the back room with a beautiful, doll-like baby wearing a lemon-coloured jumpsuit in her arms and nonchalantly places the child into the grasp of a young daughter. Lyda sits on a bench and, encouraged now by the presence of their mother, all ten children take their places in the room, which is a bit of a crush, and the parents visibly warm to the gathering of their own fecundity.

Serge takes the packet of saucissons he has just purchased and spills the defrosting meat onto a white plate. He pushes the ten raw sausages across the table towards me.

'Please eat, I bought… for you.'

I look down at the ten sweating pink fingers. I then glance back up at Serge, his wife and the little football team staring at me, all wondering how an Englishman eats his sausages.

'But they're raw, Serge. Generally in England we tend to… eat them cooked.'

'Please, what is "cooked"?'

'Cooked is not raw. *Saucisse chaud.*'

'Ah, "hot". My wife she make a fire. No problem.'

Lyda, now cradling the newborn in her arms again, doesn't look in any fit state to be making fires for sausages.

'No, really, it's OK. Save them for the kids. I just came for tea. I'm sorry, I appreciate it, Serge, but I don't think I can eat them.'

After a pause of mental translation he asks, 'Please, what is "appreciate"?'

As the sausages point accusingly, we both stare down at the plate with our own thoughts: Serge perhaps searching for some words in English to express his teatime disillusionment, me hoping the ground will open up and swallow me. I sip the last of the warm tea. The silence, as thick as blood, is heavy with disappointment.

Serge changes tack and says, 'I have for you something more.'

He digs into a bag and places on the table a plastic bottle of long-life milk. He flips the lid.

'You have milk with your tea in England, yes?'

'Well, milk in the tea, actually. I already used the powdered milk you gave me earlier.'

The words coming out of my mouth sound so unkind.

'Take it with, please,' he says, handing me the open bottle.

'No, Serge, I'm fine... save it for the children. They need it. It should be kept cold, anyway.'

He narrows his eyes for another mental translation.

'Have you got a fridge?' I ask.

We both look over towards the silent refrigerator but we say nothing. First the sausages and now the milk; I'm beginning to see this tea lark from a whole new perspective. To me, tea is as cheap a prepared drink as you could possibly share. Here, Serge has gone to significant expense to indulge me in a social ritual he is as baffled by as he is determined to get right. Oh, Serge, Serge, I wish you hadn't. I invite myself for tea and you go and blow the weekly food budget on a bottle of milk and a packet of frozen sausages – a terse indictment of the distance between us.

The two tea bags have now been used and I'm feeling a sickly wave of guilt – and the Brew Ha-Ha is not meant to leave anyone feeling guilty. But Serge, for all that you have done, for the extraordinary man that you are, and for making this part of the journey unforgettable, the Brew Ha-Ha salutes you.

15
NDENDÉ, WITHOUT RAISING THE SPIRITS

Never lose sight of the blinding light.
Mike Finnigan

Seven weeks after I left Mouila on that wet morning of 9 December I get ready to leave the town and take the same road to Ndendé once more. A dark page has been turned; another is about to be written.

With more rain during the night and after unsuccessfully scouring the town for tea, I do not leave Mouila in an optimistic mood. More than that, I have to take the Ndendé road to the bogey town which some thought I should never go to because my family had not raised the protective spirits.

The way through the three-metre high elephant grass is muddy and churned up, and beyond ten kilometres from town there is very little activity along the road, let alone traffic. As it's my first day back on the bike since the accident, it takes some getting used to having my arm outstretched all the time. The position is not too sore, but if I make any sudden movements to correct the bike as it heads for a rut the pain is otherworldly. If I stay upright I should be OK.

The most important word in that whole paragraph is 'if'.

After two hours it becomes clear that either I have returned to the Brew Ha-Ha too soon or the road is one of the worst yet. I reach a long stretch of muddy track that is being made worse by a rough terrain excavator that has left deep ruts. It doesn't take long before the bike goes over and I break my fall with my right hand, shooting a sickening pain into the collarbone. The fused break – that tender knitting of bone to bone – has already eased slightly apart. The ugly lump under the skin just got bigger and it's moving about in a very worrying manner.

I feel such a fraud to be back on the trip, as I don't have the strength to get the bike through this terrain. It's an ignominious restart to the Brew Ha-Ha. I flag down a truck. Eight of us lift the bike onto the open back and I jump in next to it. We continue on towards Ndendé with the bike on its side bouncing around like a pinball for the next three hours. Perhaps the spirits were right after all...

RAP RAP RAP RAP RAP!

Who the bloody hell is that?

'*Le professeur d'anglais est ici,*' says the voice through the door of my hotel room.

An English teacher here? In Ndendé?

I go to the bar of the petrol station where I'm staying where a little fellow in trainers stands up and extends his hand.

'Mister Alan, I think, yes? So very pleased to meet you. I am teacher of English here. The manager of the hotel he called to say he had a real Englishman staying and I hope you don't mind but we have come to welcome you to Ndendé.'

We? He steps aside and presents a group of shy twenty something-year-old students in school uniforms sitting in the corner of the bar drinking pineapple sodas.

'They have been learning English for three years but have never actually met someone from your remarkable country and would love to hear how it should be spoken.'

He gives a modest little laugh: 'I too. They have some questions for you if you have the time.'

'Delighted!'

It's the most English I've heard for an age. Tati, for that is the teacher's name, has a smile so big he appears to have swallowed a banana widthways. He chooses his words with care and enunciates the words a, little, too, clearly, but it's a joy, all, the, same.

'Would you like to join us for a drink?'

'Sure, tea'd be great.'

'Tea, of courrrse,' he says.

The students are bashful but when I tell them I'm an English teacher – pretending to be a social worker took too much explaining – I get the third degree on how the English education system works.

The courteous way Tati and his students address each other is astounding. Perhaps I am now able to hear the politeness of social engagement for the first time in Central Africa. It is charming. Tati is a joy and must be a great teacher. He has a habit of re-emphasising every point I make with both seriousness and care as if it was an opinion he has long held but had somehow neglected to mention – 'Yes, I've often felt that... That's true, so true... O, yes, I do agree.'

'What have you learned on your journey so far, Mister Alan?'

'Just "Alan" is fine.'

'Yes, how true, Alan, I always find "Mister" too formal.'

'I've learned that it rains a lot in Central Africa...'

Everybody laughs.

'Yes, perhaps like the dogs and the cats, as you say,' says Tati.

'... and that there is nowhere quite like Africa in the world.'

'O yes, home sweet home, as you might say.'

This is great stuff. Everybody's engrossed in how Tati's colloquialisms are used in conversation, although I'm not sure they can all keep up. After taking some pictures of themselves on the bike with their cellphones we stroll back up to our drinks where the African Cup of Nations on TV has got the whole bar gripped. I ask the students what they plan to do after they leave college. There is no shortage of ambition: nurse, teacher, businessman ('because I want to make money'), policeman ('because I want to make money, too') and accountant ('because I want to use other people's money!').

Tati asks, 'May I ask you, as a teacher, do you have any heroes?'

He really is interviewing me now.

'Only one in English literature: James Joyce.'

'They won't know who he is,' he says.

'Why don't you introduce them to *Ulysses*, it's an unforgettable read.'

'Perhaps I will, perhaps I will...'

That should keep them all busy until the next English speaker drops by.

The students politely end the conversation with 'The best of luck' 'All the best, my friend' and 'Until the next time'.

Tati says, 'I would take my hat off to you in your quest – if I had one!'

The mention of Joyce gets me thinking about my own trip in Odyssean terms: my delayed return to Ithaca/Eccles Street, or in my case a pot of tea at Original Tea Bag Designs; the countless obstacles to be overcome, circumvented or conquered; the setbacks with my chosen mode of transport; and finally, a welcome from my own Penelope/Molly in Cape Town. In that story Odysseus successfully returns home, of course – maybe he never lost sight of his blinding light.

Tomorrow – Congo!

The following morning I immediately put my mind to my own odyssey and ask the hotel manager about the state of the road ahead towards Congo.

'Il est mauvais à Nyanga, après Nyanga c'est bon.'

Nyanga is the first town of any size over the border, so I prepare myself for poor roads until then. I manage quite well on the sixty kilometres to the frontier; I buy my visa for 25,000 CFA and sail through the polite Gabon frontier without delay. On the Congo side I enter a shack housing an immigration officer in fatigues armed to the teeth. His rusty Kalashnikov rifle hangs on a nail behind his head and when I sit down I inadvertently kick a wooden container on the floor under the desk. He apologises then boots the open box of ammunition away with his foot. As the soldier notes down the details from my passport in a ledger I scan the wooden shed, which is basically an arms depot for the frontier post: rifles lean up against all four walls and stacked ammo boxes spill over in one corner. If an invasion were to happen right now we'd go up like a box of fireworks.

The ragged border post is a magnet for women with babies attached at the hip who beg for money or food of any kind, anything to take away the metallic taste of hunger. Some of them are in a bad way. A famished woman wearing only an ankle-length skirt on which is printed the image of President Bongo stares at me with a look of such despair I wonder if she might expire in front of me. The woman's face is deeply lined and sallow and she barely has the strength to support her own weight, let alone the baby she is clutching. She walks with me to the bike and I offer her the remainder of a carton of mango juice, the only edible thing I have. She takes it lightly, avoiding my eye, and scuffs off barefoot back to her spot in the shade.

I get on the road to Nyanga and, hopefully, to Dolisie. The route is lined by scratchy bike-high yellow grass and people in tiny ragged settlements with expressions that seem to be crying out for some compassion. I ride by along with the rest of the world.

The bike is overheating – probably a combination of the Mouila crash and the time spent on its side in the back of the truck. It's so hot I have to ride with my knees outstretched so my legs don't scorch. That's not good.

I meet two men on a small moto going in my direction. The rider is wearing a jumpsuit and dark sunglasses with oversized headphones covering his ears. I try to keep up with them but after twenty minutes they clear a police checkpoint quickly and don't wait for me. Alone again.

The road gets wetter and the puddles deeper with every immersion, and I'm now permanently wet from the knees down. As it reaches the hottest part of the day, I ease the bike into a thirty-metre stretch of standing water. Halfway in the bike hits a rock under the surface that stops it dead in the water. I put my foot down to steady it but my boot sinks into the soft mud; the bike is going, O NO!... beyond the point of no return, it's gone. I manage to get my leg out from under the falling machine but lose my footing and splash backwards up to my neck. After thrashing about like a baby having his first bath I manage to stand up when all I can do is stare at the bike – submerged except for most of the right pannier and the exhaust – slowly sinking with a taunting gurgle as the pannier fills up with water.

I've got to get it upright immediately. But how? I try to move the bike enough to get the submerged pannier out from underneath. My shoulder and collarbone feel as if they are about to burst. I look back down the road, nothing; I look up the road – I can see someone standing facing in my direction... a child, I think. Frantically, I wave one-armed, but the figure runs in the opposite direction.

'NO! DON'T RUN AWAY, COME BACK!' I yell helplessly.

Christ, now I'm stuffed. There is no way I can shift the bike even an inch. The gurgling has stopped and I stand blinking at my whole world lying in the muddy water.

I look back up the road again, but this time I see a small crowd running towards me. The child in red is leading the group down the hill – about a dozen other children and one adult, a man. They wade into the water and know immediately what to do.

'*Un, deux, trois*, HEAVE!...' I implore.

The bike has already settled deep in the mud.

'*Un, deux, trois*, HEEEAVE!'

The bike is up. Now to move it.

'*Un, deux, trois,* PUUUSH!'

Nothing.

I take everything off the bike and dump it in the water to make it easier to move the beast. Once it is on solid ground I lift one of the panniers onto dry ground and open the lid. It's full to the brim with brown water. I push it on to its side to drain it and quickly take out the laptop, all my clothes, my camera, other essential gear. The tank bag is also soaked through with all my paperwork inside – the carnet, passport, bike documentation. I feel numb. Everything, all the important stuff, looks ruined. I press the shutter to see if the camera is working. It's dead. I flip open the laptop but the screen is already pitting. I look for something dry to remove the excess water; futilely, I wipe it on my sopping shirt.

My mind is blank. The children stare at me staring at my gear. I have to do something. I pick up the clothes and squeeze out the dirty water as best I can. The children copy me.

'*Avez-vous de l'eau?*' Fresh water.

'*Oui... là,*' they all point in the direction from whence they came.

The children pick up a bag or package each and stride off up the hill; one teenage girl lifts the 20 kg pannier onto her head. I put the bike in neutral and press the starter. After half a minute it coughs like a sixty-a-day pensioner over breakfast and bursts into life.

'Thank Christ for that!'

I swing a wet leg over the bike and ride up to a clearing in front of a hut; someone runs with a bucket for some fresh water. The children take each item of clothing, squeeze out the excess muddy water, then rinse it in clean water – which soon becomes equally muddy, of course – and spread it out on low bushes and trees. Everyone is agog at my stuff – the playing cards, tools, books and paperwork, the camera, laptop, charger, clothes, first aid kit, toiletries, malaria tablets – laid out like this, indecently smug in the mud, it looks an obscene amount of riches for one man to be carrying through Africa.

Some of the documentation and all the precious collected tea bags are kept in a blue folder which is sopping, so I ask a young girl to take everything out and lay it on the ground in the sun. She upends the folder and all the tea bags plop out like soggy, brown samosas. After noting the grimace on my face, the girl shakes the folder again and a wad of 10,000 CFA notes fall to the ground. She emits a little scream.

'AH!'

So do I.

'AH! Bloody hell!' I exclaim, genuinely astounded.

Where did that come from? I must have put it there for emergencies. From every disaster... I may have lost a laptop and the camera, but I think my cash worries are over, for the time being anyway. I peel apart ten beautiful 10,000 CFA notes and put them in my pocket.

I am so grateful to these good people and briefly consider what the outcome of this fall may have been had they not found me. All I can think about now is getting to Nyanga, as if it were Xanadu. I've got to focus on getting out of this mess. I thank each one of my helpful gang – especially the little girl in the red dress – and throw the wet stuff back into the panniers helter-skelter and load up the bike. I tell the kids they can keep the playing cards now distributed around the place; to the man I give an unworn pair of Nike shorts and some spare change.

I plug on. After another ten kilometres I have used up all my drinking water: I'm now simultaneously wet through and dry as dust. The huge puddles come thick and fast, about every fifty metres, and like waves on the beach every seventh one is formidable. I have to swallow hard, breathe deeply, brace my shoulder and go for it, but to be honest my confidence is waning.

I reach another expanse of water. I'm not even sure if it's a river or a puddle; it doesn't matter anymore, it's all water. I slowly inch forward, paddling at walking pace. I hit a large rock under the surface. Not again, not now, please; I struggle to keep upright pulling the bars with all the strength left in my shoulders. I gently ease the bike up onto the rock and... it stays right there. I'm revving like a madman but the bike is going nowhere; it is now perfectly balanced on the bash plate with both wheels off the bottom. I'm helpless, but at least I haven't dropped the bike.

I wait it out, with the water up over my boots, feeling a bit like a survivor on a desert island waiting for a passing ship. But there hasn't been another vehicle in over an hour in either direction so my prospects aren't exactly glowing.

After a short time, rather incongruously, a line of children walk down the road dressed in pristine uniforms: the boys in crisp white shirts and grey trousers, the girls in new blue skirts. They begin having some fun with me, teasing *le blanc* and my predicament stuck on a rock in Congo. They strut about as teenagers do, hands on hips at the edge of the water, and I imagine they are saying something like '... and if you think I'm going into that mud hole to help you in these clothes, think again...'

But after equal measures of flattery, cajoling and a direct appeal to their sympathetic natures, I get them to take off their shoes – those who are wearing them – and wade into the water to gently rock the bike. They are careful not to splash their spotless uniforms as I urge more kids watching on the side to push the bike from behind, pleading, 'S'il vous plaît, mes amis, s'il vous plaît.'

I get a decent push and sense this is the time to give it some stick. I know precisely what's going to happen when the tyre makes contact with something solid but regardless of the consequences I twist open the throttle; the rear wheel finds the rock and the bike shoots forward sending titanic spurts of water into the air behind. Every child is caught in the backwash and is now drenched from head to foot in the muddy water. White blouses are soaked through, grey flannel trousers are now brown and stunned faces are dripping with water. They turn to one another pointing unbelievingly. Some children start to run after the bike splashing the water at me but I decide that it's best I keep moving. I stand on the pegs, look over my shoulder and shout, 'Merci beaucoup, au revoir, mes amis' to which I get a mixture of cheers and jeers as I fishtail off through the water.

Less than five kilometres further on there is another enormous pool of standing water. I take it carefully; I don't want to fall in the drink or get shipwrecked again. This time I take it so slowly that I stall the engine as soon as it meets a rock under the surface. And now the bloody thing won't start. I don't believe it. I am balanced with my submerged feet planted in the mud right enough, but I can't get off the bike to investigate the problem. I am well and truly stranded for the third time today. I keep trying the starter and when I get to the point that the battery starts suffering, a small moto appears around the bend up ahead. It's the guy in the orange jumpsuit, sunglasses and headphones, and he's got a different passenger riding pillion. Out of curiosity he stops. Silently, he helps me push the bike onto a dry piece of ground where he tries the ignition for himself.

'*Buges?*' he asks.

A man of few words, obviously.

I soon discover that *buges* are spark plugs. I indicate that I have some spare and the tool to remove the old plugs. That's all he needs to know to start stripping the fairing off in search of the faulty *buges*. We soon have a crowd who stop on their way from somewhere down the road to somewhere up the road and have nothing better to do than stand around watching us fiddle with the bike. By the time we fit the three new plugs it is approaching six thirty – an hour in which not one person in the crowd has moved.

Occasionally, we hear distant airborne cheers.

'What is that?' I ask.

'Football.'

And it's an important match; Congo's near neighbours Cameroon are in the quarter-final. Mr Orange indicates that he was on his way home to watch the game when he saw me and – I'm sure he regrets it now – stopped to help. But nothing in his manner indicates irritation. He calmly works on replacing the tank and all the connections and the fairing. It is soon dark on this lonely track enclosed by tall grasses. Creepy as a crypt, and with the distant cheers making us all feel rather forgotten, it's a grim last half hour. Our audience is still there at the end, two hours later. It is now pitch dark, and all we have to guide us is a miniature pocket torch, so we spend an age on our hands and knees searching for lost screws and washers in the sandy earth. The bike fires into life at the first time of asking, coughing a loud, satisfying expectoration into the black night. I am relieved that the guy can now get on his way to watch the end of the match, at which point he offers to take me to his village – back the way I came – to spend the night.

Considering the shape I'm in, the soaking wet clothes, all my stuff steaming in the panniers, the state of the road and the sinister darkness that has now engulfed us, I think it best I spend the night in the nearby village full of football fans. He agrees and leads me up the track lit from above by the occasional star marking out the colossal sky; it is an eerie feeling riding into the void.

Shortly I see a group of people on the side of the track, most of them carrying petrol storm lanterns. I stop. To the right are a small number of shacks set a few metres back from the road. To the left facing an outside wall is a tight cluster of faces illuminated by the light of a television screen next to a satellite dish. A loud cheer goes up as they stand and wave their arms, some applauding. Cameroon have scored again. And I think I have as well.

Mr Orange is standing next to his passenger and holding another man by the arm.

Before I get off my bike he says, 'This my brother. Everything OK!'

He refuses to accept a few thousand CFA for his help and jumps back on his little bike with his remarkably patient pillion passenger and plunges back into the blackness.

I am so relieved I have to laugh, and I shake the brother's hand like he is a long-lost uncle or something. The brother is delightful and delighted to see me in equal measure and immediately walks off towards an incomplete concrete building. He enters, then shortly after pops his head out from behind a curtain and beckons me in. I park up at the door of the building, which I now realise is his home. I emit an audible sigh of relief and temporarily forget about the wet gear and all the documentation (which is probably cementing itself together into a block of paper at this very moment) because never was anyone so looking forward to spending a night in a lean-to.

The brother pulls aside the doorway curtain to reveal a one-room windowless shack with a double bed, a two-legged table leaning against one wall and a hissing lamp which sets the intimate scene perfectly. At head height there is a piece of string stretched across the room on which is hanging some laundry. After I show him the state of my clothes, he immediately pulls his laundry off the line and indicates I should replace his dry things with my soggy stuff. There isn't room for everything so we distribute the remainder around the shack.

I can't believe this is a spare 'guest shack' and ask, *'Cette lit – votre lit?'*

'Oui.'

Good grief, he's giving me his bed for the night.

'Pas de problème,' he says, as he sweeps a proud hand over the ill-fitting sheet stretched across the rectangle of foam. Castro, for that is his name, leaves the shack but soon appears at the door with a plastic bucket of water.

'Douche?'

Oh God, more water!

After a bucket shower I am desperate for a cuppa. I start fixating on tea. If only I had a cup of tea the outlook would seem brighter, I could relax a little and make some sense of today.

'Avez vous du thé ici?'

'Non,' he replies with a fused look of disappointment and incredulity. That *'non'* spoke volumes: it said, *'Non,* white man, if you can find tea here, you're welcome to it'; it said *'Non,* white man, where do you think you are, the Savoy?'

I try again. I ask if he has any food.

'Non,' says Castro with disappointment but no incredulity this time.

'À la village?'

'Non,' he repeats plainly.

That's what I like, a straight answer to a straight question. The village has absolutely no food on offer.

Last try.

'Avez vous un bière ici?'

'Oui!'

'Où?'

'À la boutique.'

Bloody hell, they've got a boutique. There's no light, no food, a haphazard collection of shacks, goats running amok and half the village cheering for the Cameroon football team off in the darkness, and I'm being invited to a boutique for a nightcap.

Castro leads the way carefully, lighting the ground for me with the arc of the storm lantern. The match on TV comes to an end and someone decides to fill the void with the unmistakable rhythm of Central Africa – speaker-blowing Congolese dance music.

The happy football crowd (Cameroon beat Sudan 3–0) disperses around the village. One supporter is another of Castro's brothers who goes to the back of a kiosk-sized building and re-emerges by swinging a hatch open and wedging it with a length of wood against a three-foot-wide counter that has flopped down to provide a convenient bar. He places a storm light on the counter and gives us a cheery grin indicating he's open for business, as if he was the publican at the Fox and Hounds.

Castro smiles a warm welcome-to-my-world grin: *'La boutique!'*

'DEUX BIÈRES!' I call out cheerfully above the music.

The barman goes to a chest freezer – which I doubt has been troubled by electricity this century – and takes out two large tepid beers for Castro and me. It hits the bottom of my stomach with a click and I order again. With the alcohol in me I relax enough to allow myself a brief feeling of well-being, but then the jagged memory of the day returns: the state of all my belongings, the lost computer and camera, and I fret that all my notes and photographs from the trip are lost. I try to calm myself with 'whatever happens to me on the trip *is* the trip' but I'm not very convincing. I zoom back to immediate concerns – for now, I am so grateful to this man who has given up his bed for me and wants to share a pint.

We walk back to Castro's home and I sit down on the edge of the bed surrounded by all my gear. He asks if I would like him to sleep outside next to the bike to ensure it is not stolen in the night. Who by, the bogey man?

I say, '*Non, non, pas nécessaire,*' at which he immediately jumps up on the bed next to me – he wants to share. I suggest that we sleep head to tail, an arrangement he is just as happy with. I begin to get undressed and slip into bed (*avec pantalon*).

Castro comes to bed a little later after watching the late film and surfing the Internet for an hour, as is his normal routine, after which he brings me up a mug of Earl Grey and two Jaffa cakes.

Some hope. In fact, after ordering two more beers on my tab from *la boutique* he scuffs in, kicks the door shut and locks us in with a padlock, hanging the key on a piece of string around his neck. Somehow pitch black just got darker.

I try to review the incredible day I've just lived through. I seem to have crammed in so much, while Africa, once again, has grabbed victory from the jaws of defeat. After the experience of the last few hours, the enduring – and paradoxical – feeling is strengthened that I somehow belong in this wild, unpredictable place. Despite my traumas, the day has been a success merely because I have reached the end of it. That's the African in me speaking.

The events of the day happened over a period of only twelve hours, which shows that time is a malleable notion in Africa. In the west we tend to view time as a constant, scientifically provable concept that orders our lives. It's a comfort to have a watch and plan life by its predictability. In Africa, time moves at different speeds – and so it proved today. While sometimes African days can seem endless, waiting for someone to arrive or something to happen, at other times so much can be achieved in an instant that it makes my head spin. The minutes when the bike was submerged in the water seemed like a lifetime, yet the amazing welcome to the village tonight seemed to happen instantaneously. But there is no way to slow down or speed up a process that takes a finite length of time on this continent. I've learned that certain things – like waiting for a pot of tea to brew – can never be rushed.

We both lie in the bed listening to the wet clothes dripping around us.

I ask Castro, *'La nom de cette village?'*

'Byongo.'

'Bonne nuit, Castro; bonne nuit, Byongo.'

'Bonne nuit, l'homme blanc.'

16
'WHEN IN DOUBT, TURN RIGHT'

Don't ride a bike in shorts.
John Clayton

As soon as I wake, and watched by the entire village, I begin the depressing task of repacking all the damp items back into the panniers. Castro has been a terrific host and I would dearly love to have tea with him, but now as I look around Byongo in the light of day I see the people here are desperately poor and a pot of tea would be a fantasy. At times like this I wish I had brought my own tea so that I could bring the joys of sharing a pot to these remote places, and I chide myself for asking for it on my arrival last night. I pay off the bar tab at *la boutique* and after some brief but sincere thank yous, I load up and press on.

For an hour the track continues in the potholed, sandy, gravelly, wet and uneven mode all the way to Nyanga, about thirty kilometres away, a no-horse town huddled around a crossroads. So much for Xanadu; the place doesn't even have a petrol pump – a local measure of sophistication. Instead, I make do with the usual iffy gasoline poured from ancient liquor bottles.

My arrival attracts a crowd and an English speaker directs me to a place for breakfast. I say I don't want much, just some tea and a slice or two of bread and maybe an omelette.

He laughs.

'English,' he says, 'the sense of humour, always. And tea! Hah!'

He takes me to a shop.

'I thought we were going to a restaurant.'

'First we buy food, then we take it to restaurant,' he says as if stating the obvious. 'You want bread, and something for the bread?'

'Yes.'

'You must buy here,' he says.

We enter a breezeblock building where I choose a dense disc of bread the shape and size of a cow pat and a tin of sardines, the only food readily edible. We walk across the dusty road to a shack where five or six men are chowing down on *fou-fou* and greens. My companion orders coffee for me before stepping outside.

Within, the restaurant is a dank, dark space with wooden benches laid out around three walls and a few wobbly tables. The man who runs the dirt floor operation rinses off a glass dish in a bucket, then pours in my drink from a dirty plastic jug and hands it to me. It is undrinkable. I am not sure what the brown liquid is but it is not coffee, and somehow I feel debased slurping it out of a scratchy Pyrex dish.

The other diners eye me sideways and say nothing ostentatiously. The atmosphere in the room is stifling, smoky

– with what, I cannot say, as there is nothing cooking. We are all subject to the begging of sombre women who enter and exit the tiny space – in one door and out the other – like some appalling starving relay in the hope of scavenging some scraps. But everybody looks away or stares at their bowls of food with full mouths and clear consciences; I have neither. I nibble hastily on the sardines and a corner of the bread and finish with a sip of the warm brown liquid to dilute the taste of sawdust and oil. A woman lurks in the doorway with a baby on her back so I offer her my remaining bread, which she accepts gratefully, but I'm sure the offering means little set against the wider truth of her predicament. (Starvation as a predicament? Words fail me.) The suppressed need of the women and the soundless, mocking indifference of the men are depressing. I leave.

The English speaker is waiting for me on the low bench outside.

'The route to Kibangou is good?' I ask, holding out for another minor miracle.

'*Àpres Kibangou*. After one hundred kilometres.'

That's what they said about Nyanga.

The track is no better than yesterday's and with the heat building by eleven o'clock I have to stop exhausted under a tree. I ask a teenage boy for water or a drink of any kind as I give the bike, which is still scorching my legs, a chance to cool down. The village chief joins me and tries to make small talk as the rest of the villagers stare open-mouthed at the Triumph. To my astonishment the boy arrives with a hot bottle of Coke and I drink the sickly liquid with enthusiasm. Once that's gone I get a hunger on. As if he were reading my mind, the chief offers me a scrawny corn on the cob and a small handful of groundnuts.

It is not even noon but I'm so exhausted I'm ready to call it a day. The third day back on the road is no easier than the first two; the sheer energy needed to keep the bike upright over the gallops is gruelling. My thoughts turn, as they often do now, to the very real possibility of not finishing this trip, of throwing in the towel; the persistent maggot of doubt has not yet been killed off. Perhaps I could leave the bike here in Congo in the care of this chief and return at some time in the future to continue on when the collarbone has fully set and I've forgotten how bloody hard it is. But that scenario – one in which I weigh up all the options and do the sensible thing for a change – leaves me too open to ridicule, or worse – sympathy.

The chief keeps pouring groundnuts into my palm, encouraging me to throw them playfully into my mouth as he is doing himself. The effect of the tiny bit of food makes a huge difference to my state of mind and after thirty minutes' rest and with his best wishes I press on.

Following one more occasion when I need to be rescued from the granddaddy of all water-filled potholes – this stuck-in-water stuff is starting to become a habit – I reach Kibangou, after which the route improves considerably. It is now a not-too-bad dirt road; there are even a few minute patches of, no doubt colonial, tarmac poking through, and the surface firms up throughout the whole afternoon. The improved road gives me a chance to look at the countryside in between the trees and villages strung along the route. When a vista appears I see a benign mix of low hills carpeted with thick bush and the occasional path through the tall grass to a settlement, perhaps, just out of view.

I am enjoying the level road so much that when I see some street lights ahead all I perceive are wondrous metallic shapes in the sky – it doesn't register that I am approaching a town. The front wheel hits something very hard while I am lost in a world of my own; when I look down, I realise I am on a paved road. I look back to see I have just slammed into a huge lip between the dirt road and the tarmac – I'M ON TARMAC – and the street lights are switched on. I try to remember the last time I saw that in West or Central Africa; I can't.

In a state of some excitement I ask the policeman at the last checkpoint into town to recommend a hotel and he suggests Hotel Gabriella. He seems a garrulous type so I quiz him about my onward journey to Brazzaville.

'Brazzaville, no good. *La moto, non!* The road is too bad, the water, and too dangerous!' he says, and shakes his head conclusively.

Sounds like the onward journey is going to be a scream.

I check in at the hotel and explain the situation with all my wet belongings, which by now must be growing their own life forms. Without a flicker the guy on reception offers to wash all my clothes. Rather you than me. He even sells me one of his old T-shirts so I don't have to wait around naked for the clean laundry. I'm happy enough with the arrangement and go to the restaurant in his soiled shirt, order fish, then charge the waiter's cellphone to call home as it has been some time since I spoke to Olive. It is a difficult conversation. I am struck dumb by an inability to describe the last few days, the people I've met, the effort involved in travelling just a few kilometres; I say nothing of my own doubts about reaching Cape Town.

As I come to pay for the meal I realise I have left the wet 100,000 CFA that the little girl discovered in the bike jacket sent for washing. The woman scrubbing the clothes can hardly believe her eyes when I retrieve the money soaking in the stone bath.

The next day, 1 February, is the four-month anniversary of the Brew Ha-Ha. First thing, I go to a cyber café at a place called the Sala Ngolo, some kind of vocational college, to email Philip for some advice about the bike overheating and various other technical issues. I walk outside and right next door is a training workshop for mechanics. They are keen to work on the bike (or at least practise on it), so I give them a list of problems to keep them busy for a couple of hours: I'm lonely, I'm wet, my shoulder is murder, I'm shedding weight by the day... O, all right... I tell them to repair the horribly bent foot pegs; every other nut and bolt needs replacing after sheering off over the potholes; the fused chain lock needs cutting off to save weight, and various non-working dials are still filled with river water. Best not to mention the overheating problem, which I fear may be close to terminal.

Sitting in the shade I have time to consider my options for forward progress. My planned route from Dolisie is to ride east to Brazzaville, take the ferry to Kinshasa in the Democratic Republic of Congo, then ride to Matadi for the Angola visa. But even locals are warning me against using the road alone, and anyway they say it is completely washed out, as is the rail track. I feel trapped here doing nothing when I should be getting ever closer to Cape Town. But sometimes it's better to make a positive move even if that means taking an unexpected turn – in this case maybe I should listen to Mehdi Benslimane's advice, 'When in doubt, turn right.' Looking at the map, turning right would take me to Pointe

Noire on the west coast, which looks like it might be a bigger town. It's worth investigating.

When the work on the Triumph is completed to their satisfaction – all the lost screws and bolts have been replaced with mismatched ill-fitting items, they've mangled the foot pegs beyond recognition, and all the dials are still dead – the mechanics want to take the bike for a test ride, perhaps to make sure the wheels still turn.

'No, I have too much to do today. You can have a ride on my way back from Cape Town.'

'Yes boss! Yaow!'

I pay them and ride to Dolisie station to check out rail options, but the place is quiet as an empty box, so I return to the hotel. The employee who has all my clothing is chatting to another guest and they both strongly advise against road travel to Brazzaville.

'The road? No! Train is not good idea because the robbers, the bandits will be there. But now the Brazzaville rail track is washed away and all trains have stopped.'

One of the soldiers whose job it is to accompany (i.e. protect) the passengers on the train shows up and says, 'The train to Brazza may be cancelled for many days.'

It's going to be harder than I thought to get out of Dolisie. I put my thoughts to more immediate needs and ask if there is a good restaurant in town as it has been some days since I had a full meal. The laundry guy responds quickly and makes to jump on the bike. He thinks he's invited and I don't have the heart to lever him off the pillion seat. We go to a completely empty restaurant and eat in almost total silence – I can't make myself understood in French and it appears he speaks hardly a word of English. Towards the end of the meal he asks if I would like to meet '*ma femme*, my wife'. He seems quite insistent and won't let it drop, so I say yes I'd love to meet her. He asks if she can come this afternoon. This guy wants me to feed his wife as well, I can tell. We go back to the hotel and he asks me for money to call '*ma femme*' on his cellphone. Bloody cheek.

Back in the room I spread out all my wet belongings that could not be laundered – on the bed, the floor, the table, chair, door handle. I peel the documents apart and stand them up to air out a little and line up all the tea bags on the windowsill. By the time I'm finished the space looks like a modern art installation.

An hour later there's a loud knock. I open the door to a tall, slim, light-skinned woman in sunglasses, hot pants and lots of cheap jewellery. She steps forward and lifts the shades up onto her head. It instantly hits me: the laundry man used the English word 'wife' but has sent me a '*femme*' or woman.

'*Parlez-vous anglais?*' I ask.

The woman, who is leaning suggestively against the door jamb, emanates the low-level thrum of sexual promise.

'Non, Portuguese.'

Bloody hell, he's sent me an Angolan hooker.

'*Non, excusez-moi, l'homme* has made a… m-mistake,' I say, never realising that I would need to know the Portuguese for 'your pimp got the wrong end of the stick'.

She gets my drift but she's not happy. She puts her hands on her hips and asks something like, 'So does that mean you don't want me to stay?'

She's well into the room now and I'm a little tongue-tied.

'*Pardonnez-moi,*' I say, and swing the door wide open while looking at the floor. I can feel her boring holes in me as she slowly hip-swings out of the room. She clicks her heels extravagantly across the courtyard and makes her exit through the hotel reception. A few minutes later there's another knock on the door. The hotel laundryman cum pimp stands there a little confused.

'That was not your wife,' I say with terrific understatement. 'You said you were inviting your *wife*.'

'You do not want?'

'NO!'

He gives a light shrug and remains standing there. I'm sure he's waiting for a tip. I shut the door in his face.

That evening I decide to go to the hotel bar for a drink, which I think I deserve. As I walk through the little courtyard towards reception I can feel electricity in the air. I look up in time to see an inconceivably sustained lightning flash light up the whole town. As I reach the end of a long corridor there is another almighty lightning strike and all the lights go out, plunging me into pitch darkness. I try to retrace my steps back towards the open courtyard until I reach some foliage and decide to wait for another flash to see exactly where I am. There is no reflected light coming from anywhere in the town, and no moon or visible stars; all the power must be down. I can't even see myself blink.

After several minutes, the door from reception pushes open and a man holding a candle aloft comes out to the courtyard. Another shadowy figure follows behind him. I call for help to get back to my room so I can get my torch. They lead the way but once there I have second thoughts about opening the door with these two strangers in tow. Reluctantly I show them into the room by the light of the flickering candle, which illuminates enough for me to distinguish the two men, one of whom is built like a quarterback – including the protective padding. They are both extremely interested in my belongings; while I dig around the art exhibit in search of the torch they pick things up and drop them and move items about on the floor while whispering to each other. I feel suddenly very vulnerable and become more aware of my heartbeats than usual.

'I can't find it,' I say, trying to hide my anxiety as annoyance. '*Where is it?*'

The candle goes out. My mind flexes with the potential of the moment and I get a little frantic, in the dark, with these two characters both perhaps deciding which items they are going to pinch.

'Relax, you will find it,' the quarterback says in good English.

I finally lay a hand on the torch. When I light the space, they are crowding me in the doorway but I want them to leave immediately. They relight the candle and I feel the need to explain the state of the room – and at the same time somehow suggest none of it is worth stealing.

'*Je tombe à l'eau, a la moto,*' I say.

He is aghast as the penny drops.

'Your moto fall in water?'

He looks again at all my wet gear, the documents stuck together on the table, a few scanty remnants of clothing hanging around the room, the rest caked in mud. He explains my situation to the other man and then turns around, spreads his arms wide and swallows me up in an immense bear hug.

'Is terrible... but you will be fine-fine,' he says, squeezing and patting me on the back not indifferently, as if he's trying to get me to cough something up.

Once I get my face back from his chest, I say, 'It's probably not as bad as it looks.'

We both smile weakly, me out of relief at being able to breathe again as much as bereavement for all my gear.

Before he leaves he asks for my email address and writes down his own with his phone number on a slip of paper. He clearly wants to keep in touch. I can see now that he is wearing casual sports gear about which I pass a breezy remark.

He smiles and says conspiratorially, 'Yes, I am Minister for Sport.'

'Of course, and my name's Ewan McGregor!'

We laugh together as I read what he has written on the scrap of paper: KAYA BERNARD.

'Thank you, Bernard, you're a gentleman,' I say.

I am relieved at their friendliness after my initial anxiety. Perhaps the dip in the water has left me a little edgy.

The town remains in complete darkness for the whole evening. I go out to the front of the hotel where at least I can see the taxis streaming down the road at their usual breakneck speed, their headlights making eerie silhouettes of the people walking from the shanty town towards the centre of Dolisie. I chat to another hotel guest who has the same idea. I ask him about the possibility of getting to Brazzaville, which is still my preferred option.

He says, 'Brazzaville, you go? I do not think so. The road is too bad, the rain, and I think the train is stop. Maybe for days, or weeks. This is Congo, you must allow for the rain always.'

Another man joins us and sits on the stoop a little way along. The dark figure agrees with the assessment of my planned onward route.

'The bandits and the gangsters are on the train and the road. I do not like that way. It is too dangerous. There will be nobody to help if you need it. You understand, my friend?'

My options are shrinking by the second, that's what I understand. In the glow of the next taxi's headlights I see that the second man is Bernard. He is now dressed in a pair of shorts and a T-shirt, the relief of his shoulders and biceps straining through the material.

'Think very careful, Mister Alan. I am fourth dan black belt judo, but I would not go that way. You will not make it!'

The cheerless mood changes when a teenage girl walks past on the darkened street and Bernard throws what sounds like a flirtatious comment in her direction. The girl spits a curt put-down at which he responds with a theatrical guffaw.

He turns to me and asks, 'How many girls you have in Africa?'

'I have a wife in Manchester,' I say categorically.

'Yes-yes.'

The fiftysomething-year-old makes another comment into the darkness at a second teenager walking past. She responds, but not with an unqualified dismissal.

'Come on, let's go,' he says collusively.

'What did she say?' I enquire.

'She say, "If you have a message for me why don't you come here and tell me."' He winks.

The louche stroll of the girl now lit up by car headlights tempts Bernard onto his feet and he walks sharply after her. He returns a few minutes later with a look of disappointment and his hands outstretched as if to say, 'Well, you can't blame me for trying.' Sexually speaking, the man is stuck on amber. Sports minister, indeed; randy old goat.

The next morning I check my emails and get some very direct instructions from Philip who is now diagnosing the Triumph's mechanical problems in upper case ('THIS COULD BE VERY SERIOUS') and warning me about the dangers of continuing to ride the bike in its present condition. But I have a dilemma: I have to find a way to get out of Dolisie and improve my options to progress the Brew Ha-Ha, which from this town amount to precisely zero. Pointe Noire on the Congo coast might be a better option, but as there is no way to get the Angola visa there the onward road is a no-go. My last option is to continue either by air or sea.

I'm feeling trapped in Dolisie and frankly right now I'd take any form of transport to Namibia or South Africa. I feel as though I don't belong here. I stroll over to the workshop that helped repair the bike yesterday. On the way, a traditionally dressed man with a briefcase and a willing manner immediately asks if he can help in any way.

'I need to find someone who can speak good English, *s'il vous plaît*.'

'I am in your service,' he says. 'I on my way for to teach English class in private school but no matter; I will help you.'

Well, I've solved the English-speaking part of my problem. Next, I explain my predicament – which is now becoming the new word of the Brew Ha-Ha – I need to GET OUT OF HERE.

'Can you help me find some reliable information about the state of the roads and rail tracks to Brazzaville?... or anywhere?' I ask plainly.

The man has been listening to me dispassionately for the last couple of minutes; he raises his eyebrows and says, 'Why not.'

'I don't care how I travel, by plane, by truck, by train, even a boat would do it. Is it possible to go to the airport now?'

'Why not,' he says as he prepares his robes to jump on the pillion seat.

I'm wearing shorts and swing a bare leg over the seat but feel a sickening sensation like a hot iron on my thigh and immediately jump off and start hopping around on one leg. I have left the bike in the sun and the plastic seat is almost melting. After a small group of students stop laughing at the red patches on my thighs someone throws a bucket of cold water over the seat (the bike's, not mine). It dries almost instantly but cools enough to ride off. (Another piece of good advice ignored, this time from a Tea Encounter in Blackburn with John Clayton: 'Don't ride a bike in shorts.')

My pillion is soon shouting above the sound of the motor, 'My name is Galley. Severin Galley; and yours, sir?'

'Je m'appelle Alan. Enchanté!'

First stop: Dolisie Airport. I park the bike right outside the chaotic and frankly rather distressing airport terminal. I could be kind and say it is in the middle of renovation, but more probably it is just falling to pieces. The place is full of mean-looking female soldiers and sweating people sitting behind fold-up tables used as check-in desks with hand-written signs indicating the 'airline' they represent. Severin finds one that he thinks can take both me and the bike to Pointe Noire, but the price is prohibitive. I'm secretly thrilled.

On the way out I notice a smartly-dressed party of people exiting the shambolic arrivals hall being snapped by a photographer. In the middle of the group is a familiar muscular frame, the thick neck and monumental face dressed now in an immaculate blue pinstriped suit, red shirt with oversized gold cufflinks and a bubblegum pink tie. It is Bernard Kaya, latter-day Romeo to the lonely girls of Dolisie.

'Oh, look who it is...' I say.

'You know this man?' asks Severin.

'Yes, I met him last night at the hotel.'

'It is good to know this man.'

'Why?' I ask.

'Because he is Minister for Sport.'

Bloody hell, he is the Minister for Sport.

Bernard is chatting to his companions in his usual engaging manner when he sees me across the roadway – I'm not hard to spot, admittedly. He strides self-assuredly over, extends a beautifully-tailored arm – with the label still attached to his jacket sleeve, Congo style – and shakes my hand as if we were old pals. He then greets Severin, who is visibly impressed with my friends in high places. I explain to Bernard what I'm trying to do.

He says, 'I agree with your friend, Mister Alan, Pointe Noire will give you more options out of Congo than Dolisie. If there is nothing here for you then go elsewhere! Good luck.'

He then turns back to the photographer. If Bernard stayed in the hotel last night, this 'arrival' scene at the airport must be a PR stunt for a newspaper – and a chance to get dressed up in some decent clobber.

'I need time to think, Severin. In the meantime, would you like a cup of tea?'

'Why not.'

Back at the hotel Severin doesn't need much encouragement, in between slurps and bites of my leftover breakfast, to talk about his beloved Congo.

'To improve Africa we must reduce the birthings, and as a rich country, naturally speaking, we must respect the earth and make better use of our raw materials. We must also not worry about politics too much, otherwise it may lead to more wars.'

'Civil wars?'

'Of course.'

'When, exactly?'

'Nineteen ninety-three...'

'Was there much...'

'and nineteen ninety-seven...'

'... fighting here in Dolisie?'

'and two thousand... and often in between. In Dolisie there was a lot of struggle, it was most terrible.'

Looking out from the hotel reception it is hard to believe these sleepy streets were the scenes of some of the worst intertribal fighting over the last decade.

'We must argue less about politics and listen more to others' advice wherever we go,' Severin says. 'We have a saying here: "If the locals dance with one foot then you should do the same."'

I allow some silence to settle before my mind inevitably returns to the feeling of incarceration in this town.

'Do you think there is a way out of Dolisie?' I ask.

He detects the desperation in my voice.

'Of course,' he says. 'We are able to find solutions to our problems; it is what makes us different from the animals.'

'Shall we head back to the station?' I ask.

I already know the answer to that.

Everyone on the platform has a different opinion about if and when the next train will appear and in which direction it will head, so we go into the grimy freight office for an update on my travel options. After a brief consideration the freight guard suggests I go to Brazzaville a roundabout way by taking the Pointe Noire train in the opposite direction to ensure my space for the return journey back through Dolisie to Brazza – assuming the tracks are passable by then. This option would take several days and seems unnecessarily complicated, but at least it would get me to Pointe Noire in the first instance, where I could enquire about onward options for the duration of the stopover. I have nothing to lose except the quoted 41,000 CFA, which I can ill afford, as lately I seem to be losing money like a boy with holes in every pocket. My cash problems are further compounded by the guidebook advising there are no ATMs in Congo; there certainly aren't any in Dolisie.

Taking the train seems at once a rashly desperate yet oddly sensible thing to do. I know I have to get out of this stifling town, so on that count at least I should perk up a little, and I would feel as though I were doing something positive instead of scuffing along these dirty streets waiting for the Minister for Sport to pick up the next passing underage pedestrian.

We sit on the crumbling station platform, now deserted. Severin has been a rock all afternoon: encouraging, optimistic, enlightening, amusing. I think about the English class he abandoned for my sake and those students eager to gain a skill to fight their way out of here. Now I have to do some fighting of my own. I make a decision.

'Right,' I say, 'I'll take my chances on the Pointe Noire train in the morning, although nobody seems to know what time it will leave. That sounds OK, doesn't it?'

'Why not. Be here no later than six.'

I allow the decisive change of direction to fire me into a little action and hurriedly ride back to the hotel to pack up all my gear for the morning train.

17
ESCAPE ROUTE TO
POINTE NOIRE?

There will be real dangers.
Pauline Waterhouse

The following morning I do precisely what I meant not to
do. I oversleep. I throw my gear onto the bike at 5.45 a.m.
in a panic and speed through the town towards the station
believing the Pointe Noire train is about to leave. On the
way I overtake an open-backed military truck full of armed
soldiers. They give chase. I don't know what to do for the
best: stop and plead my case or pretend I didn't see them and
try to outrun them. I open the throttle and skid around the
next bend. I park up outside the station and run inside – to
a completely deserted platform. A few porters are sleeping,
waiting for work, but there is no sign of the train that will
take me out of Dolisie.

I walk back outside to see the truck has caught up with
me. The senior officer jumps down in a fury then lays it on
all heavy.

'*Pourquoi vous n'êtes pas arrêté pour les militaires? Qui êtes-vous?*'

He wants to know why I didn't stop. I plead ignorance and change the subject to the train timetable and my urgency to get to Pointe Noire.

'*Je suis un touriste!*' I say without any conviction.

The officer looks me up and down.

'From Blackburn!' I say, at which the truck full of restless soldiers suddenly turns into a football terrace with shouts of 'Black-bairn Rovers *êtes-vous?*' 'Chelsi! Chelsi!' 'Arsenarl, Meester!' 'Leevairpull!' as they wave their Kalashnikovs in the air.

The mood lightens considerably and the officer accepts that I am not planning a violent coup with a band of biker mercenaries. Before he leaves he assesses my chances getting to Pointe Noire in one piece.

'You know, this Pointe Noire train is dangerous, for the Europeans, and for the Africans. Two weeks past the train is stop by gangsters, bandits, ninjas, and everything is taken, all the freight. And they rob everyone. Be careful, my friend, be careful.'

Gulp.

The advice from Pauline Waterhouse in Blackpool over tea suddenly hits me – 'There will be real dangers.'

By eleven o'clock, more than five hours after I arrived, I haven't moved and the platform is looking like some kind of refugee reception camp. In fact, it couldn't look any less like a train station. There are extended families of eight, nine and ten members, women, children, small groups of men, and of course the animals, live chickens and goats, some on short tethers bleating helplessly, others with legs bound slung over muscular shoulders. Belongings are carried in rudimentary sacks tied with string or nailed boxes, or in blankets slung around the waist.

People spread themselves and their throws over the scorching platform to give themselves enough room to eat, drink, sleep, clean soiled babies, talk, yell, gesticulate, laugh and sweat in the pitiless heat. It's a colourful, smelly and occasionally volatile place. Two vicious arguments have played themselves out on the edge of the platform and a fist fight has just been broken up.

Nobody knows when or if the train will arrive or leave and, to be honest, no one looks as if they're all that bothered as the sun reaches its zenith and the crushing crowd does its best to huddle in the diminishing shade up against the station wall.

'When will the train leave?' I ask.

'When it comes.'

Curious women strike up odd conversations with me, and when they notice I am recovering from an injury they solicit my medication for ailments of their own while men and boys surround the bike and stare at it silently, sometimes for as much as an hour without uttering a word, their eyes committing the image to memory. All the while food vendors hopscotch their way through the crowd selling withered ears of corn, grilled chicken on sticks, the ubiquitous groundnuts wrapped in pages ripped from inky exercise books and cloudy water in small knotted plastic bags. But quite categorically, there's no tea.

As the train approaches people stake their positions on the very edge of the platform. Before the train has even halted, parents push their children through open windows and stuff in their baggage to anyone who will take it. They then run to the open doors and jump in, eager to grab a spot on board.

Getting the bike onto the train is a per-usual bunfight. The guys who are detailed to help me bounce the bike down fifty metres of sleepers and then over the rails to the freight wagon at the rear of the train.

As we reach the open boxcar the atmosphere quickly turns from a lazy carelessness to fraught chaos. People are shouting, about what I have no idea, and waving their arms frantically as a sea of hands covers my gear and the bike. The gear goes flying over the heads of everyone into the wagon: bags, tyres, panniers. All the while the boxcar guard is screaming directions at the top of his lungs, his spittle landing on those around him. Then the bike slowly rises above the crowd as porters throw sacks of avocadoes, crates of mangoes and bags of vegetables into the wagon. Some people jump inside to guide the bike's front wheel onto the boxcar floor, but just as they prepare to heave up the rear wheel a fight breaks out in the car between two bare-chested men. Two porters holding the bike join in, prompting an almighty scuffle in amongst the fruit and veg. I look away, bracing myself for the bike to hit the tracks. I scream at anyone who is there to grab something on the bike, 'DON'T LET GO!' They save the bike and, almost as an afterthought when they decide they've had enough, the pugilists haul it unceremoniously into the car and wedge it in amongst the freight.

There is more than a little confusion about whether I should actually be in the boxcar at all. But I am not keen to leave the bike and all my gear for the long journey ahead; with freight being loaded (and unloaded) at lonely sidings, and the need to keep the bike upright, I insist I have to be here. People suggest I move to *la voiture* (passenger car) but I play dumb and say nothing. Others ask for my *billet* (ticket) at which I pat my pocket as if I have one; I'm an old hand at this stowaway lark. I find a discreet spot in the boxcar, wedge myself in and pray the train leaves soon.

When the conductor is busy, more stowaways make a leap for the open door and scramble aboard. There is only around three square metres of floor space left, and they have to pick their way through the bundles, bags, sacks and crates to find a place to perch. The rusting tin can is soon crammed full of sweating bodies – a dishevelled gang with not one word of English between them.

The guard shouts a warning, which sends everyone scurrying over the avocados in fear of detection. I am left alone at the sliding door and feel terribly exposed, so I follow my boxcar companions and dive for cover behind the crates on the far side of the carriage. There are stage whispers about my dramatic leap over the mangoes, followed by suppressed laughter, the kind you hear in church. The *chef de gare* takes a cursory look into the carriage. He idly acknowledges *le blanc* peeping out from behind the fruit – everything OK here – and moves on down the track. The stowaways clearly appreciate my act of solidarity in my dash for cover. What they don't know is, like them, I am ticketless.

We're all relieved when the train jolts to a start towards Pointe Noire at half past one, the very hottest part of the day. But not all have made it: some stragglers run after the boxcar down the track; hands are extended; some make it, some give up.

Shortly after, the train stops. The guard who was earlier negotiating the packing of all the crates runs back from another carriage and negotiates with the stowaways over unofficial payment (OK then, bribes). There is much lively argument about the value of the ride as I keep my head down, hoping it doesn't turn into another punch-up. Everybody seems to pay a different amount. Some regulars are known to the guard – maybe they flash a frequent stowaway card – while others, like me, are first-timers. I am not included in the negotiations; maybe my novelty value has paid my way.

The train picks up speed again and I settle into the syncopated rhythm of square wheels over loose tracks. I am instantly hungry, but there is no way I can eat my meagre rations – chocolate chip cookie anyone? – without incurring envious stares from everybody, so I hand the biscuits round. They're an instant hit and after the packet is returned to me empty my fellow stowaways decide I should sample some of their food. It is the start of a feast of which I wouldn't have thought the Congo capable. The stowaways lean out of the wagon to buy everything from women and small children who run to the train as it trundles through ragged villages. We feast on grilled fish, boiled eggs and cassava wrapped in its own leaves, we suck multicoloured frozen ice in plastic bags, nibble at corn on the cob, savour a strange sour cooked fruit on the end of a stick and eaten like an ice cream mivvi, we chew more unidentifiable fruits with the taste of pineapple and guava, and to finish we gorge ourselves on the sweating mangoes and tomatoes that surround us in the boxcar. As I finish one mango the size of a melon with a blissful '*fantastique!*' the guard throws me two more stolen from a crate which I gorge on until my teeth are stringy from the flesh and my lap dripping with juice. It's the greatest meal of my life – fourteen courses and no hectic bill at the end of it – and I begin to feel like a character in a Tom Waits song.

The Congo countryside is stunning as the train shunts through some untouched low hills with open vistas and lush vegetation. After the claustrophobic jungle in Cameroon and Gabon it's a welcome delight for the eyes. The sound of rushing water from countless waterfalls and a thousand shades of green bolster my mood and, coupled with a full belly, inject me with some fresh optimism. The scenery helps me take my mind off the airless carriage, the temperature increasing measurably every time somebody stands in front of the two open sliding doors. We cross at least a dozen rickety wooden bridges spanning swollen rivers, sometimes hundreds of feet below. One embankment we cross especially slowly, and a stowaway points out the aftermath of a head-on collision. On both sides of the track, like two train sets gone awry, the mangled engines and carriages lie appallingly down a steep ravine where they came to rest. A stone memorial commemorates the date and death toll of the disaster, one of two head-on smashes at this spot within the last fifteen years.

The train reaches the outskirts of Pointe Noire after six o'clock. It's a beautiful ride in to town through patchwork farms and small plantations with a reddening sky to the west and a gorgeous sensual quality in the air. As we approach Tie-Tie, the junction before the main terminal, the stowaways prepare to exit and urge me to leave too as they grab their few possessions. It's all right for them, but I have to negotiate the despatch of a 250 kg bike.

The train shudders and squeals to a halt and people throw their bags onto the narrow platform. One of the stowaways tells me to get down and watch their gear for fear of thieves – *'les voleurs, les voleurs!'* They throw my stuff on top and I do my best to keep an eye on everything until the bike is handed down. There is no fuss, no negotiating for a fee, no fist fights, just much good-natured joshing.

'À *bientôt, à midi,'* one says.

'*Douze heures?'*

'*Oui, pour les expeditions.'*

They say that if I plan to return tomorrow I have to book the bike in at noon for the four o'clock train back to Dolisie and on to Brazzaville (if the tracks are passable), which only gives me about three hours in the morning to find an alternative route out of Pointe Noire.

I ride into town hopefully, only to realise I'm back in Libreville territory – a surprising number of white people and predictably expensive accommodation. There are thousands of French expats working around the port or servicing European oil companies, the new four-by-fours testifying to the industry's importance in the region. I notice a Visa sign on the door of a hotel, which encourages me to hope the guide book might be wrong about Congo not accepting credit cards. This could solve so many problems, as I am running seriously short of cash. I ride down the main street and stop at a bank with a guard outside. Visa, I love you. The cash machine dispenses wads of precious local currency and I look for a hotel with my immediate money worries solved. I find a place that is asking an absurd amount for a tiny room, but it's next to a French patisserie so it's not a total washout.

By nine o'clock next morning I ride to a line of shipping companies in the Pointe Noire port district and choose one at random. Sometimes doing the seemingly insignificant moves the journey on in leaps, for in the very office I walk into I meet a French sales director who happens to be a biker. I explain my situation.

He says, 'Angola is not possible by road from here but there are always options.'

I'm all ears.

'Unfortunately, you have missed a ship that left yesterday for Cape Town. But why not fly? You say you have taken African trains before, why not a plane?'

He's right. Why not?

He makes numerous telephone calls on my behalf to enquire about options and prices and discovers that the Angolan national carrier, TAAG, flies freight south.

By the time I find the freight company, they have already worked out a price to get me and the bike to Windhoek in Namibia, leapfrogging the DR Congo and Angola. They tell me that if the bike is delivered to the depot tomorrow, I can fly the following day. It is still only eleven o'clock. African time seems to have expanded to suit me once again.

Although the flight will put me back on course to meet my tea party deadline in Cape Town, there is a nagging feeling that the Brew Ha-Ha will be tarnished if I continue by air. I order a coffee at a sidewalk café and debate the dilemma with myself. I swing between justifying the flight because of the accident and the days wasted with the worn clutch on the one hand and devastating disappointment for not being able to ride through Angola on the other. But finally I decide that meeting the deadline on 22 February is my prime concern;

that was always my blinding light and I intend to be guided by it.

I use the convenience of a large city to eat and wash some clothes as I approach the moment I have been dreading ever since all my gear was submerged under water: the camera and laptop were ruined – that I can live with – but what of the precious stored images on the flash drive? Have I lost my only pictures of Tabot, Serge and all the other remarkable people I have met so far? It takes me most of the day to summon up the courage to go to a cyber café and plug it in. It's fantastic news. I celebrate by eating a pizza and leaving a huge tip for the delighted waiter.

In the TAAG depot next morning, rather than crate the bike, the freight handlers merely wrap it in used cardboard boxes and newspapers held on with an entire roll of sticky tape.

I ask when the mummified bike will arrive in Windhoek.

'Before you get there.'

18
MANICURED DESOLATION

Take care, and take a few spares.
Clifford Baskerville

The next day I meet all the TAAG freight guys who wrapped up the bike in old *Les Dépêches de Brazzaville* newspapers. They are checking in the bags at the airport and are delighted to tell me the bike went on the morning flight. But later I realise they don't mention where the flight was going.

I reach 'security', a small airless room with a customs officer, an inactive security scanner and a bored policeman on the other side of the glass divide. The room lacks the traditional electric hum of an airport and I feel strangely vulnerable alone in the space. The customs officer, who has apparently left his sense of humour in his other suit, demands to know how much cash I have in CFA – I say a thousand – and euros – I say none. It doesn't seem like the sort of place I should admit that I'm loaded with crisp notes from the ATM. He lets me pass. On the other side of the non-working scanner the policeman checks every pocket and zipper of my bag before discovering my wallet from which he gleefully liberates 12,000 CFA (useless anywhere else) and a few hundred euros. He calls back to the customs fellow, who is already in the throes of apoplexy.

After he has calmed down to a panic he shouts, '*Dix mille francs!* You pay fine for false declaration!'

'*Non,*' I say, recoiling at the prospect of parting with 10,000 CFA. He tells me there is an export limit of 700 CFA, about 80p (which is news to me). I offer the customs officer 3,000, but he refuses to indulge in any negotiation. Then I suggest I go back out to the terminal to change the remainder of the CFA into euros, but he insists I cannot go back out through security. I'm stuck in no-man's land. We argue for a little while before he writes the citation, snatches my passport and walks off.

As he disappears out the door, he says, 'You no pay, you no go anywhere!'

I can't believe that after the thousands of kilometres and hundreds of checkpoints and immigration posts I have passed through I finally get caught out at a bloody airport. I stand there wondering what to do next when there is a power failure. I'm now standing in the dark wondering what to do next.

The officer returns after half an hour with a set jaw. He sits down and says, 'If you no pay…'

'I'll pay,' I interrupt.

'If you no…'

'OK, I'll pay! Just get me out of here.'

Looking down at Africa from 30,000 feet, it seems like the path of the tea tour is taking a very odd dog-leg; I never expected to fly into Namibia, but then has anything happened on this trip that I was expecting? I suppose the question is: Is the integrity of the African Brew Ha-Ha being challenged? Sat here on a plane, it certainly feels like it, especially when the flight attendant brings me a paper cup of tepid tea.

I arrive in an eerily quiet Windhoek airport. Other than a young man who politely asks if I would care to take a taxi into the city, nobody hassles me, or tries to grab my bag, or even approaches in any way. It feels as if something is missing.

I walk straight to the freight depot to check on the bike – which hasn't arrived. The major part of me is not surprised.

'But the bike left Pointe Noire before me,' I say.

The look I get in reply says 'So?'

I take a taxi into town and the driver finds me accommodation in a neighbourhood of spotless sidewalks, trimmed hedges and gleaming street furniture. I had forgotten what hygienic looks like. I could eat off these pavements; this place is clean-clean. The hotel-pension is pristine and I wonder if it's because of an outbreak of something nasty that everything has been clinically scrubbed.

I go to the TAAG office to enquire about the whereabouts of the Triumph.

'I don't know where your bike is but it should arrive on Tuesday from Luanda,' says the stroppy woman behind a desk.

'Luanda? In *Angola*?' I blurt out.

She ignores me and answers a ringing phone. There are only ten days to go before the tea party in Cape Town and I get a little unsettled at the news that the bike is not due here for at least four of them – and has gone to the wrong country.

The capital of Namibia, a modern city sited at mile-high altitude, is a big shock: the tarmac, the Afrikaans and English speakers, the pavements, the Western brand names, the blotchy white skin, the unsmiling faces, the lack of personal greetings on the street. It is as if I am seeing these things for the first time. Incurious shop assistants refuse to look me in the eye, I get begrudging 'hellos' 'goodbyes' and 'thank yous', people whoosh past in polished four-by-fours with windows up, air conditioning on, eyes focused ahead – 'get out of my way'. The houses in the white neighbourhoods have high walls, bars on the windows and obsessively trimmed lawns – manicured desolation, it seems to my eyes.

Frankly, I'm missing Africa, or what I have come to know as Africa over the last few months: the curiosity of the people, their openness, the easy smile and wit, the physicality of the people, their attractiveness, the colour, the music blaring from every taxi. I'm even missing the touts and hangers-on, and the way warm-blooded life is played out in all its glory on the street. But in Windhoek people have more important concerns: keeping themselves to themselves.

I mooch around the city waiting for the bike to arrive, more in hope than expectation. I buy a replacement camera, go to the movies, eat a steak in a restaurant with a tablecloth and a wine list, the explosion of tastes in my mouth a marvellous revelation. Despite the comforts, I seem to be mourning the end of the trip again. Being without the bike is extremely frustrating.

It is difficult to reconcile the indifference of everyone here to my experiences over the last few months with my own sense of anti-climax. After believing I relied on my own ingenuity for the past five months to get me through the sand and the mud and the potholes, I have come to realise that it was the people who succeeded, who made the journey happen and ensured my search for the ultimate cuppa would not fail if they had anything to do with it. The people became the trip, and now they have been taken away from me. The times people helped pick up the bike, divided their food without a thought about their own diminished share, the sheer joy in their faces when they heard about my trip; these are memories that cannot be articulated here in Windhoek. Maybe the stories are so thickly accumulated they will never truly be told. I am left with clipped hedges and lawn sprinklers.

Windhoek is pleasant enough, set amongst beautiful hills with a gentle pace of life. But for my time there it rains almost every day. One evening the lightning illuminates the sky for twenty-five minutes; it's so bright and prolonged I can read by its light in the bar in which I am happily ensconced. But in the north of the country rain is not so benign; people are desperate in the villages where there is no drainage. People stand outside their huts knee-deep in water, staring out from the front page of *The Namibian* newspaper living very different lives from those shopping in the malls and eating lunch under parasols.

As a territory once administered by South Africa, Namibia still wears its legacy of apartheid like weirdly unfashionable clothing. Those contemptible divisions between black and white are still apparent: whites stick with whites, blacks with blacks and coloureds with coloureds. Whites drive new cars, blacks use the shared taxis or walk; whites, with a few exceptions, are in positions of authority in shops, restaurants and offices. Whites own the pension in which I stay, blacks make the beds; Italians run my first night's restaurant in the city centre, while blacks and coloureds run around carrying plates of pasta. Although there is a European sensibility about the place, it is blacks and coloureds who sit behind the tills at the supermarkets, who carry shopping to customers' cars and who fill petrol tanks at the garages. Blacks treat me with arrogance and bitterness masked as surly indifference; whites treat me with coolness.

And there is another difference from the rest of this continent: 'black' seems to be a derogatory term in Namibia – unlike in most of black Africa. And for all the 'white man, white man' and casual references to me as *le blanc*, there is a different power struggle here for the right to use the words 'black' and 'white' without political overtones. Language can be a wickedly divisive instrument: black, white, black, white, black. Somehow, the further south the black family drifts, the lower their social standing, the more loaded the word 'black' becomes, because they are living in a white world. But that does not stop them coming for some kind of future for themselves.

The bike arrives within a few days, and with a mechanic's help and some Blackpool Tea Encounter advice from Clifford Baskerville – 'Take care, and take a few spares' – we strip the Triumph down and replace or repair what we can, and what we can't we 'make do'.

As soon as I believe we have done everything possible to make the bike roadworthy for the remaining few thousand kilometres, I leave Windhoek in a rainstorm and head for Mariental on the edge of the Kalahari Desert. I reach the crest of a hill on the outskirts of the capital as the rain eases and see stretched out before me the last chapter of my journey – a week on the road in beautiful Namibia and South Africa, countries I am already familiar with. Looking forward to some planned and unplanned Tea Encounters I open up the throttle and press on. The immaculate tarmac is like a narrow motorway through semi-desert, and by the time I reach Mariental the sun is blinding.

19
TABLE MOUNTAIN IN SIGHT

If you have the right attitude
you can tackle almost anything.
Gavin Lesch

15 February (seven days to go before the tea party)

Mariental is a small town boiling in the sun, and if it were not for the main tarmac road running through it would get few visitors, I'm sure. With a panorama to every horizon, the huge sky seems to swallow the town like a souvenir snow globe covering a toy village – with sand rather than snow shaken up in the atmosphere. The salmon pink sand beneath my feet and the reserved politeness of the people signal a new location and a new culture.

Jeremy Muller, described by his wife as 'a so-called coloured', prefers to be known simply as 'a Capetonian'. Out of some people's mouths the word 'coloured' has negative connotations from the old days of apartheid, when ethnic groups were categorised for legal purposes. 'Coloured', 'Cape coloured' or 'Cape Malay' are terms used to describe people with ancestry that goes back to the slave labourers imported by the Dutch in the seventeenth and eighteenth centuries, often from Indonesia and Malaysia. But there was more ethnic integration than the architects of apartheid would have credited, so the skin tones of people known as coloured can range from a deep hazelnut sheen to ruddy, pale pinky-orange, not unlike my own.

Jeremy escaped the Mother City to the tranquil and dusty streets of Mariental some years ago. As national programme manager for the Namibia Development Trust he helps local people establish small businesses, often in tourism. Currently, a fair number of tourists – many South African – drive through the country in swish four-by-fours to stay in equally swish game lodges run by other white people, with local blacks serving the food, making the beds and fetching and carrying – the old story. Jeremy intends to change that by encouraging local tribes and coloured communities to get a slice of the action.

'With some help who knows what we can achieve? Now, we don't have a "tea ritual" as you call it. You get rooibos in a mug with us,' says Jeremy, as he hands me some 'red bush' tea.

The rooibos – a uniquely South African caffeine-free tea – is the very colour of its name. I sit down in Jeremy's comfortable lounge and take a sip of the earthy brew as he draws the curtains to keep out the sun.

He is keen to talk about Africa's problems.

'Although you will notice there is more money in Namibia than in many of the countries you've visited in Africa, the gap between the richest and the poorest is shocking, even here in Mariental. Many people have next to nothing, while others live a very good life. The thing that would change Africa the most is if people would use their democratic rights to vote governments out that do not serve them. Why do people vote in crooks like Mugabe in Zimbabwe?'

I shake my head in wonder, 'It makes no sense to a European.'

'It makes no sense to a Capetonian, either!'

It is a short encounter as it is already approaching half past three and I want to reach the next town tonight. Jeremy leaves me with some advice: 'Enjoy the time you have left; don't speed down to Cape Town at 140 kph.'

So I speed off to Keetmanshoop. On a road as smooth as marble, for the first time in months I can calculate how long it will take to ride to each town. The 200-kilometre stretch south to Keetmanshoop takes me a predictable two hours. The heat is predictable, too – it's debilitating. The hot air rushing under the visor is burning my eyes, which are now stinging and streaming. The sensation reminds me of drifting across the road in the Sahara with my eyes shut. There is nothing between towns and little in the way of actual traffic; I see another vehicle every ten or fifteen minutes.

16 February (six days to go)

The next day I make Grünau, a place whose name is its most interesting feature. It is little more than a railway siding with a dirt road leading to the touristy Fish River Canyon, a huge ravine only beaten in size by Arizona's Grand Canyon. I stay at the appallingly naff Grünau Country Hotel, which looks like a cross between a caravan park and an Afrikaner detention centre. The reception is plastered with oversized signs telling me what not to do: No Swearing in the Ladies' Bar; Order Dinner Before 6 p.m.; No Animals WHATSOEVER! What are they expecting? Hyenas? And the receptionist needs to know now exactly what I would like for tomorrow's breakfast. 'A fry-up with one egg, two rashers of bacon, three grilled tomatoes and thirty-one baked beans, *asseblief*!'

17 February (five days to go)

I get a very early start. After a few hours I reach the last frontier crossing on the trip with conflicting emotions. I am aware of an inner capsule of euphoria in my heart as I roll into South Africa, but sadly it also signals the end of the Brew Ha-Ha now speeding towards me. The advertising hoardings and the giant electricity pylons linking arms across the country all convey to me that the adventure part of the holiday is over. As much as I thought I missed the comforts of my life in Britain during the tough miles in Cameroon and Gabon and Congo, I now find myself regretting the passing of the unpredictability of West and Central Africa. It's a strange sensation, very much how I felt in Kumba after Tabot and I conquered the mud.

I step into the border control where there is a short queue of people waiting to get their documentation stamped. In front of me is a British couple who have driven down the east coast of Africa in an old Landy. Their clothes are unironed, their hair knotted, their faces burnished and scaly with sunken cheeks, and there's a wild look in their eyes – but I can also see the achievement. Perhaps they notice the same in me.

Over the border I speed through a vast open landscape east towards Johannesburg and my last planned Tea Encounter a thousand kilometres away – an important one that the workers at Original Tea Bag Designs will be thrilled to hear about. Johannesburg, where Olive was brought up, was always on my planned route, but now it seems an absurdly long way to go for tea. If it wasn't tarmac all the way I would have made my excuses.

In a neat symmetry, one of my first Tea Encounters in Britain was with Sir Tom Finney, left-winger and all-round greatest living Prestonian. Now, one of my last encounters is with an African sporting great who has also achieved legendary status in a football-loving nation: Kaizer Motaung, chairman of the Kaizer Chiefs team. Olive's sister, Dara, who works for Amakhosi – Zulu for 'Chiefs' – has arranged the meeting, so I don't want to let her down.

The football club, still largely a family business, was created in the 1970s in the dark days of apartheid, when black teams were forbidden from playing at the best stadia because they were located in 'white' areas. In the late 1960s, while playing for the Atlanta Chiefs in the US, Kaizer was persuaded to return to his home country and build a new team. He was greatly admired in South Africa, so the team's popularity grew quickly. During the early days, Orlando Pirates lost some of their squad to the Chiefs, which sparked a rivalry that exists to this day, and even divides fans along political lines. But then sometimes, to foreign eyes, it seems everything here is divided along political lines.

With the 2010 World Cup in South Africa approaching, the country is struggling to meet both the demands of a rising population and its own economic growth. Kaizer and I, now sitting in a darkened boardroom within a free kick of Soweto, are made very aware of those demands as we endure a power cut, one of many that have blighted Johannesburg for the past few weeks. Luckily the kettle has recently boiled – it's not the first time my tea has been no more than lukewarm, but it's welcome all the same.

A little embarrassed, the soft-spoken Kaizer says, 'There are worries about the problem of power and other issues for the World Cup, and also the impact on Africa's image in the world. For the sake of Africa we must get it right.'

The conversation turns from footballing matters to politics, always just under the surface in this country.

'What most African countries have in common, the common denominator, seems to be a need for good governance,' Kaizer says. 'Those in power make decisions based on what's good for themselves rather than what's good for their country. In South Africa we seem to have got it about right, and as the last country to get real independence we have benefited from an excellent infrastructure left to us by the previous regime.'

Notwithstanding the power cut, it is an infrastructure that has greatly benefited the club, Kaizer Motaung and his family. I look out towards Soweto and the famous painted cooling towers and speculate how many people living in shacks think the same way.

I am invited to have lunch with the players following training. The PR spiel about this being a family club and their mission statement 'Amakhosi 4 Life – Love and Peace' is borne out when every single player notices the new face in the dining room and comes up to shake my hand. I can't see that ever happening at Chelsea. The atmosphere is warm and friendly, and the players treat each other with respect.

Sitting amongst the players is their own *amakhosi*, the manager Muhsin Ertuğral, a famously irascible touchline tantrum thrower, but he is a gentleman off the pitch.

18–19 February (three days to go)

I leave Johannesburg with 1,200 kilometres ahead of me to Cape Town. I ride on a black corridor of tarmac to the west coast through some glorious country – wide open vistas, fields of plenty and misty blue mountains in the middle distance; a feast for the senses. Making up more time than I had anticipated, I spend a night at a roadhouse near Richmond in the Karoo (Afrikaans for 'Land of Thirst'), the semi-desert heartland of this vast country in Northern Cape province. In the morning I continue south-west. With the Western Cape within touching distance, I relax a bit and admire this gorgeous country – to my eyes the most beautiful on the journey.

The vistas seem never-ending: there are unfenced merino sheep nibbling at stony ground, breathtaking roads that sweep down to fertile villages like oases and a sense that time here stands still; I squint and pretend I can see a Bushman.

Then I reach the Western Cape. After the virgin wildness of large parts of Africa I have seen, it's a fantastic, fertile scene: tractors – tractors! – kicking up clouds of dust with each turn in the field; orchards of olives, apples and oranges, nectarines and peaches; ostriches racing each other across the *veldt*; huge skips filled with fat grapes pulled behind slow-moving vehicles wince under the weight on their way to the winery, the smell of fermenting grape juice in the air, a heady concoction; burned figures in floppy hats bent over for months tending the vines, lovingly pruning, for this one moment, this one supreme moment of harvest and the anticipation of creating one of the bottled joys of the world – Cape wine.

'No officer, I haven't had a drink, I just took a deep breath on the R45!'

Hoping to avoid tourists in the trendy west-coast resorts, I decide to stay at one of the least fashionable towns by the sea – Saldanha, a wide, sheltered port with a gritty character located on a huge natural bay. I dump my stuff at a B&B and ride along the beautiful coast to Paternoster, a twee and creepily empty village on a gorgeous sandy bay. The whitewashed houses all look as if they have been recently built but never occupied.

In reality, I'm treading water in Saldanha so that I arrive at the tea party on the agreed date, but I'm enjoying having little to do except eat and readjust my mental clocks to Western time. I take advantage of a slow evening and have my fourth haircut on the Brew Ha-Ha. In Western Sahara I stepped out of the barber's without a single hair out of place exactly like the locals. In Yaoundé, Cameroon, the lady barber and two young female onlookers could not contain their giggles when she had to admit, 'You are my first white man!' Then there was the young lad in Douala who, when I asked for a shampoo, went out into the street with a bucket for the water and then rinsed my hair over the unconnected sink and soaked my feet. The water swirled out underneath the wall of the shack back into the street from whence it came.

A visit to the Saldanha barber is meant to be a quick tidy-up before my arrival in Hout Bay. But, this being South Africa, the sight of a white in a black barber's causes not a little disquiet. In my experience, most African barbers use clippers and shavers rather than scissors, so as the three young stylists get close to finishing their own clients with cool buzz cuts and shaved styles I sense them all stretching it out to avoid tackling the white man's greying, stringy locks. The youngest loses the slow cut race and gets me next. I ask him not to use the razor if he can avoid it, but the only alternative is a pair of kitchen scissors and he seems very ill at ease wielding them around my head. He isn't the only one.

20–21 February (two days to go)

The last two days of the Brew Ha-Ha are spent in Worcester in the beautiful Breede River Valley in the Cape Winelands. I choose Worcester partly because it is where Nobel Prize–winning novelist J. M. Coetzee spent part of his childhood. He has long been a favourite of mine, and although he doesn't write very glowingly about the place I am curious enough to make the diversion. The centre of town is litter-free and well-ordered with wide boulevards and exists to serve the wine and fruit farms hereabouts under a brutal heat. But there's also something eerie about the gabled buildings, sleepily tree-lined streets and whitewashed churches – conventionally pretty on the outside maybe, but if I were to set a thriller in a town with a hidden dark side, this would be it.

In Saldanha yesterday I picked up a tiny brochure in a bar that had a telephone number of someone in Worcester who offers something called 'home stay'. It sounded more interesting than just a bed and breakfast because the host takes responsibility for showing the guest around their home town. I rang the place, called Anne's Corner; Anne said, 'Come on over.'

The route to Anne's Corner takes me through a run-down neighbourhood (the Mr Hyde part of the dual-personality town), with people slumped in front of *drankwinkels* – liquor stores – and uninviting shops with bars across the windows. I keep going and am pleased to see my destination is in a quiet residential neighbourhood.

Anne Lesch is a half-size woman with a full-size personality. The pensioner, an ex-teacher, had a stroke a couple of years back but still welcomes the occasional traveller to her home. And I do mean occasional – the last person to sign her guestbook did so in 2001. There is another person in the house, a woman who maids for another family but lives with Anne. She says nothing to me in the entire forty-eight hours I am under Anne's roof but stares dolefully with eyes that give nothing away, watching my every move as she hugs herself with her brown arms. My attempts to engage her in conversation are shyly rebuffed. I'm not sure if she speaks any English, or if she's just bashful. Either way, she only speaks to Anne in Afrikaans.

Anne insists on introducing me to everyone she knows. We spend the time either welcoming other retired friends to her home for tea or visiting others – for more tea. It's a fantastic boost to the tea quotient on the Brew Ha-Ha and partly makes up for all the dry days in Central Africa when it was scarce.

Late on the first afternoon Anne picks up her car keys and says she'll drive me to the mall to buy a Coetzee novel. All three of us get in the car. Anne can't reach to buckle her seat belt so hooks the strap around the hand brake and sets off.

Apart from stalling the car and clipping the kerb a couple of times, stopping at every side street even though we have right of way and crawling over speed bumps as if they were landmines, we manage to get there in one piece.

Strolling around the shopping mall is the most surreal experience of the trip so far. It is as if I am watching a freakishly dazzling TV advertisement, my eyes flitting from item to item in the shop windows. These alluring commodities once represented my life, but I'm not sure they will again after the past few months.

I buy a book – *In the Heart of the Country* – then tell Anne I will make my own way back to the house.

'No, you won't. I don't want you walking in Worcester – it's too dangerous. And anyway I've made dinner for us.'

She seems to be taking me under her wing and, even though I survived the last five months on my own in darkest Africa, Anne is determined that nothing should happen to me on her watch. I suppose an opportunity to put back some of the weight I've lost on the trip – around two stone – should not be dismissed lightly.

On the way home we stop at her son's house. She leaves me there to have more tea while she goes home to prepare dinner. Her son Gavin and daughter-in-law Paulina are wonderfully welcoming.

'Does she give this treatment to everybody who stays with her?' I ask.

'Yes,' Gavin answers with more pride than embarrassment.

Gavin inherited the teaching gene from his mother and teaches at the local high school, where he is also heavily involved in sports, especially cricket. All round, he seems a very civic-minded person and a favoured subject of his is the transformation of the country from a divided to a united one but, as a coloured man, he is also keenly aware of the many problems still facing his students. He responds quickly when I ask him what one thing would make the biggest difference to Africa.

'Attitude. If you have the right attitude you can tackle almost anything. That's what's lacking in a lot of my pupils.'

Gavin gives me a lift back to his mother's home the long way to show me where many of his pupils live. The neighbourhoods have generally gone to seed, with many street lights out and a mildly threatening air coming from the groups of kids hanging around on corners.

'Our classes have about forty pupils; some of them come from bad homes,' Gavin tells me. 'They see older family members who don't work driving nice cars – who knows how they got them – and they want the same. They don't care what they do to get it. The problems we have start at home; there is only so much a teacher can do. I always say it is easier for one parent to discipline a child than for one teacher to discipline forty children.'

That's difficult to argue against. Gavin turns a corner and points out his school.

'The schools, generally, are more integrated since we got democracy in 1994, but white children do not come to our previously black or coloured schools, though blacks and coloureds do go to the previously white schools because they still have better facilities.'

Before dropping me off, Gavin gives me some advice for the remainder of the trip: 'Treat others as you would wish to be treated. It's simple advice but I try to live by it.'

I step through the iron security gates into Anne's porchway where the table is set for a feast of chicken and rice – the best *poulet et riz* on the entire trip. I set a warm bottle of Cape wine down onto the table beside three glasses into which we add an ice cube each – Anne, me and the silent one.

Later, Veronica, a teacher friend of Anne's, comes by. I give her a flavour of my journey in South Africa and mention that I visited Paternoster, the quaint fishing village near Saldanha.

Veronica puts down her tea cup and says disdainfully, 'More coloureds thrown out of their houses by rich whites!'

'It looks a bit like a Hollywood set, almost too beautiful for real life.'

'Yes. It is unreal. The houses are going for a small fortune!' Veronica says. 'The more they move in the less the local coloureds can afford to stay. During the week it's a ghost town 'cause they're mostly second homes. It's a shame.'

She is right. I was one of only a handful of people walking about the village while the excellent restaurant in which I ate served only four other people, all tourists. The one person on the roadway below was a coloured man illegally selling fresh crayfish at 30 rand (£2) a pop.

Veronica hasn't finished.

'The coloureds are always the ones to lose out. Under apartheid we were not white enough and now under the new regime we're not black enough! We can't win. But they forget the contribution we made towards ending apartheid and fighting for equal rights.'

Anne concurs with a nod of her head.

'Many black businesses only hire blacks. What about us? Where do we fit in in the new South Africa?' Veronica asks.

I mention that I had tea at the Kaizer Chiefs the other day, which presses another of Veronica's buttons: 'Football – ha! Another business run by the black mafia!'

21 February (one day to go)

Next morning after breakfast and tea with two more neighbours, Anne takes me to the Nuwe Hoop Centre for the deaf, the school from which she recently retired. It's both a day and boarding school of about 400 kids who are predominantly deaf or hard of hearing but also with many children who have behavioural problems or who are just 'uncategorised' – square pegs in the round-holed education system. The school is fairly well equipped – there are a few computers – and children wear uniforms, but there is an element of teenage anarchy about some of the classrooms.

At the end of my tour, principal Basil Davids, a small, neatly dressed man with tea-coloured skin, welcomes us into his office for a cuppa. I comment on the fact that almost all the children are either black or coloured.

'For many poor children we are the last resort. Some come from small villages in remote areas and struggle to pay the fees, even though they are very low. The families are extremely impoverished so when the school closes at the end of term many parents cannot even afford to come and pick up their kids. So they remain in the school throughout the holidays. It's heartbreaking.'

22 February

It's the last morning of the African Brew Ha-Ha... and I suppose, looking back, it has been a brouhaha on many levels: the sheer distance, the mechanical breakdowns, the time waiting for visas, the accident (bloody goats), the hospital stays and all the rest. But looking back over the whole trip, those things will not be remembered. It's been, so far as the things that matter are concerned, five months of pure joy: the feeling of freedom, possibility and hope, the landscape, the bigness of Africa, the remarkable people and their attitudes to life, the optimism, the friendliness and the thousands and thousands of guileless smiling faces. And the tea, of course.

Most of all, the trip has woken me from my westernised stupor by opening a window of clarity into my own life. Africa has made me feel alive and in touch with my own emotions and of those around me. And it has reminded me how dramatic life can be; not the superficial Western faux drama that I am used to – and which occasionally makes a sane man ride a bike through Africa on a tea quest – but the drama of struggling for life's necessities day in, day out. When each day is a grand endeavour to satisfy even basic needs, life cannot help but become a poignant drama. The sensations and challenges on the continent are extreme, but doesn't that make life all the more precious and worthwhile?

The longer the trip has continued the more I have learned not to view the continent as one uniform entity. Far from being an homogeneous whole, Africa is a many-shaded field. It is impossible to compare the life of the Berbers with that of the Zulus, or Dakarites with the Touaregs of Tombouctou, or link the ambitions of the streetwise in Pointe Noire with those of the people in the mud on the heartbreaking Mamfé road. Some, in North Africa, declined to be classed as 'African' at all, fearing, I would suspect, they may be confused with being black-skinned. So too, in South Africa, many whites who have spent their entire lives here have asked me 'what was Africa like?' as if they had never set foot in the place. But this has been part of the experience – to tease out those differences.

The search for the ultimate cuppa came out of an interest in the tea ritual, but of course the main purpose of sharing a pot of tea is to spend time with another person, time to talk and feel connected, and these are the things that I will remember long after the memory of the drink is lost: Pastor Samuel's wife, who brought the brew in a plastic bucket, the lukewarm tea that Serge served with the frozen sausages and his ten children looking on, the many teas with the fabulous Benslimane family in Casablanca, the rocket fuel brewed by Bwedra in the tent in the Sahara, tea on the sidewalk with the Carlton cooks, Tabot's one-night stand returning with a flask the morning after, Kaizer Motaung, Madame Mathey Boo and all the rest, these are the encounters I will remember most because I will never forget the people. How could I?

And before I even arrived in Africa I had six months of drinking tea with Brits, who were no less welcoming. It's not as if I didn't come equipped for the journey, remember; I was armed with all the advice from my British Tea Encounters, which got me out of the odd dodgy situation – and occasionally taunted me after I ignored it. In fact, they were essential to the whole journey. I'm not sure I could have done it without the encouragement from Mike Finnigan, Hazel Harding, Dave Edmundson and others, the shared insights from Doctors Alex McMinn and George Ogola and the expertise of Philip Youles in Blackburn, Lancashire – where there are still four thousand holes. I will never forget asking

Philip if the bike in its road set-up could make it to Cape Town – 'It'll be reet,' he said, which terrified me at the time but... he was reet.

Before I left I was curious to know if Africans performed the tea ritual as we do in Britain, and whether it played such a central role in daily life. The simple answer is yes. Tea was offered to me in friendship and as a celebration, a comforter, a pick-me-up and a consolation. Where people were clearly struggling to make ends meet, tea became even more important to their lives. I could see that despite having few material possessions it can be a great comfort to tend a miniature brazier with a tripod standing over it and a battered teapot slowly warming.

So, was there an ultimate cuppa? In a sense, the quest is a lifelong odyssey and for as long as I drink tea it will go on. But the pot of tea shared with the old man on the Kayes-Bamako route in Mali comes closest for a number of reasons. The whole point of the trip was to chance upon people to share a pot – you could call it serendipi-tea – so I was astonished that at the very point I realised I was in too far to turn back, the first time I truly felt out of my depth in Africa and needed the reassurance of another human being to bring some perspective to my predicament and set me right, I stumbled upon somebody brewing up. If I wasn't alone, I would have thought somebody had set it up. The man's advice will stay with me forever: *'Manger, du thé, reposer'* – 'Eat, drink tea, rest.' The mixture of timing, location, the right person and the perfectly expressed sentiment forced me to invest so much hope into that one glass of tea. But the Tea Encounter worked its magic – I got back on the bike and finished the day in the boxcar of the Bamako train, one of the most memorable days of my life.

The man's welcome was a wonderful example of how many people throughout Africa value helping and sharing, which they will do down to their last handful of manioc. He could probably guess that the value of my bike alone could feed his family for most of the rest of his life but that mattered not when he saw what a state I was in and how much I needed the tea and an encouraging word.

There have been many other times on my journey when I have been astonished by people who have shared their time, food and ingenuity – there are a hundred examples I could give. And the sharing is always given with disproportionate joy. What is important to them is that God has put me in their path, so they accept the responsibility to help. If they become needy, someone else will provide, somehow, further down the line.

Necessarily, in the act of retelling the African Brew Ha-Ha in book form, I have had to leave out much of the random nature of the trip, which in many ways is what made the journey so unforgettable: a glance, a smile, a helpful lift of the bike, a delighted child, a curious immigration officer, a generous *maman* by the roadside, a big-hearted sweaty hug, a talented mechanic and all the time the ingenuous smiles in the villages and towns and along the roadside. How do they do it? Three months before I left, the advice from one of my Tea Encounters was to bring a smile with me; well, that wasn't too difficult on this astonishing continent.

In this and in many other ways, Africa has never failed to surprise (more than the word, as Tabot would say). I may not have been able to rely on systems, institutions, timetables, road signs, the law, embassies, petrol stations, brand names, medication, plumbing, electricity supplies or opening times… but I could rely on the people. And I'm fully aware of that paradox. Essentially, I have learned to expect the best out of people – someone who has fallen over and needed rescuing as many times as I have can reach no other conclusion.

I have had no less a welcome in Worcester. Anne is as excited about the finale to my trip as anyone I have met along the way, and she is plying me with so much tea that I almost commit Brew Ha-Ha sacrilege on the very last morning and ask for coffee.

I take the last of the used souvenir tea bags from the kitchen counter and put them with the other twenty or so I've collected since 1 October, then get on the N1 for the Mother City two and a half hours away and my 2.30 p.m. appointment for tea.

The highway unreels before me like a perfect concrete corridor through vineyards and abundant farms. The nearer I get to the city the more I ease off the throttle to put off the inevitable end to the journey; by the time I see Table Mountain poking out from behind some poorly timed clouds, I'm down to around 70 kph. Although I ponder the idea of returning to Europe via the east coast, I know I am physically exhausted and will have to fly the bike home in a crate.

Cape Town is an appropriately spectacular end to a journey through Africa, as it has been for European explorers and seafarers over the centuries (Sir Francis Drake called it 'the fairest cape', which I cannot contradict). The sight of the beautiful city, huddled around the slopes of Table Mountain and Lion's Head and spilling down to Table Bay, has made the trip worthwhile.

I ride to the Triumph dealership in the city for a prearranged cuppa and they release a couple of salesmen to escort me down the coast. Olive meets me at the top of the mountain above Hout Bay where people are selling local crafts in a lay-by and there is much incredulous laughter at the absurdity of what I have achieved.

'You've done it!'

'I bloody have, haven't I?'

We both hug and then hug again as the hawkers and a couple of tourists look on. We then both stare incredulously at the Triumph.

'Fifteen thousand miles!' says Olive.

'Actually, the speedo and odometer haven't worked since the Congo, so who knows?'

We both laugh. The two guys on the Triumphs laugh too.

I ride down the mountain, put the headlights on, keep my thumb on the horn and freewheel into the courtyard of Original Tea Bag Designs, where I am amazed to see around a hundred people waiting for the crazy English guy who rode a bike through Africa. Even the British High Commissioner Paul Boateng is there. It instantly reminds me of the Mad Hatter's Tea Party in Blackburn before I left. Perhaps this is a little more polite. I take off my helmet for the last time as applause rings out around the courtyard; workers from the township and strangers come up and shake my hand, and Jill Heyes gives me an immense hug. I look at my watch. It's 2.45 p.m. – I'm fifteen minutes late.

Jill has some entertainment lined up: after Paul Boateng gives a mildly embarrassing speech about grit, determination and what makes Britain great, Mumsey Mongwe's all-girl dance troupe in new costumes, headscarfs and face paint perform a Zulu dance; then a group of schoolboys do a hilarious take on the mineworkers' gumboot dance, which has everyone in stitches – except the po-faced representatives from the South African Tourist Board.

I try to thank everyone in the courtyard for coming out for tea. People say they have been following the blog all the way since 1 October, which is astonishing to hear because sometimes I have felt as if the trip existed only in my head – one insignificant journey out of six billion occurring simultaneously on the planet. But now I know it is real. I did it, and Africa did it.

The African pool that I plunged into five months ago has kept me buoyed and moving south. Although I have felt like a skimming stone on the surface of Africa for the past few months, there is a belief that I have left a few ripples along the way. I came to Africa not because I belonged but because I wanted to belong, and the continent has not let me down. I'll never forget the people I met, and I hope they never forget *le blanc* who came wobbling past once upon a time on a big black Tree-oomph.

Tea bag workers Donna, Medica, Nicholas, Sweetness, Russell, Graciouse, T-Man, Peggy, Elaine, Rachel, Nomsa, Mavis, Daysman and Agnes form themselves into a choir and break into song. I choke. I am guided over to a trestle table bowing under the weight of éclairs and scones and sandwiches and a warm teapot, and Jill asks, 'Will you have a cup o' tea?'

Have you enjoyed this book?
If so, why not write a review on your favourite website?
Thanks very much for buying this Summersdale book.

www.summersdale.com